BATTLE THUNDER

The Story of Britain's Artillery

BATTLE THUNDER

The Story of Britain's Artillery

KENNETH BROOKES

OSPREY

First published in 1973 by
Osprey Publishing Ltd, P.O. Box 25
707 Oxford Road, Reading, Berkshire

ISBN 0 85045 160 4

For Jo and Trevor

Printed in Great Britain by
Cox & Wyman Ltd, London, Fakenham and Reading

Contents

Illustrations

Preface

This attempt to tell the story of a great military corps has been made possible through the generous help of a number of British Army officers, civilian officials, and others.

Acknowledgment for extremely kind encouragement and advice must be made to the staff of the Royal Artillery Institution at Woolwich, including Brigadier P. W. Mead, editor of the regimental journal. I am particularly indebted to Major R. G. Bartelot, Assistant Secretary (Historical) of the Institution, for reading my script as a check on factual accuracy – though it should be understood that responsibility for any opinions that are expressed is mine alone.

In Malta, where this book was written, I was greatly assisted by the grant of facilities by the Command Library at Headquarters, British Troops, where the librarian, Mr G. Crockford, kindly arranged for the loan and despatch of works from the Army Central Library in London.

Information has also been supplied by Mr Charles Andrews, of the Military Historical Society.

RIGHT OF THE LINE

'War, that mad game the world so loves to play.' – *Swift*

There is a regiment in the British Army which has no distinctive flag of its own, no battle honours displayed after the manner of other corps; yet it claims to be entitled, by virtue of privileges granted long ago to certain of its members, to take official precedence over all other branches of the service, however old or distinguished.

The Royal Regiment of Artillery is able to maintain – not simply as a matter of tradition, but on the basis of definite acknowledgments in black and white – that if detachments from every unit in the entire Army were to be drawn up for ceremonial review, the Royal Horse Artillery, when parading with guns, should hold the ancient post of honour, the right of the line, on all occasions.

A gunner, if he could be induced to put into words things that are usually left unspoken, might tell you something like this: 'Standards and colours were for others, the cavalry and the infantry as symbols and as rallying points in battle. We do not need them. We have the guns, our pride and our trust, on which we rally, and which, as a point of honour, must be prevented at all costs from falling intact into the hands of the enemy. The guns are the colours or standards of the Royal Artillery.

'As for honours, no flag would be large enough to hold the list of ours, for we have served in every battle that the Army has ever fought. On the little scrolls beneath the grenades on our old brass collar-badges you will see just one word – *Ubique*, meaning "Everywhere".'

One does not find the Royal Artillery at the head of the Army List, and it is far from being the oldest in the land forces of the Crown. It cannot compare in antiquity, as a regiment, with the Household Cavalry and the Guards battalions that were formed soon after the Restoration, to say nothing of such an almost legendary body of infantry as the Royal Scots (Royal Regiment, or 1st Foot), which was originally raised in 1633 by order of Charles I, and which can trace its descent from Scottish regiments that served in the famous Green Brigade under Gustavus Adolphus of Sweden in the Thirty Years War. The artillery was not formally established as a regiment until 1716; but its origins lie much further back, in the earliest days of the use of firearms by fighting men in the English service.

The circumstances of the regiment's foundation were quite different in nature from those attending the birth of the most famous cavalry and infantry corps. In the accepted sense, the first forerunners of the British gunners of today were not soldiers at all. The first colonel of the Royal Artillery – one of the finest officers it has ever had – was a foreign soldier of fortune, serving under the Board of Ordnance, a venerable institution standing apart from the main structure of military organization, such as it was in those days. For well over a century, by reason of its origin and characteristics, the artillery in the British Army developed as something of a distinct entity, almost a separate force, with its own rules and channels of command dividing it, both for good and ill, from the rest of the troops; and the regiment did not finally come under the full control of the War Office and the commander-in-chief until after the Crimean War.

The Royal Artillery has long ceased to be a regiment in the tactical sense; indeed, it would be almost true to say that it never was one. For more than a hundred years now, after sloughing off the caparisons of Ordnance Board overlordship, it has been a large and highly diversified specialist corps, supplying by constantly changing means, and in an almost endless variety of settings, one fundamental unchanging need – the provision of fire power above and beyond the capacity of infantry weapons. But the circumstances of its infancy left their mark upon it, some vestiges of which lingered at least until the first part of the present century.

There must be many thousands of men (and some women) now living, who have served in the artillery at one time or another, without ever coming to know more than the sketchiest fragments about the origin of the regiment and its early history. All but a few devoted students of the records would probably be surprised to learn that, for a considerable period, artillery officers – qualified men of skill and experience – were looked at askance as outsiders by many holding commissions in other branches of the service, and that, as comparatively late as in the American War of Independence, a dispute arose on whether a general whose regimental service had been with the guns should be permitted to exercise command over a force including troops of all arms.

The social climate in which Royal Artillery officers, as such, were liable to be cold-shouldered in military circles as not quite gentlemen will strike most people nowadays as being so hopelessly antediluvian as to be almost incredible, but it was real enough while it lasted. This obstacle, like many others, was eventually overcome. It would perhaps be fair to say, however, that for a long time there existed in some quarters a rather broader prejudice, or distrust, against the artillery as a body of pampered specialists – favoured creatures enjoying a certain privileged status and functioning, even on the battlefield, in conditions of relative comfort and safety in comparison with the mud, toil and blood which were the inescapable lot of the long-suffering foot soldier, who did the hard and dirty work while others gained the glory. Anyone who has talked with ex-infantrymen (particularly the veterans of the First World War, perhaps) will no doubt have heard wry stories of well-sheltered artillerymen, at a respectable distance behind the front line, loosing off in leisurely fashion their allotted quota of rounds, while the infantry in the trenches crouched in filth and misery beneath the lash of enemy bombardment, and sometimes also of British shells that fell short.

Old grudges and complaints tend to die hard in the Army, but a good deal of this kind of feeling has probably vanished together with other myths. Few infantrymen who have worked in close contact with the gunners can be under any illusions about the arduous nature of the artillery service or the degree of hardship and danger that its members are called upon to share with other soldiers; nor would any artilleryman be so bigoted, or so ignorant, as to seek to belittle in any way the importance of the infantry – the one abiding and essential basic factor, the men who are always needed for the duties that no others can perform, and on whom, in the last resort, everything depends.

Rivalries within a service are inevitable, and healthy enough up to a point, but there is something bigger to which they must give way, as they have done in the main. Battles are won, not by one branch of the Army alone, but by the closest cooperation between all arms. All are vital, none is self-sufficing. Historically the classic role of the British artillery, apart from the defence of our own fortifications and the assailing of enemy strongholds, has always been the support of the infantry, both in attack and in retreat. In the fulfilment of this task, comradeship between the artillery and the infantry has been forged, and mutual respect has been earned, in hundreds of tough engagements.

On more than a few occasions gunners have turned for the moment from their own weapons to go to the aid of the hard-pressed regiments of foot. They have fought beside them rifle in hand, there have been times when they made sorties with the infantry or mounted into the breach with the storming parties. Likewise, the Royal Artillery has reason to be grateful to a good many soldiers of the cavalry and infantry who have stepped forward to take the place of dead or wounded artillerymen, to keep the guns in action or save them from the enemy. But it has not always been so. Time and again, on obscure ravaged corners of the earth when the tide of war was running against the British and skies were blackest, the artillery – sometimes a single battery – has stood alone, because there was no possible source of help within reach, and the fight has been carried on to the end, good or ill, by a handful of desperately strained and weary men who would not leave their guns.

This book is not a technical study, nor does it make any pretension to be a complete detailed history of the Royal Artillery, which would entail a specialized survey, far beyond the scope of a single volume intended for the general reader, of every war in which Britain has been involved. In the past this task, formidable enough, has been tackled with diligence and thoroughness by a series of regimental historians, though never for many years by any writer in a form embracing the whole story of the gunners from before the birth of the regiment. The present intention is to attempt a broadly outlined picture of the early artillery, and from it to trace the growth and achievements of the Royal Regiment down to the present day, including some reference to the principal developments in the art and tactics of gunnery, together with accounts of as many as possible of the outstanding actions by the gunners in our own time and before.

It is a task which must be approached with humility by anyone who has ever set down any kind of roots in the Royal Artillery, for the field is an enormous one, and the literature and source material that impinges on it is vast. Whole bulky segments of information, such as detailed organization of units, changes in establishments and equipment, and lists of personnel, which are of interest to the professional soldier and some value to the historian, must be omitted, or drastically compressed, in a general work. When one comes to set in their framework some of the deeds of gallantry of the artillerymen, the problem is not so much what to include, as how many can be left out without injustice to those whose names are not given. In the Crimea, the Indian Mutiny, the South African War, the two World Wars and in lesser conflicts, fifty awards of the Victoria Cross have been made to men of the Royal Artillery, as well as fourteen to gunners of the Indian Presidencies.

As our story unfolds, the reader will be able, it is hoped, to follow the long progress of the artillery from the crude fourteenth-century siege trains to the weapons of today with all their complexity and destructive potential. We shall see the artillerymen proving their worth in the eighteenth-century struggle with France, when wars raged across three continents; defending Gibraltar in the three-year siege; playing their part in decisive battles against Napoleon's armies in the Peninsula and at Waterloo; holding firm amidst the chaos and wretchedness of the Crimea; and learning hard lessons at the hands of the Boers.

Then will come the illimitable tragic drama of the 'Great War' – the fighting retreat in 1914, and later the colossal bombardments during the terrible years of deadlock on the western front – to be followed in turn by the wide-ranging sweep and action of mobile warfare in 1939–45, with the Western Desert battles and the advance into Hitler's Germany.

Today, in the flux and uncertainty of a riven world, the Royal Artillery stands strong and efficient, adapting itself once again to new ways and new weapons, in the age of guided missiles and nuclear warfare. The record of the artillery, like that of other regiments, has not all been glory. We shall read of defeat and disaster as well as shining victories, of muddle and disorganization behind the fighting men in addition to devoted service. Being human, the gunners have made mistakes. They would be the first to admit that sometimes they have fallen short, not always through any fault of their own, of the level which they would set for themselves, and which would be expected of them. But, judged by any criterion, the measure of what has been achieved is truly great, and should not be forgotten.

There are tales to be told not only of the pomp and circumstance of war, but also of little human oddities, disinterred from musty old files and records, giving a glimpse into the down-to-earth realities of army life that go on, with very few major changes, while empires fall and centuries pass. A place must be found for some curious episodes, most of them little known and perhaps of an unexpected kind, like the bishop who helped the gunners at Sedgemoor: the light battery that defeated an American flotilla; the English artillerymen who became caught up, against their will, in a mutiny during which the Russian flag was raised in Malta; the facts behind the bitterness between the Royal Artillery and the Duke of Wellington; and the battery which, at the end of the long day's fight at Waterloo, found itself under fire from Britain's Prussian allies.

VILLAINOUS SALTPETRE

'But for these vile guns, he would himself have been a soldier.' *– Shakespeare*

In a brief glance backward over the past of the gunners, it is worth while to remember that the term artillery is much older than the first cannon. Before gunpowder, in England and also in France 'artillery' meant bows and arrows. The weapons of the Genoese crossbowmen at Crécy in 1346 were referred to by Froissart as 'leur artillerie', and later Roger Ascham, in *Toxophilus*, wrote: 'Artillerie nowadays is taken for two things, gunnes and bows.'

But there was artillery, properly so called, thousands of years before that. As early as the reign of Uzziah, who was King of Judah in the first part of the eighth century BC, the Old Testament speaks of 'engines, invented by cunning men, to be on the towers and upon the bulwarks, to shoot arrows and great stones withal'. Uzziah's campaigns are recounted in the Second Book of Chronicles.

Among the engines of war used by the ancient were the ballista or mangonel and the catapult, utilizing the torsion of strong twisted cords (some were plaited of women's hair) or the tension of massive bows or timbers. Such machines were in extensive use by the Romans, mainly but not exclusively for siege operations. Later the principle of counterpoise was employed in the medieval trebuchet. Some of these engines were so powerful that they were not completely discarded until several decades after the introduction of guns.

The belief that the Chinese invented cannon has now lost ground, though it is known that they were familiar with the use of gunpowder, for their ever-popular firecrackers and for more lethal purposes, at an early date. In Europe, one of those mentioned as a possible originator was an obscure German monk, Berthold Schwarz, or Berthold the Black, apparently so called from his dabbling in the black art of alchemy. All that can be said with any certainty, however, is that the invention had been made by about 1320. The first known instance of a piece of artillery being fired in anger was at Metz in 1324, and there are a number of references to the use of firearms by English, Scots, Germans, Moors and others in the second quarter of the fourteenth century. According to some historians, guns were put into the field by Edward III at Crécy, and the English also had artillery at the siege of Calais in 1347.

The very earliest known specimens of gunpowder artillery seem to have been quite small. An illustration shows a grave-looking operative applying, from a respectful distance, a flaming brand to the touch-hole of a piece, shaped rather like a pot-bellied vase, from whose neck protrudes a dart-like projectile. These pioneer efforts were in cast bronze or brass. Soon afterwards guns of wrought iron appeared, but not of cast iron, as the technique of castings with ferrous metals was not mastered until the fifteenth century.

At the siege of Harfleur in 1415 Henry V had some of the latest German-made cannon. In his artillery train were twenty-five master gunners, apparently including some Germans, and fifty 'servitour gunners', having under their charge ten cannon, three of which were exceptionally large, with names such as 'London' and the 'King's Daughter'. The chief engineer, Master Giles, organized a day-and-night bombardment, concentrated on the walls flanking one gate. After twenty-seven days the gate and barbican were in ruins. Giles then set alight the woodwork with an incendiary missile, and as the breach was stormed the town surrendered, the garrison begging the king to make his gunners cease, 'for the fire was to them intolerable'.

A number of enormous bombards, that still rank among the largest guns ever made, were manufactured during the fifteenth century. Edinburgh Castle's 'Mons Meg', probably built before 1500, weighed 5 tons and could throw a 19½-inch ball of iron for nearly a mile. 'Dulle Griete', the 13-ton bombard of Ghent, had a calibre of 25 inches and fired a stone weighing 700 pounds. The biggest of which there is an authentic record was the 'Great Gun' of Moscow, cast in 1694. According to the *Voyage de Deux Francais*, this weighed 2,400 pounds. It was 16 French feet long and 4 feet, 3 inches in diameter, deducting 16 inches for the thickness of the piece.

There are reports, however, of an even bulkier piece of ordnance more than a century earlier at the siege of Constantinople by the Turks. A Hungarian engineer, Urban, had approached the Emperor Constantine, declaring that he could make the best cannon in the world, but he failed to come to terms with the emperor, and Urban then went over to the sultan. By early in 1453 the Hungarian had succeeded in producing at Adrianople the largest piece of artillery yet seen, nearly 27 feet long and capable of hurling stone balls of over 1,000 pounds for a distance of a mile. According to an account quoted in Field-Marshal Montgomery's *History of Warfare*, when the gun was tested the noise 'caused pregnant women 12 miles away to have miscarriages'. This monster set out for Constantinople, drawn by a team of sixty oxen. At the siege it 'broke down'.

Almost all guns up to this time were smoothbore muzzle-loaders, though there were some experiments with breech-loading, using a primitive kind of plug device, but the basic difficulty, that of ensuring a safe gas-tight seal, was not satisfactorily solved until much later. Apart from siege work and the defence of castles, the early cannon were of very limited practical value, owing to their unpredictable behaviour, lack of mobility, and slowness in operation. They were cumbrous hulks of metal, rigidly fixed to frameworks of stout timber, with no means of changing aim by alterations in bearing and elevation, except by laborious manhandling of the entire gun and carriage. Anything approaching accuracy was out of the question, save at the shortest range, and the main effect in the field seems to have been that of a new and horrific weapon to spread general alarm and despondency in the enemy ranks.

Sometimes they may have had a different effect, by discouraging the men on their own side. While the armoured knights, whose battlefield supremacy was doomed by the English long-bow and by gunpowder, loathed the new weapons as a beastly and unchivalrous form of warfare, the foot soldiers regarded their own commanders' artillery with the utmost suspicion.

English soldiers have usually been among the most conservative of people, in many ways, and they instinctively resented the appearance of these strange new engines, manned, as likely as not, by interlopers who were not Englishmen at all, yet who received rather better pay than the ordinary foot soldier's pittance.

Worst of all, in the eyes of the archers and pikemen, the fellows who worked the guns were not even soldiers, though the actual commander of the artillery was usually an officer of some experience, often a foreigner. In many cases the guns were not the property of the king waging the war, but of some master gunner whose services he had obtained at an agreed price, and who brought with him a band of 'civilian artists' or 'artificers' who had no real allegiance to the prince, save as an employer. To haul the guns, great numbers of oxen, mules or horses were needed. Drivers were hired, on contract for the campaign or as required, from among carters, farm hands, or at a pinch any available peasants who could handle a whip, and who (a sore point with the soldiers) had a tendency to run away at the first opportunity.

All in all, it can be understood if the English soldier was at first inclined to think that the cannon were less trouble and menace to the enemy than to himself, now that he faced an added risk from the dangers of bursting gun barrels and accidental explosions among the powder kegs. Many would have agreed with the lordling quoted by Hotspur:

> 'It was great pity, so it was,
> This villainous saltpetre should be digged
> Out of the bowels of the harmless earth,
> Which many a good tall fellow has destroyed
> So cowardly.'

But the gunners multiplied. During the Wars of the Roses, Richard Duke of York is said to have had a great train of ordnance with many gunners at Dartmouth in 1452. As artillerymen became more numerous, they commanded a lower price.

The first great patron and innovator of the artillery in England was that prince of many talents, Henry VIII. His country had been a late starter in the making of guns. When the king decided that he must have 'cannon enough to conquer hell' he was forced by the lack of a home industry to employ a Fleming, Hans Poppenruyter, who supplied him with nearly 150 pieces of different calibres, including a set of bombards known as the 'Twelve Apostles'. These made their appearance at the siege of Tournai, where the one named after St John unfortunately stuck in the mud and was captured.

Through the king's initiative, the art of the gun founder was being practised in England before long. The first mention of the casting of 'great brass cannon and culverins' in this country is in 1521, when Francis Arcanus began to make them. The first English iron guns were made from 1541 onwards, it is said, by the Rev. William Levett in Ashdown Forest and by three foreigners at Buckstead, Sussex.

Not content with the usual solid shot of the period, Henry took steps to augment them with crude types of shell. These were described by a contemporary as, 'hollow shot of cast iron, stuffed with fireworks or wildfire; whereas the biggest sort for the same had screws of iron to receive the match to carry fire kindled, that the firework might be set on fire to break in small pieces the same hollow shot, whereof the smallest piece hitting any man would kill or spoil him'.

At first, in addition to buying all his cannon from abroad, mainly from Flanders, Henry had also employed foreign gunners, but as early as 1514 Lord Darcy was making a plea for the employment of native-born artillerymen, and soon Englishmen were being appointed. They now received the ordinary soldier's pay of sixpence a day.

By 1528 King Henry must have had a fair number of guns, for in that year he was able to give nineteen bronze cannon and more than a thousand roundshot to help to arm the Knights of St John as champions of Christendom against the Turks in the Mediterranean. The presentation was made to Philip de l'Isle Adam, Grand Master of the Order of St John of Jerusalem, when he was received in London by the king and Cardinal Wolsey. The visit came about five years after the fall of Rhodes, the former stronghold of the knights, and two years before they were established in the Maltese islands. Some of the cannon from England may have done good service in the Great Siege of 1565, in which the Order held out through four months of fierce attack by the forces of Suleiman the Magnificent; other guns had been used earlier in the unsuccessful defence of Tripoli.

Henry VIII was the first to establish a permanent corps of gunners to garrison the defences of his realm. From this, temporary 'trains of artillery' were formed and sent out in time of war. All artillerymen, as well as every kind of equipment for them, came under the direct administration of the master-general of the ordnance, who later signed all commissions for artillery and engineer officers below field rank. The post of master-general was one of the great offices of state, dating back at least to 1483, perhaps earlier. Between the Glorious Revolution and Waterloo, its holders were to include seven dukes, two marquesses, six earls and three viscounts, few of whom had any practical experience as artillery officers. Besides manufacturing and supplying cannon for both the Navy and the Army, the Ordnance Board was responsible for providing stores of almost every description, from muskets to camp kettles, and also maps.

From its headquarters at the Tower of London, the board, of which a good deal more will be heard later, ruled over a multifarious and unwieldy domain, peopled largely by dim civilian functionaries, swathed in red tape and almost totally divorced from real contact with the facts of life in an army. At its best their work was pedantically exact, though painfully slow; at its worst it was an almost incredible mixture of obscurantism, ignorance, and downright neglect, according to its severest critics – though this is a point on which there is some difference of opinion.

The permanent manning of the royal castles and fortresses, excellent in theory, had lamentable deficiencies in practice. Too often these defences degenerated into convenient posts of duty, or havens of refuge, for worn-out old soldiers, a number of whom at a later period came from the Royal Artillery's 'invalid battalions'. In the reign of Elizabeth some of the Tower gunners are said to have been over ninety years of age, and much later, during the period of neglect after the Peace of Utrecht, forty-six guns at Pendennis Castle in 1743 were found to be in the charge of one feeble old master gunner, with a youth as assistant. Here, however, volunteers from the 'marching companies' came forward with great enthusiasm.

During the reign of Henry VIII an attempt was made to set

up a corps of drivers or wagoners for the artillery, though the problem was not permanently solved. The men were to wear white coats with the red cross of St George, and to be mustered and paid once a month. It is a commentary on the system of stoppages (the perennial bugbear of the soldier) that it was thought necessary, for the protection of the drivers, to order that the paymaster should exact from them nothing more than one penny a month per man.

Although English cannon were highly esteemed, under Charles I England was still buying guns abroad, from Holland now. The theory and tactics of artillery were neglected, but the training of the individual gunner received close attention. Already there was an approved drill, with thirteen separate commands for the wielding of ladle, sponge and rammer. To withdraw the smallest quantity of powder with the ladle after loading, or to spill even a few grains on the ground, was considered 'a foul fault for a gunner to commit'. Every gunner was exhorted to 'set forth himself with as comely a posture and grace as he can possibly; for the agility and comely carriage of a man in handling his ladle and sponge is such an outward action as doth give great content to the standers-by'.

The English were not leaders in the effective use of mobile guns with troops. Bartolommeo Coleoni, the Italian soldier of fortune, who died in 1475, is credited with being the first captain to work out a true field artillery tactic, placing light guns to the rear of other elements, and firing through gaps that were opened at a signal.

The first great commander to make systematic use of field guns on a fairly large scale, spaced at intervals between blocks of pikemen and musketeers, was Gustavus Adolphus. The Swedish king had a Scottish artillerist, Sir Alexander Hamilton, one of whose experiments produced the celebrated 'leather guns'. These apparently had a thin copper tube over which hempen cord was tightly bound, the whole being covered with varnished leather. They were easily portable, but Gustavus discarded them on finding that they would last for only ten or twelve rounds; however, the guns (known as 'Sandy's stoups' after their inventor), were used by Scots against the English in 1640 at the battle of Newburn in Northumberland.

At the time of the Civil War the English artillery, though

less mobile than the Swedish, was probably more accurate. There were at least seven sizes of field guns, from the culverin, which fired an 18-pound shot to an extreme range of 2,100 paces at the rate of one every six minutes, to the drake, a 3-pounder which could be discharged once every four minutes. On occasion the artillery did good service, though never decisively in battle, and Cromwell made effective use of siege guns.

After the Restoration, for some years the artillery seems to have lagged behind in the various moves for the establishment of a national army. Even such organization as existed in Parliament's New Model Army apparently disappeared, so far as the gunners were concerned, though the Commonwealth had made a point of keeping one train ready for the field. Gunners were now left as small semi-independent bodies in scattered garrisons, while field guns were allotted, usually in pairs, to battalions of infantry – a 'penny numbers' system which has always been anathema to all right-minded artillerymen, though it is fair to add that something on rather similar lines has been tried at much later dates, and not only in the British Army.

If organization was still weak, the artillerymen were already taking on the outward trappings marking them as persons of consequence. An inventory for the clothing of a 'trayne' in Scotland in 1662 shows that the coat for the gunner (meaning presumably master gunner) was of 'fine scarlet cloth laced with black velvet as the Yeomen of the Guard at London, embroidered with a thistle and crown and two cannons on the breast and one on the back, and gunner's badges of silver'. One of the largest artillery trains would include not only the necessary ammunition and store wagons, with all their attendants, but also a pair of kettle drums, mounted on a specially designed carriage with raised seats for the drummer and driver. The artillery does not seem to have followed the fashion of the cavalry, who had Negro kettle drummers, wearing small white turbans wound about blue cloth caps with hanging hoods or bags, but the gunners' chief purveyor of warlike music was sufficiently resplendent, in crimson coat with blue cuffs, heavily laced with broad bands of gold and silver, and bearing the royal crown and cipher on chest and back – a dress similar to that worn today on state occasions by the trumpeters of the Household Cavalry. Nor were the artillery kettle drums kept only for grand parades in London; they went on campaign to Ireland, and also to the continent during the wars of William III and Marlborough.

In 1682 the control of the Ordnance Board, which had lapsed for a time, was officially reasserted over the 'fee'd gunners' at the Tower, who were reduced in number from a hundred to sixty, brought under military discipline, and exercised regularly in their duties. Three years later a warrant of James II was issued for the raising of companies of fusiliers or 'firelocks' to serve with the artillery. This document mentions a hundred aprons for each company, from which it may be taken that the fusiliers were expected to carry out a certain amount of manual labour, such as the construction of chevaux-de-frise and other defences; but their duties appear to have included not only the protection of the guns, but also the keeping of a watchful eye on the detachments, particularly to discourage the civilian drivers from taking to their heels.

The personal equipment for a train under the orders of the Earl of Feversham in 1685, the year of Monmouth's rebellion, has been listed as follows: 'two gunners' mates and thirty-two gunners, each a field stave or linstock; thirty-two matrosses [gunners' assistants], each a half pike, hanger [short sword] and belt; the pioneer sergeant, a partizan, hanger and belt; pioneer corporal, a halberd, hanger and belt; twenty pioneers, each a hanger and belt and either a spade, a shovel or pick, and were dressed in red jackets and red caps; a drummer with his drum, hanger and belt; the artificers wore red clothes laced; the conductors, wheelers, carpenters, coopers, smiths and collar makers, each a hanger and belt'. Conductors were assistants to the commissary of stores.

This train was so desperately short of draught animals that Dr Peter Mews, Bishop of Winchester, who was with the king's forces and who had been a Guards captain in the Civil War, lent the horses from his coach to help to drag the guns into position for the battle of Sedgemoor. Coach horses were by no means uncommon for the artillery; on several occasions the hackney drivers of London were pressed into service. The bishop is said to have supervised the deployment of the cannon, and in the battle he received a wound from which he suffered for the rest of his life. After the defeat of the rebels, four worried farmers, whose oxen had been requisitioned to haul away the artillery train, petitioned for the return of the animals, which had been taken as far as Devizes, 40 miles from their owners.

A warrant in 1686 created a new artillery rank, that of bombardier, to come directly under the fireworkers, or firemasters' assistants, for specialized duty with mortars, and later in bomb vessels. This special enlistment subsequently lapsed, and the term was applied to junior NCOS. Nowadays, wearers of one stripe or two in the Royal Artillery intensely dislike being addressed by the uninitiated as 'corporal', and are rightly proud of their distinctive title, which in its Italian form of 'bombardiero' can be found in continental records at least as early as the sixteenth century; but not all of them may know that 'corporal' did also exist as an artillery rank, and survived until 1920, coming below sergeant and above bombardier.

In 1688, faced with the growing threat of invasion by the supporters of William of Orange, James II ordered the preparation of the largest artillery train yet known, or at least the most lavishly officered. It was proposed that, in the event of the king accompanying the train in person, he should have with him the lieutenant-general of the ordnance, the comptroller-general, the principal engineer, the master gunner of England and his clerks, the chief firemaster and his mate, the keepers and makers of the royal tents and their assistants. There would also be the commissary of ammunition (at ten shillings a day), the paymaster, engineer, wagon master, quartermaster, surveyor, provost marshal, chief petardier, bridge master, gentlemen of the ordnance (four at five shillings each), the chief-conductor, the captain of pioneers, and a surgeon, all in addition to the gunners (thirty at two shillings each) and matrosses (forty at one shilling and sixpence each). The lesser functionaries, whose number gives an idea of the remarkable variety of paraphernalia with which the gunners set out to war, included a tinman, ladle maker, master farrier (with four servants), master carpenter, master wheelwright, master collar maker, cooper and gunsmith.

This train never took the field for James. The king fled, William landed at Torbay, and under his rule, after a brief interregnum, the Ordnance Board moved on with somewhat enhanced vigour under a new master-general, that seasoned campaigner the Duke of Schomberg.

Changes were made in the board, and Dutch, German and even French names may be noted among the new officials. Great trouble was experienced over the provision of arms and transport, and over the derelict condition of some of the old forts. Schomberg may have felt some relief when he left behind the cares of office in London for service in Ireland. For this there was a train of 147 gunners and matrosses, with 200 carters. The gunners and tradesmen were dressed in 'coats of blue, with brass buttons, and lined with orange bass . . . the money to be deducted by equal proportions out of their pay by the Treasurer of the Train'.

A few years later, in the Flanders train of 1695–97, we find the gunners in crimson coats faced with blue, already wearing (though in reverse order of prominence) the colours that were to be retained right down to the present day in the dress uniforms of the Royal Artillery.

The first short-lived establishment for English artillery in regimental form came in 1699, partly because of a growing awareness of the dangers inherent in the lack of a permanent force, and partly owing to the existence of a considerable number of fairly experienced gunners, available and unemployed after the Peace of Ryswick. The regiment was to consist of four companies with only thirty gunners each, at an estimated annual cost of £4,482, in addition to the pay that some of the men would draw as part of the old ordnance establishment. Within a year the little regiment was disbanded, only meagre provision being made for its officers.

Seventeen years were to pass before the stamp of permanence was set on the artillery, and it was then due mainly to the care and insight of one of his country's greatest masters of war, a man who understood and valued artillery – John Churchill, first Duke of Marlborough, who was appointed master-general of the ordnance, as well as captain-general of the forces, soon after the accession of Queen Anne in 1702.

UNDER MARLBOROUGH

'It is with artillery that one makes war.' – *Napoleon*

The gunners owe a lasting debt to Marlborough, who also did so much both for the efficiency and the welfare of the rest of the Army, particularly the infantry. In his campaigns during the War of the Spanish Succession, in which England, Holland and the emperor faced France, Spain and their lesser allies, for the first time the artillery found itself raised before the eyes of Europe, and of its own country, as a battle-winning factor of first-rate importance. Victories were gained and prestige was immeasurably heightened, though with material which in the main, continued to be of an imperfect, rough-and-ready kind.

War at the beginning of the eighteenth century was still conducted, to a large extent, at the deliberate, almost courtly pace of a bygone age. Campaigns were fought, particularly as regards siege operations, in accordance with a rigid set of time-hallowed principles and conventions, with which few generals cared to take liberties. They were always extremely conscious that, in the absence of full-scale conscription, the reservoir of readily available manpower behind their armies was small, and that losses could not easily or quickly be made good. Most of them therefore manœuvred and counter-manœuvred with caution, showing a natural if sometimes short-sighted reluctance to face the possibility of heavy casualties in pitched battles, unless conditions were exceptionally favourable. Marlborough stood out from his contemporaries by his readiness to take grave risks if there was a reasonable chance of great results, and also by his capacity to seize and exploit the element of surprise.

The English artillery contingent for the opening campaign of the war was a small one, being composed of thirty-four pieces – fourteen sakers, sixteen 3-pounders and four howitzers – with two companies of gunners; additions were made later. The ordnance columns continued, for the time being, to be swollen and tied down in pace by the ponderous bulk of much non-artillery material, such as a pontoon section, under a captain of the boats, and a detachment of miners, besides carrying a proportion of the small-arms ammunition for the Army as a whole. With the trains went the engineer officers from whom a separate corps was to be developed later. The ordnance trains, in fact, were expected to serve multiple purposes which in modern times would be considered those of the Royal Artillery, Royal Engineers, Royal Army Ordnance Corps, and the Transport Corps.

Some of Marlborough's most dazzling successes were triumphs of organization rather than of brilliant strategy or any new tactical methods. Of nothing is this more true than his famous march to the Danube, a feat crowned by the great victory of Blenheim.

Marlborough knew that he could never gain Dutch consent for a move to counter the French-Bavarian threat to Vienna if this had the appearance of leaving Holland unprotected. He therefore made a pretence of mounting a flank attack on Marshal Villeroi's force in Alsace, but, after a feint at crossing the Rhine at Mannheim, he pushed on across country into Bavaria, taking with his troops an artillery train that had by this time been strongly reinforced.

Eye-witnesses, both English and foreign, were unanimous in praising the tireless efforts of both officers and men in getting the cumbrous pieces over the abominable roads between the Rhine and the Danube. For six weeks the Army advanced at an average rate of about ten miles a day. The duke's secretary, Hare, wrote in his journal of the gunners having overcome difficulties which the French had believed insuperable. Often the ascent of a single hill cost the artillery a whole day of toil. We have it on the authority of Uncle Toby that our troops 'swore terribly in Flanders'. It may be taken for granted that the artillerymen also did their share on some of those hills.

After joining hands with the Margrave of Baden's Army, the first important move by Marlborough's force was to secure the Schellenberg, an entrenched hill with a protecting wood and a fort dating back to the days of Gustavus Adolphus. In this action the English had thirty-six guns, all fairly light field pieces, but of excellent quality. A witness to the accuracy of their fire was M. de la Colonie, Commanding Officer of a French grenadier battalion. His men were drawn up on high ground behind a breastwork which gave no effective protection against the guns. At the first discharge, he writes in his memoirs, he was spattered with the blood and brains of a company commander who, together with twelve grenadiers, was crushed by a single round-shot. The battalion lost five officers and eighty men, out of a strength of perhaps six hundred, before a musket shot was fired by either side.

Before this, in the campaign of 1702, the work of the artillery-men had been officially described as being carried out with 'as much order, despatch and success as ever before was seen'. Now the field artillery's first great battle was at hand.

Among Marlborough's guns at Blenheim on 13 August 1704, were some 36-pounders and even 60-pounders. Such heavy metal was exceptional; guns larger than 24-pounders had seldom been brought into the field, even for siege work. The movements of the artillery before the battle were superintended by Colonel Holcroft Blood, an engineer officer who was chief of the ordnance train, and who was subsequently promoted to brigadier-general. On the field the duke himself saw to the placing of the batteries. He spent the hours of waiting, before the infantry joined battle, in conversing with artillery officers and watching their men serve the guns. During the afternoon, when the whole of the left wing had crossed the stream in front of the village of Blenheim, he ordered Colonel Blood to take a battery over the pontoons in support of the infantry. These guns went forward to within about a hundred yards of the enemy, and caused much slaughter, 'ensuring the success of our troops'.

In numbers the artillery at Blenheim was not strong; the proportion worked out at about one gun to every 1,000 bayonets. But it had been enough to administer an unpleasant shock to the marshals of Louis XIV, whose successor was to order that all his cannon should bear in bold lettering the words *Ultima ratio regum* (the final argument of kings).

Four years after Blenheim, in 1708, the artillery train for the siege of Lille consisted of a hundred guns, sixty mortars of calibres up to 15 inches, and more than 15,000 horses, taking up when on the march a total road space of about fifteen miles. The approach from Brussels was completed without the loss of a single wagon.

At Malplaquet (11 September 1709), Marlborough showed his mastery in the handling of cannon by the massing of forty pieces in one central battery, and by their subsequent advance, divided left and right into two groups, to support the infantry by cross-fire. It was a hard-fought victory, gained at a cost of 20,000 casualties as against about 11,000 French killed or wounded.

After peace had been made with the French in 1713, the military organization that had been built up was allowed, as so often before and since, to crumble away. This was made lamentably clear at the time of the Jacobite rebellion in 1715, when the Ordnance Board, on being ordered to fit out a train for service in Scotland, proved utterly incapable of doing so. A 'very confused' selection of field pieces from Edinburgh was to join the train. Harassed officers managed to get some of these cannon as far as Dundee, where orders were received to bring them all back to Edinburgh by sea, this forming part of a general process of the kind which is usually summed up as 'order, counter-order, disorder'.

This fiasco did more than anything else to convince those in authority that they dare no longer delay the formation of a permanent artillery force on a regimental basis, to be made possible by certain reductions and economies in other sections of the Ordnance Board's realm. The new corps was estimated to cost £15,539 a year. Under royal warrant dated 26 May 1716 – with Marlborough again master-general, after a spell of political disfavour – sanction was at last given for the establishment of four permanent companies of artillery. This action is now generally regarded as marking officially the birth of the regiment, though the title 'Royal Regiment of Artillery' was not conferred until 1722. At first only two companies were actually formed, at a cost of £4,891 a year, and with a total strength of 192 men, but the two other companies were added in 1727.

In the same year as the creation of the regiment, the office of master gunner of England was abolished after an existence of nearly five centuries. This left two principal subordinates, the master gunners of Whitehall and of St James's Park, but the former soon dropped out, and by the end of the eighteenth century the latter office had taken on its modern form by the appointment to it of a general officer of the Royal Artillery. The master gunner is selected by the sovereign personally, as captain-general, from among the colonels commandant. Although he is not necessarily the senior of these, as deputy for the captain-general he takes his place as head of all regimental institutions, chooses the representative colonel commandant for the year (with the sovereign's sanction) and recommends officers for appointment to that status. The master gunner has no operational powers (it is now customary to confer the honour on a distinguished retired officer), but his prestige and influence, as symbol and guardian of tradition, are almost unrivalled.

The first colonel of the regiment was Albert Borgard, a Dane by birth, who began his military career under the King of Denmark and also soldiered in the service of Prussia and Poland. Before he was induced by William III to enter the English service in 1692 (in time to fight at Steenkirk and Landen) he had already taken part in more than twenty battles and sieges, from Norway to the Rhine and from Namur to Hungary. He was adjutant of the first short-lived regiment of gunners under King William, and in 1715 had the thankless job of trying to make ready for the field an artillery train in the midst of 'such confusion as cannot be expressed', as he wrote in his diary.

At the siege of Valencia in 1705 Borgard had lost his left arm. In other actions he was wounded several times, in addition to receiving severe injuries in an explosion which killed seventeen onlookers during the recasting of some brass guns at the Windmill Hill foundry in 1716. Despite this he lived to be ninety-two, and when he died in 1751 he had given almost a lifetime of skilled, devoted service to the British Army, his last commission being as a lieutenant-general in 1739. A number of his descendants have been Royal Artillery officers.

1. *Artillery, Warlike Machines and Soldiers of the Fifteenth Century.* From an artist's impression by C.H.S., etched by L. A. Atkinson, aquatinted by Hill (British Museum)

2. 'Mons Meg', the famous sixteenth-century cannon of Edinburgh Castle (Crown Copyright, reproduced by permission of the Controller of H.M. Stationery Office)

3. The royal arms and regimental badge, heading the charter establishing the Royal Regiment of Artillery in 1716 (Royal Artillery Museum, Woolwich)

4. The royal warrant issued by George I on 26 May, 1716, for the establishment of the Royal Regiment of Artillery. From the facsimile in the R.A. Museum, Woolwich

George R 26 May 1716

Whereas Our Rt Trusty and Right Entirely beloved Cousin & Councellour John Duke of Marlboro Mast. General of Our Ordnance hath laid before us a Representation of Our Principall Officers of Our Ordnance setting forth the Inconveniences & Defects of the present Establishment of the Military Branch of Our sd Office amounting to £[illegible] and therein a Scheme Shewing that a greater Number of Gunners Engineers & other proper Officers may be Maintained for less than the present Expence And Whereas by Our Warrant of the 27 of November 1715 Two Compas of Gunners & Mattrosses were raised for the Service of Our Artillery sent upon the late Expedition to North Brittain And having been found always necessary that a sufficient Number of Gunners with proper Officers should be maintained & kept ready for Our Service And Whereas it hath been represented unto Us by Our said Master General of Our Ordnance that there are several Sallarys now vacant of the present Old Establishment which are not necessary and that other savings may be made by which part of the Two said Companys may at present be Maintained It is therefore Our Will & Pleasure that the said vacancys & savings be immediately applyed for the payment & Maintenance of One Serjeant Three Corporals Three Bombardrs Thirty Gunners & Fortyfive Mattrosses being such as have served well abroad during the late Wars & are no otherwise provided for and as other Sallarys shall become vacant in the said Military Branch That you apply the same to compleat the pay of the rest of the Officers & others according to the annexed List which with their respective Pays We do hereby approve and Establish and for so doing this shall be as well to you as to the Auditors of Our Imprests and all other Officers concerned a sufficient Warrant Given at Our Court at St James's the 26th Day of May 1716 In the Second Year of Our Reign

By his Matys Command
James Stanhope

To Our Rt Trusty & Rt Entirely beloved Cousin & Councellour John Duke of Marlborough Master General of Our Ordnance

THE ROUGH ROAD

'Trust in God, and keep your powder dry.' – Cromwell

Colonel Borgard's first active service with the artillery as a regiment was in 1719, when he went with Lord Cobham's force against Spain and bombarded Vigo, using 'forty-six great and small mortars of my own projection, which answered their intended end'. After troops had been landed, Vigo soon capitulated.

The regiment's first defensive operation came in 1727 when 20,000 Spaniards besieged Gibraltar, which had been in English hands since 1704. Lieutenant-Colonel Jonas Watson, whose service had started in the Flanders campaign of 1694, was sent out from England to take charge of about fifty-two artillerymen, who played the dominant role, assisted with much vigour by bomb vessels which enfiladed the enemy's entrenchments. After suffering heavy casualties, the Spanish force abandoned the siege at the end of four months.

Successes did not continue for long without a break. The organization of the artillery as a regiment had been one of the few redeeming features in a period of military cutbacks, political corruption, inefficiency and weakened morale. The Army was in fact at a low ebb during the twenty-five years of peace, or absence of major war, between the Treaty of Utrecht and the outbreak in 1740 of the War of the Austrian Succession, and the gunners did not escape involvement.

The first large-scale overseas operation in which the Royal Artillery took part, and its first appearance on the other side of the Atlantic, was an abject failure, through causes broader than any defects in the artillery itself, though these certainly existed. This was the attempt in 1741 against Cartagena, on the coast of the old Spanish Main, in what is now Colombia. At the head of the British force was General Wentworth, a weak, indecisive character who accepted the command reluctantly on the death of Lord Cathcart, the original choice. Even a good commander would have been hard taxed to accomplish anything with the material placed at this general's disposal.

Fortescue, in his monumental history of the Army, writes: 'Although the least foresight must have shown that the brunt of the work would fall upon the artillery, the gunners furnished to Wentworth were raw yokels, just caught up from the plough and wholly ignorant of their duty, while their commander was incapable and his second a drunkard. . . . Of the eight battering cannon, one was found to be unserviceable and the rest were all of different patterns, while the shells, like the hand grenades, were of bad quality.'

Wentworth bickered with Admiral Vernon, the naval commander, and nothing was achieved. Battle casualties were few, though they included Colonel Watson, killed during the bombardment of Cartagena at the age of seventy-eight; but hundreds of soldiers died wretchedly of fever on board the transports. Some of the miseries of this expedition have been described in *Roderick Random* by Tobias Smollett, who was a naval surgeon at the time.

Another feeble performance, this time much nearer to the critical eyes of the British public, occurred in 1745 as a part of the artillery side of the action against the Jacobite rebellion. For this duty the whole of the British artillery in Flanders, where by this time Britain was once more engaged in war with France, was recalled; it amounted to four companies, organization into batteries and brigades being still a thing of the future.

General Hawley, who had been appointed commander-in-chief, Scotland, to act against Prince Charles, reported that the gunners from the garrisons at Berwick and Edinburgh proved to be 'civilians who had been foisted on to the establishment for the sake of their votes, and were not intended to be of any other service'. He wrote: 'The heavy artillery is still at Newcastle for want of horses, which were sent to Carlisle for no use. The major of artillery is absent through sickness. I suspect his sickness to be a young wife; I know him. I have been obliged to hire a conductor of artillery, and seventy-odd men to act as his assistants for the field artillery. I was three days getting them from the Castle to the Palace Yard and now they are not fit to march.'

There was much futile marching and counter-marching. At

Prestonpans the guns were manned not by the Royal Artillery but by sailors. At Falkirk, 'the guns were hard and fast in a bog, and were not once in action', according to Major Francis Duncan, author of the first part of the regimental history. 'As soon as the peasant drivers, who had been engaged with the horses, saw the Royal Army waver, they promptly fled; out of the eight guns which had accompanied the king's troops, seven fell into the hands of the enemy.'

There was a different story to tell after Culloden, where the victory over the Young Pretender's clansmen may be said to have been won by the artillery. While Prince Charles's guns were ill-aimed and badly served, the Duke of Cumberland's cannon 'made dreadful lanes through some of the clan regiments. It was with extreme difficulty that the men could be kept in their places to stand this murderous fire.'

In spite of this, the fiasco at Falkirk left a bad taste; but it did serve one good purpose. As in 1715 the unwieldiness and poor equipment of ordnance trains on the old pattern had brought recognition of the need for a permanent artillery force, so in the 1745 rebellion the ignominy of Falkirk compelled the nation to see the folly of a field artillery that could not be sure even of enough transport to take the field. The seed was sown, though the harvest was to be long in ripening.

Before continuing the artillery's story in the long series of eighteenth-century wars, it is well to have clearly in mind that, despite setbacks, the Royal Regiment managed throughout this period to improve its reputation fairly steadily in all theatres. With few exceptions, however, its role in pitched battles, whenever the infantry was in an adequate state of efficiency, was still a subordinate one, the decisive weapons being the musket and bayonet (the pike had been discarded by about 1700). Massed batteries as winners of battles were not to come before the Napoleonic age. Nevertheless, the British artillery, without any revolutionary advance in equipment, increased slowly but surely in numbers and effectiveness; and it is somewhat ironic that this progress was due in large measure to the fostering shelter of the Board of Ordnance, that same creaky monolith of power whose administrative weaknesses had caused so many headaches for artillerymen in the field, and would continue to do so for many years.

With all its faults, the Ordnance Board at least enabled the gunners to develop as a corps with a body of specialized knowledge and doctrine of its own, led by officers who had learned their jobs thoroughly, both in theory and in practice. One great benefit was that the Royal Artillery escaped the evils of the purchase system, under which almost any young man of good birth, provided he was capable of riding, shooting and issuing orders with the right air, might, if he had enough money, pay his way up to the rank of captain or even lieutenant-colonel before he was twenty-one, while giving the barest minimum of time and attention to military duties in peacetime, and in wartime sometimes evading service with his regiment if it chanced to be ordered to one of the more unpopular stations, such as the West Indies.

From the start it was laid down that Royal Artillery officers should be promoted from the ranks. This practice was modified later, but a good many did come up the hard way. For an artillery officer it was never enough to be merely a dashing fellow and a hard rider, though these qualities were not despised. Even in the eighteenth century gunnery was a science, and its practitioners had to be prepared for real study, to acquire at least a grounding in many subjects – mathematics, ballistics, chemistry, as well as man-management and horse-management. As a result the artillery tended to attract men of a rather different stamp, often more serious-minded. Mostly they came from the ranks of the gentry or professional classes, but among them were men with little or no private means, who would have stood practically no chance of making headway in any of the smart, and expensive, regiments of cavalry or foot. It would not be too much to say that the artillerymen were professionals at a time before that term could be fully applied to most of the officers in other corps of the Army.

A landmark in the regiment's history was the founding in 1741 of the Royal Military Academy, not only for the practical and theoretical instruction of cadets, who already existed, but for the professional education of 'all the raw and inexperienced belonging to the military branch of the ordnance'. Classes were attended by all officers and men off duty, as well as by the gentlemen cadets. From its birth the RMA ('the Shop'), which later extended its scope to include engineer cadets, did work of great value in raising the professional level of the artillery, and the standard was maintained after the foundation of the Royal Military College at Sandhurst.

With the founding of the Academy, Woolwich, which was already a centre for the manufacture of guns and explosives, took on added importance as the home and focus of the regiment. All the home-based artillery companies, except one which was detached at Greenwich when the Warren was overcrowded, were stationed there. Most of the men were billeted out (this was before the existence of a general barrack system), and each night after roll-call the orderly corporals were required to make the rounds of all quarters, 'those in private lodgings, as well as those billeted in public houses, and make a report to the officer of the guard of those who are absent'. Captains were to 'advertise all their deserters in the newspapers'.

Old standing orders, preserved in the regimental records, give many other glimpses into the details of army routine from about 1740 onwards. Great attention was paid to correct clothing and the care of it. It was laid down that 'when any man is discharged he is not to take his coat or hat with him, unless he has worn them a year'. No soldiers must be allowed to go out walking 'without their hats being well cocked'. On no account must they 'carry their victuals from the bakers or any other weight on their regimental hats', nor should they work in their blue uniform coats, but in 'frocks or surtouts'. As for the officers, they were enjoined to wear on parade hats 'cocked in the Cumberland manner', and no others. They were 'not to appear under arms in bob wigs', and were ordered 'to provide proper wigs for such of their respective men that do not wear their hair, as soon as possible'. All troops below commissioned rank were forbidden 'to wear ruffles on the wrists when under arms, or any duty whatsoever'.

For a special parade, a guard of forty men was ordered, 'to consist of ten of the handsomest fellows in each of the companies'. In the early days all recruits for the artillery had to be at least 5 feet 9 inches tall; this requirement was later reduced.

Junior officers, and their batmen, apparently had a watchful eye kept on them. It was provided that 'no subaltern officer is for the future to have a servant out of any of the companies. . . . All the officers' servants who are awkward at the exercise of the small arms to be out every afternoon with the awkward men, and the rest of them to attend the exercise of the gun. . . . The captain or commanding officers of companies are not to give leave of absence to any of their recruits or awkward men. . . . That none of the lieutenants go to London, stay all night out of quarters, change his guard, or any other duty without the general's or commanding officer's leave'. Officers responsible for squads were to inspect them once a week 'to see that every man has four good shirts, four stocks, four pairs of stockings, two pair of white and one pair of black spatterdashes, two pairs of shoes, etc. and that their arms, accoutrements and clothes are in the best order. . . . The captains are to give directions to their pay-masters to see that the initial letters of every man's name are marked with ink in the collar of their shirts'.

The cadets, in the earliest days of the Academy, and before, did not wear uniform, and were notorious for indiscipline. So unruly were these youths (they joined between the ages of fourteen and fifteen and a half) that one of the tasks of the duty officer at the Warren was to make occasional visits to the class-rooms and make sure that the masters were not being plagued or even pelted. An order dated 10 October 1740, said: 'Complaints having been made to the Board that the following persons belonging to the Company of Gentlemen Cadets in the Royal Regiment of Artillery have been very negligent of their duty, viz., Francis Volloton, Archibald Douglas, etc. etc. . . . and that Francis Volloton has been absent about twelve months, and not so much as attended the muster, and has otherwise misbehaved himself, it is the Board's order that the said Francis Volloton be broke, and the rest suspended from their pay till they show cause to the contrary.'

High spirits were apparently not confined to the cadets. Another order, issued twice, gave warning that 'none of the men play at long bullet on Plumstead Road, of which they are all to be acquainted'. In the event of graver misconduct, it was laid down that 'if any non-commissioned officer or gunner makes himself unfit for the king's duty, either by drinking, whoring, or any other bad practice, he [the officer] will send them to the hospital at London for cure, and discharge them out of the regiment'.

Some idea of the sternness of discipline may be obtained from a series of orders in April 1749, concerning preparations for a parade in Green Park, at which the regiment was to be reviewed, for the first time, by the king. One paragraph said: 'The first man that is seen drunk, or the least in liquor, he shall be immediately brought to the halberts and there receive 300 lashes and afterwards be drummed out of the regiment with a rope about his neck. The guard to mount tomorrow in black spatterdashes, and the officers in boots.'

When Britain sent an expedition to Flanders in 1742, in support of Maria Theresa of Austria against the French, the artillery contingent amounted to two companies, with sixty-four gunners and 140 matrosses. Later another company went out, and twenty-four 3-pounders were present on 27 June 1743, at Dettingen, the last battle in which a King of England led his troops in person. The battle is remembered for the gallant conduct of George II and the stubborn bravery of the infantry; the artillery's share was small.

The gunners showed up to better advantage in 1745 at Fontenoy, where Lord Charles Hay of the Guards is supposed (probably incorrectly) to have offered his famous invitation: 'Gentlemen of the French Guards, fire first.' It was a French victory, after hard fighting. The battalion guns, served by artillerymen and hauled on drag-ropes in the front line of the attack to within thirty yards of the enemy, gave the infantry gallant support, while the 6-pounders, though heavily outnumbered, tackled the French batteries; but efforts were hampered by the fact that, once again, the civilian drivers had taken themselves off, with their horses, early in the day. Among the artillery subalterns at Fontenoy was Forbes Macbean, who had joined the regiment as a 'cadet matross'.

After the drain-off of resources to meet the Jacobite rebellion, there was a delayed but substantial increase both in men and guns, and the regiment received the thanks of the Duke of Cumberland for its bravery at Val, where the artillery had thirty men killed, nineteen wounded, and twenty-five taken prisoner. Fourteen more were killed at the siege of Bergen-op-Zoom.

Before the war dwindled to an end in 1748, the diminutive 1½-pounders had been discarded, and 9-pounders and 12-pounders were introduced, but the standard field gun was still the 6-pounder, which normally had with it a hundred round-shot and thirty rounds of grape. Howitzers of 8-inch and 10-inch calibre were also in use, firing shell like the mortars. One new custom which the gunners brought back from the continent was the addition of fifers to the regimental drummers. The fifers, said to be the first in the Army, were taught by John Ulrich, a Hanoverian brought from Flanders by Colonel Belford.

In 1751 the vexed question of the Army status of artillery officers was officially settled in a declaration by the king, stating 'the rank of the officers of the Royal Regiment of Artillery to be the same as that of the other officers of his Army of the same rank, notwithstanding their commissions having been hitherto signed by the master-general, the lieutenant-general, or the principal officers of the ordnance'. From this time, all artillery commissions were signed by the Sovereign.

Four years later, in 1755, the number of companies, which had been reduced from its wartime peak of thirteen to ten, was raised to sixteen. In the same year a sharp reminder that not all campaigns would be fought in familiar European conditions was administered with the disastrous end of General Braddock's expedition aimed at Fort Duquesne in French Canada. For this attempt there was an artillery contingent of about a hundred of all ranks, with ten light guns, accompanied by twenty-one civilian attendants of the train, also 'ten servants and six necessary women'. A contemporary diagram shows the guns spaced out at intervals along the column of infantry, store wagons and pack horses. Ambushed in the woods beside the Monongahela, Braddock's force was cut to pieces, the stiffly drilled infantry being quite incapable of any effective reply to the well-aimed fire poured in by the French-Canadians and their Indians from the shelter of the trees. For a time the artillerymen stood firm and 'sent round after round crashing uselessly into the forest', but in the end all the guns had to be abandoned. Among the ablest officers present at this desperate affair was George Washington, fighting for the English with the same cool courage that he was later to use so memorably against them.

A tonic for regimental pride was given at home in the following year, 1756, when it was laid down that 'the artillery takes the right of all foot on all parades'. It has been said that this privilege was probably based on the position of the man-hauled 3-pounders on the right of each battalion when in action, though any such rigid precedency in deployment (on the lines of the old cavalry and infantry, which actually claimed and took position in battle according to seniority) had already ceased to make practical sense so far as artillery was concerned.

More to the point, in practical terms, was the enlargement of the regiment to twenty-four companies, now grouped into two battalions, with brigades of four to six guns each, all of the same type, as the normal tactical unit. By 1757, after its first practice camp at Byfleet, the regiment had a total strength of 2,531. All this, and more, was to be needed for the stern tests that lay ahead in Europe, North America and the East.

VICTORY AND DEFEAT

'The fortunes of war are always doubtful.' – Seneca

The battle of Minden, the allies' first telling blow in the Seven Years War, will be remembered above all, for at least as long as there is an Army, for the six British regiments – the 12th Foot (Suffolks), 37th (Hampshires), 23rd (Royal Welch Fusiliers), 20th (Lancashire Fusiliers), 51st (King's Own Yorkshire Light Infantry), and 25th (King's Own Scottish Borderers) – which, with three Hanoverian battalions, marched steadily through the crossfire of sixty cannon towards the mass of French cavalry, halted within close range and then, when the enemy squadrons moved against them, tore them to pieces with volleys of musketry at a distance of a few yards. But the contribution of the artillery was scarcely less outstanding, and the battle is notable as demonstrating once for all the value of concentration and of mobile action by the field batteries. It should have sounded the death knell of the battalion guns, though in fact their end was not yet.

The three companies of British artillery were under Captain William Phillips, who joined as a cadet gunner in 1746, and he had with him three other captains, Forbes Macbean, Duncan Drummond and Edward Foy. Before the battle their units had been skilfully concentrated by the Count of Lippe Buckeburg. A French commentator later bore witness that the British guns were by far the cleanest and best maintained in the Allied Army. At Minden on 1 August 1759, the gunners showed that they were not just spit-and-polish soldiers.

Macbean's brigade of ten 12-pounders was so well handled that the guns on the enemy's left flank were silenced. Towards the end of a hard day of counter-battery and infantry support work, it fell to Macbean and Foy to gather the laurels of the pursuit once the French had broken. Limbering up, they moved their guns 'with astonishing rapidity' along the fringe of the Minden marsh, halting from time to time to hammer the retreating enemy, until finally the British took post opposite the bridges of the Bastau, where they punished the fugitives so severely that they could not be rallied until they had fled far beyond their camp. Forty-three French guns and all the baggage were captured.

General Westphalen, Chief of Staff to Ferdinand of Brunswick, the allied commander, wrote afterwards that, while every battery had done well, those of the English had worked wonders. Prince Ferdinand gave instructions that the following gratuities should be paid: Phillips, 1,000 crowns; Macbean, Drummond and Foy, 500 crowns each.

One strange episode at Minden, concerning the cavalry, is of some artillery interest because it involved an officer who subsequently became master-general of the ordnance – John Manners, Marquis of Granby. In the battle, Granby, as colonel of the Blues, was subordinate to Lord George Sackville, the cavalry commander. At a crucial stage Sackville, for reasons best known to himself, refused despite repeated orders, until it was too late, to attack with the cavalry. Granby protested, unavailingly; Sackville returned to England under a cloud. After being court-martialled at his own request, he was declared by eleven lieutenant-generals and four major-generals to be unfit to serve His Majesty in any military capacity whatever, and the king with his own hand deleted Sackville's name from the list of privy councillors. Later, under his new name of Lord George Germain, he came to the fore again, was appointed secretary of state for the colonies in spite of objections, and was responsible for a good deal of the harassing interference which plagued British senior officers in America during the War of Independence.

Granby, very naturally, was furious about the Sackville incident at Minden. His chance to redeem the name of the cavalry came before long, at Warburg on 31 July 1760, when he led a brilliant charge by twenty-two squadrons. Before the final gallop the cavalrymen covered two miles at the trot, the guns accompanying them 'at a speed which amazed all beholders'. Somewhere during the long hard ride Lord Granby's hat and wig flew off, but he pushed on regardless, his bald pate shining in the sunlight, amidst roars of delight from the troopers pounding along behind him. Later the British batteries, at the gallop, swept down to the River Dymel, unlimbered on the bank, and harassed the retreating French, who lost in the battle a total of at least 6,000 dead, wounded or captured.

Granby, that stout warrior of the old school, was appointed master-general of the ordnance in 1763, and commander-in-chief three years later, also serving as governor of the Royal Military Academy and colonel-in-chief of the corps of artillery and engineers. Today he is known by title, if nothing else, to all who patronize the many English public houses named after him.

One of the last actions of the war in Europe in which the artillery figured prominently was the siege of Fritzlar in February 1761. Here Forbes Macbean, now a brevet major, shelled the town with howitzers. After it capitulated, Macbean received Prince Ferdinand's personal thanks, and the citizens of Fritzlar were ordered to pay him 4,000 crowns in lieu of their bells, which were regarded as a perquisite of the artillery commander at a successful siege. This is the last known instance of successful enforcement of this traditional privilege, which dates back to the middle ages; the practice was officially discountenanced, and dropped, after a claim to indemnity for the bells of Flushing in the Walcheren expedition of 1809.

Across the Atlantic, three companies of the Royal Artillery, manning 150 guns, had taken part in the capture of Louisburg in 1758. In the year of Minden, the fall of Quebec assured British overlordship of the whole vast territory of Canada. Wolfe's defeat of Montcalm was a triumph of the infantry volley; but one artillery subaltern, Lieutenant J. Yorke, with a few gunners, contrived to drag a single piece up the steep, narrow path to the Heights of Abraham. By the time the French attempted to retake Quebec, in 1760, Brigadier Murray had a fine train of artillery. The ammunition supply failed, however, the wagons being stuck in snowdrifts. Some of the guns were spiked and abandoned in deep snow and mud, but the survivors of the contingent were brought safely back to Quebec.

Thousands of miles to the east, under the burning skies of India, in battles against the French and their inconstant native allies, British dominance was being asserted over the greater part of the sub-continent. In these actions the fire support was supplied, in the main, by the artillery of the Bengal, Madras and Bombay presidencies under the East India Company, though gunners were sent out from England on occasion. The effect of the artillery was sometimes out of all proportion to its numbers. More than once a few rounds from the guns were sufficient to send thousands of the Indian irregulars fleeing in wild disorder before the French troops had been seriously engaged.

At Clive's great victory of Plassey in 1757, the field guns, served by Royal Artillery men and sailors, and firing through embrasures in an embankment, wrought much destruction. In a later battle, Sir Eyre Coote's success at Porto Novo in 1781 over the forces of Hyder Ali of Mysore, the slaughter among the dense masses of the Indians' Army was almost entirely due to the fire of the British artillery. This action, a decisive one for India, was fought with odds of at least ten to one against the British. Their losses were slight, while enemy casualties were put at not less than 3,000 dead, and twice as many wounded.

Not long after the end of the Seven Years War in 1763, cuts were made in the artillery, as in other arms, but some additions had been carried out before the outbreak of the American War of Independence, in which sixteen companies of the regiment were engaged. In this unhappy conflict, fought under severe disadvantages, soldiers shipped from England or the West Indies (with some Germans) waged as best they could, under mediocre generals, and sometimes in small forces separated by hundreds of miles, a war which few Englishmen liked, against elusive rebels and in the midst of dubious American 'loyalists', more than a few of whom turned snipers after obtaining British passes.

In rough country with bad roads, the 3-pounder, already obsolete in Europe, was found indispensable. Light 6-pounders and 12-pounders were also brought into play where possible; even for sieges nothing heavier than the 24-pounder was employed. Set-piece battles were rare, and in none of them could the power of massed artillery fire be marshalled, but on a number of occasions the gunners, in spite of all difficulties, gave a good account of themselves.

The Royal Artillery's earliest appearance in the war was at Lexington, just after the first shots had been fired in the town of Concord on 18 April 1775. Although the gunners' fire in covering the British withdrawal was effective, the commanding officer of the troops complained afterwards that the artillery had been inadequately supplied with ammunition, having only twenty-four rounds per gun. Colonel Cleaveland, RA, in an indignant letter to the master-general of the ordnance, wrote: 'I had a wagon with 140 rounds on the parade, and Lord Percy refused to take it, saying it might retard their march, and that he did not imagine there would be any occasion for more than was on the side boxes.'

At Bunker's Hill, in June of the same year, twelve field guns went with the attacking force, but the support given to the infantry was poor. It has been stated that the artillery was supplied with roundshot that were too large for the guns. Fortescue writes that 'in the attack on the entrenchment and redoubt the British field guns were silent because shot of the wrong calibre had been sent across from Boston, while the officers declared it impossible to move their pieces within grapeshot range owing to a patch of swampy ground'. Colonel Cleaveland, in his official report, said merely that he 'sent sixty-six rounds to each gun, and no more than half was fired'. Whatever the reason, it seems to be a fact that only eight of the twelve guns came into action and that, partly as a consequence, the foot battalions suffered heavily under the accurate fire of the Americans, some of whom had rifles, not muskets.

Cleaveland, who had much to contend with, did obtain some results. After the evacuation of Boston he secured permission to buy 700 horses in Halifax and Annapolis and, when he protested about the 'wretches whom he had to hire as drivers', at two shillings a day, a draft of trained drivers was sent from England. Some badly-needed reinforcements of gunners also arrived, as well as a number of 3-pounders mounted in such a way that they could be carried on horses or mules. These mountings, which proved their worth, were devised by Captain Congreve, later Sir William Congreve, founder Commandant of the Royal Military Repository; it was his son who invented the type of rocket used at Waterloo.

During Cornwallis's advance into New Jersey the artillery did considerable damage, but after Washington's appearance on the scene Colonel Mawhood's detachment near Princeton had to leave behind two of its four 6-pounders, 'all the horses belonging to the guns being shot, and the axletrees of the other carriages broke by firing'.

Artillerymen fought a losing battle in General Burgoyne's hopeless thrust southward out of Canada. In the action at Bemis Heights on the Hudson (19 September 1777) the 62nd Foot had scarcely sixty men standing at the close of the combat, while the small artillery detachment, which stood to its guns until the end, lost thirty-six out of forty-eight men. In October, six guns were abandoned after every man and horse belonging to them had been shot. A few days later Burgoyne capitulated at Saratoga.

One artillery officer had distinguished himself in an unusual role earlier in this expedition. He was Captain Carter, who commanded a gunboat flotilla that gave chase to American galleys near Skenesborough. Several of the largest galleys were captured, and the colonials set fire to the rest, with considerable loss.

The post at Stony Point on the Hudson changed hands several times. A number of British, including artillerymen, were taken prisoner there in 1779. One subaltern, Lieutenant Roberts, escaped by swimming nearly a mile to the sloop *Vulture*.

Phillips, of Minden fame, who had been among those held by the Americans after the capitulation at Saratoga, was later released in an exchange of prisoners. In 1781 he was appointed major-general in Virginia to take command of a mixed force of 3,500, whose officers included Benedict Arnold, a man widely disliked as a renegade. Phillips's appointment went through after some cavilling by representatives of other arms.

A number of armed vessels had been assembled in the James River by the Americans. Two 6-pounders and two of the 3-pounders ('grasshoppers') were brought to the river bank to deal with them. This they speedily did, without a single English casualty, although they were exposed to the fire of the *Tempest* (twenty guns), the *Renown* (twenty-six), *Jefferson* (fourteen) and smaller craft, in addition to musketry from militia across the river. The ships struck their colours. Having no boats, the British were unable to secure their prizes; the Americans scuttled some of the vessels and set fire to others.

Within a short time of this action General Phillips died of a fever, after thirty-four years of exemplary service. He was the first artillery officer to attain high rank in command of a force of all arms.

For about two years during the British occupation the commandant of the city and garrison of New York was an artilleryman, James Pattison, Colonel in the Royal Artillery, Major-General in His Majesty's forces in America. He was the second son of a London merchant who owned an estate at Woolwich and Plumstead, and he had married a daughter of Colonel Borgard. From a house at the foot of Broadway, near the point still known as the Battery, Pattison, a kindly and urbane man, governed the city with tact as well as efficiency. He successfully formed a militia of several thousand loyalists for part-time guard duties, and a company of Virginia blacks was also enrolled for work with the artillery and in the ordnance yard.

The winter of 1779 was so severe that the water between Manhattan and Staten Island froze, and guns were carried across on sledges. From official correspondence it appears that the artillerymen, like other soldiers, had no greatcoats, except a few for wear on sentry duty. An appeal for an issue of coats had been made in 1777; the request was granted in 1786 (three years after the war had ended), but only for ten to each company. Two years later this was increased to fifteen.

A large proportion of the gunners in New York were sent out for the siege of Charleston in South Carolina. One of the transports carrying equipment, with an artillery detachment under Captain Collins, foundered in a gale, but the troops and stores, including 1,000 barrels of powder, were rescued by a privateer. A total of 167 Royal Artillery men were with Cornwallis's force in the capitulation at Yorktown on 19 October 1781, which shattered the last hopes of victory over the colonials.

From this melancholy record one may turn with relief to a historic feat of endurance and ingenuity – the defence of Gibraltar during a blockade and siege by the Spaniards and French that lasted three years, seven months and twelve days. At the outset in September 1779, the governor, Sir George Eliott (afterwards Baron Heathfield), who had served for a time in the artillery, found the number of gunners quite inadequate – only twenty-five officers and 460 other ranks to man 452 guns and mortars. Soldiers from the infantry were attached to help out.

Shellproof batteries were hewn within the solid bulk of the Rock, each provided with grates for the heating of shot, while the governor's aide-de-camp, Lieutenant Koehler, designed new carriages enabling guns to be depressed to an angle of 70 degrees. After the enemy bombardment began in April 1781, continuing almost day and night for eighteen months, the garrison was often under fire from 200 guns on the landward side and 212 in specially built battering ships.

As a result of the blockade rations ran short. In Gibraltar town best tea fetched £2 5s 6d a pound, a goose thirty shillings, a live pig £9 14s 9d, and a sow in pig more than £29. Scurvy broke out, and the arrival of a ship with a cargo of lemons was a great event.

On 27 November 1781, a sortie was ordered against the advanced works of the besiegers, three-quarters of a mile from the Rock and within a few hundred yards of the main enemy lines. With the 12th Foot (one of the Minden regiments) who made this sortie went 114 men of the Royal Artillery, split up into small parties and charged with a special mission to spike the guns, destroy the magazines, and burn the enemy's defence works. Drinkwater in his history of the siege writes: 'The exertions of the workmen, and the artillery, were wonderful. The batteries were soon in a state for the fire faggots to operate; and flames spread with astonishing rapidity into every part.'

Colonel Abraham Tovey, the artillery commander (he had joined the regiment as a matross) did not live to receive the report on this success. For some time he had been a sick man, and he died before the sally force returned.

At the height of the great attack in September 1782, the artillerymen loaded with red-hot shot which set on fire at least six of the floating batteries. Towards evening most of the exhausted gunners were relieved, on the governor's orders, by a hundred men from the Marine Brigade. So parched with thirst were the artillerymen that they drank the water in which the gun sponges had been rinsed.

At last, on 2 February 1783, the guns fell silent, and letters were sent by the Spaniards to the governor, announcing that preliminaries for a peace had been signed. The Royal Artillery had lost, in dead and wounded, 196 men, almost 40 per cent of the total strength. The garrison had fired 57,163 shot, 129,151 shell, and 12,681 charges of grape – altogether nearly 200,000 rounds, using 8,000 barrels of powder. For their part in the defence, the thanks of King George III were conveyed to the regiment by the Duke of Richmond, Master-General of the Ordnance.

NEW MEN, NEW WAYS

'The principal foundations of all states are good laws and good arms.' – *Machiavelli*

Immediately after the peace treaty of 1783 the Army was once more cut down, the Royal Artillery, which had reached a strength of 5,337, being reduced by more than 2,000, leaving each company with only sixty-seven men. In the few years of peace that lay ahead, the regiment was able to make a number of internal changes. Barracks had been built at Woolwich; dress and personal arms became slightly more practical; officers no longer bore the fusil (short musket) and sergeants ceased to carry halberds. The rank of matross was abolished, all enlistments being made as gunners.

A greater need was for the fuller application of scientific knowledge to gunnery. Here, fortunately, it was possible to build on solid foundations before the onset of the struggle with revolutionary and Napoleonic France, which was to plunge Europe into twenty-three years of almost unbroken war.

Benjamin Robbins, mathematician and military engineer, the son of a Quaker, had laid the groundwork for modern ordnance theory and practice in his *New Principles of Gunnery*, published as early as 1742. This swept away much old myth and guesswork about the nature and use of gunpowder and the laws governing the flight of shot. It was Robbins who invented the ballistic pendulum, an ingenious device for measuring the velocity of a projectile. The tangent sight was introduced in or about 1779.

At the royal powder factory at Waltham, Sir William Congreve greatly improved the quality of gunpowder, which in earlier days had been supplied by contractors. At the Woolwich repository he also supervised a school of instruction in mounting and dismounting ordnance, crossing obstacles, and generally overcoming difficulties by the resourceful use of simple means. Congreve is credited with being the first to allot numbers to the men of gun detachments to distinguish their duties.

Work of a broader kind to standardize the drill of the Army as a whole was that of Sir David Dundas, an artillery officer who as a young man was so poor that he walked from Edinburgh to Woolwich to be enrolled as a lieutenant fireworker. Dundas later transferred to the 56th Foot and rose to be commander-in-chief in 1809. His new 'Rules and regulations for the formation, field exercise and manœuvres of His Majesty's forces', brought into operation in 1792, were based in part on impressions gained as an observer at the last manœuvres held under the eyes of Frederick the Great. Not surprisingly, they retained a fair amount of Prussian stiffness, but they had the merit of sweeping away the old anomalies under which many regiments had obstinately continued to drill and move according to systems of their own individual choice.

A young officer who was busy about this time on labours of great significance was Lieutenant Shrapnel, later Lieutenant-General Sir Henry Shrapnel, inventor of the shell named after him, which was largely to supplant other types of field artillery ammunition for well over a century. Shrapnel was commissioned in 1779. It was in 1784 that he began, at his own expense, the experiments which ultimately produced the shrapnel shell – a spherical case containing small shot, with a bursting charge to scatter them in a deadly hail on the enemy. Almost from the first these shells were widely acclaimed, though they had at least one critic of high rank, as we shall see. Shrapnel also produced the brass tangent slide, invented certain fuses, compiled range tables, and improved the construction of mortars and howitzers.

Another subaltern, engaged on efforts of a quite different kind, was William Mudge, RA – 'Mudge of the Maps'. He was the son of a Plymouth doctor, and one of his godfathers was Dr Johnson, who presented him with a book and a guinea as reward for his diligence after entering the Royal Military

Academy. On being commissioned, Mudge went out to join the troops fighting the American colonists. At the end of the campaign he returned to England, studied higher mathematics, and was appointed to the Ordnance Survey in 1791.

The project for a general survey of England was being pushed forward energetically through realization of its military value in the event of renewed war with France. Within a few years Mudge became director of the survey, and settled down to his great work – a series of detailed maps covering the entire country on the scale of one inch to the mile. Mudge reached the rank of major-general, but died at fifty-eight, worn out by incessant work. His career is probably the classic example of an artillery officer of the more studious type achieving results of lasting practical value to the nation.

At Woolwich, one of the duties of the senior officers was the testing of inventions submitted by both artillerymen and civilians. Some of their offerings were curious ones, and many got no further than the testing ground. In 1790 the field officers were repeatedly called together to consider the merits of a 3-pounder leather gun, devised by Sir John Sinclair, and bringing to mind 'Sandy's stoups' in the seventeenth century. One of the most prolific inventors was a Mr Wiggins, who produced rifled guns to fire spherical shot, fed in on a belt. Wiggins had some success with his smaller pieces, a 1-pounder and 9-pounder, but when he exhibited before the board an 18-pounder, 'on the second round it burst into a great number of pieces'.

Although officers were available for duties of this kind, any move to interfere with the manufacturing departments at the Arsenal, which came under a separate body of Ordnance Board officials, was sternly discouraged. Attempts by successive commandants to obtain control over the Arsenal met with no success.

A great step forward for the regiment was taken with the introduction of the Royal Horse Artillery, the first two units being formed on 1 February 1793. (There were already horse artillery batteries in the Prussian, French and Swedish armies.) All field guns of this period were, of course, horse-drawn. The essential difference between the two types was that, while in the ordinary field batteries some of the gunners rode on the limbers and wagons, in the RHA, to lighten the load and give added speed, all the detachment, whether drivers or gunners, were on horseback, at least from about 1830 onwards.

From the start the Horse Artillery was an élite corps, with extra pay, the best horses, and the pick of the recruits joining the regiment. Officers vied with one another to be accepted by this favoured body, the embodiment of dash and efficiency, which has retained its special prestige right down to the twentieth century, in which the old RHA batteries, now mechanized, have served with the armoured divisions as their forerunners did with the cavalry. The unofficial watchword has always been: 'Quick into action; once engaged, as few moves as possible; all moves at top speed.'

One great advantage, even in the beginning, was that the Horse Artillery had its own trained soldier-drivers; it was never bedevilled by the antiquated nonsense of hired civilians. The rest of the artillery had to wait a little longer, until 1794, for the establishment of a military Driver Corps. Even then, this was an *additional* corps, not part of the Royal Artillery. Until after Waterloo its officers were drawn from a different source and, for as long as the Driver Corps survived, its members were never artillerymen. Four years after the corps had been formed, it was still noticeable that at a Woolwich parade in 1798 the field battery guns 'each drawn by three horses in single file, were driven by contract drivers on foot, hired for the occasion, dressed in white smocks with blue collars and cuffs, and armed with long carters' whips of the ordinary farm pattern'.

Naturally, time was needed to bring the RHA to peak condition, and the first appearances of the artillery in expeditions against the forces of the French Republic were made principally by old-model batteries, sometimes with poorer mobility than in earlier campaigns. Through years of neglect, the field guns were inferior to those of the Austrian and Prussian allies. Ammunition wagons were heavy and clumsy, and their horses were still harnessed one before the other, instead of two abreast, which made them difficult to control and took up much road space. Both harness and wagons were, in fact, practically unchanged since Marlborough's time.

The Duke of York's Army in the Flanders campaign of 1793 was still burdened with the pernicious system of battalion guns, which weakened the field batteries and encumbered the infantry without yielding any worth-while fire-power. An attempt to take Dunkirk was a failure.

The duke had been expecting transports with heavy artillery and other material for the siege, and also a fleet to cover his right flank, which had been harassed by enemy gunboats. Henry Dundas, one of the ministers chiefly responsible for the conduct of the war, had said he was preparing a siege train, but there was a great shortage of gunners in England. At last transports arrived – with gunners, but without guns. In desperation, the duke had a frigate at Nieuport stripped of her cannon, which were brought up to arm batteries not only towards the town, but facing seaward to drive off the gunboats. It was not enough.

In the withdrawal along the coast Lieutenant Shrapnel, who had been wounded during the siege, came to the fore, making two suggestions which were successfully adopted. One was to lock the wheels of gun-carriages and skid them over the sands; the other was to light decoy fires at night so that enemy fire could be wastefully diverted while the British slipped away. Some guns were saved, but thirty-two of the larger calibres had to be left behind.

Later in the same year a Royal Artillery contingent from Gibraltar, under Major Koehler, formed part of the British force sent to hold Toulon on behalf of the French royalists, but although British ministers had known for two months about the occupation of the city, no stores were sent from England, and no field guns had been provided for the men disembarked by Admiral Hood. After considerable losses the defence was given up as impracticable. In the evacuation, the key position of Fort La Malgue was held by Koehler and 200 gunners, who left after spiking the guns and seeing the last man of the main body safely embarked. Among the artillery officers opposing the British during the siege was a twenty-four-year-old Corsican *chef de bataillon* named Napoleon Bonaparte.

A few weeks later, after Britain had accepted an invitation from Corsican nationalists that their homeland should be placed under the king's protection, Major Koehler was sent to the island with Lieutenant-Colonel John Moore to weigh up the possibilities. When the fleet sailed with troops to drive the French out of Corsica, the British, in the aftermath of Toulon, still had no artillery except four light howitzers and two mortars, sent from Gibraltar, and not one item of ordnance stores had been received from London. After the disembarkation in the Gulf of San Fiorenzo and the capture of a tower, the army commander despaired of being able to move forward over rugged country the heavy naval guns that were needed to attack a redoubt. Koehler and Moore, however, urged that the attempt should be made. It succeeded, and before long the French capitulated, in spite of dissension between the British naval and military leaders. Koehler wrote to Lord Grenville: 'We never should have had any footing in Corsica but for the perseverence of myself and Moore. This Lord Hood declared to me on the public parade at San Fiorenzo.'

After the outbreak of the revolt in La Vendée, vague plans were made in London for a descent on the French coast to aid the royalists. Lord Moira, who had been named to command the expedition, asked for 12,000 troops, including 200 artillerymen with twenty guns. Not more than a hundred gunners, one-third of whom were recruits, were collected for him. Moira declared that, if he must face deficiencies such as this, he thought the ministers had better arrange the expedition without consulting him, as he could not accept responsibility. Henry Dundas then wrote begging that the Duke of York might spare a company of gunners; but the duke himself was so short of men that he had been obliged to lay up two of his field howitzers to make up the number for the defence of Nieuport. Eventually, Moira was persuaded to make do with something over a hundred gunners. These were to have been made available at Portsmouth, but they were not forthcoming. 'The confusion here is indescribable,' wrote Moira from the port. Airy promises were made to the unfortunate French royalists, but no steps to help them were taken until it was too late.

In the Low Countries, at the outset of the campaign of 1794, which produced some extremely hard fighting, it was discovered, some weeks after the Duke of York had asked for a siege train, that the application had been mislaid at the Ordnance Office. Artillery drivers were still so scarce in England that the master-general tried, without success, to hire some from Hanover. Lord Moira had now come out, bringing with him guns, but no drivers. Only two captains were available to supervise a mass of horses; thus artillery which had been sent to replace cannon lost at Tourcoing became an embarrassment rather than a help. When some of the new corps of wagoners did arrive, it was found that many of them, recruited in London, were wretched specimens. Colonel James Craig, the Duke's Chief of Staff, said: 'A greater set of scoundrels never disgraced an army. I believe it to be true that half of them, if not taken from the hulks, have at times visited them. . . . They have committed every species of villainy, and treat their horses badly.'

This was at a time when the French had already done much to put their military house in order after the chaos of the revolution's terrorist period. Their horse artillery, within a year of its formation, had been augmented to 8,000 men, and the field batteries, including detachments for battalion guns, had been given an establishment raised to 26,000.

In 1795 it was decided to forestall the French by seizing Cape Colony from the Dutch. About 500 men of the 78th Foot were put on board ships of a naval squadron; Major-General Craig pleaded for at least a couple of battalion guns to go with them, but was told that none could be spared. Disembarking at False Bay, the troops and two battalions of seamen, making a total of 1,600, set out to march northward along the coast from Simonstown – still without a single field gun, while the Dutch had plenty of artillery. Protected by a gunboat and the launches of the fleet, armed with carronades, the small force managed to seize a Dutch battery with two heavy guns and an advanced post in which were two howitzers and a field gun, so that when the Dutch attacked next morning they were received with fire from the captured cannon. A British sloop from St Helena arrived on the following day with 400 men and nine field pieces, but little ammunition.

Stores were landed and a depot established, after which the main body advanced on Cape Town. As no draught animals of any kind could be obtained, the guns were dragged by volunteers from the ships. The men, who were on short rations, had on them four days' supplies, and all other stores and ammunition also had to be carried by the seamen and soldiers. A march of six miles was made with a loss of one man killed and seventeen wounded. Alarmed by the entry of three ships into Table Bay, the Dutch capitulated with little further resistance.

Two years later, about the time of the naval mutinies at Spithead and the Nore, there were isolated cases of disaffection among artillerymen at Woolwich, but these were publicly disavowed by the majority of the gunners. Shortly after this, in May 1797, the Government suddenly granted to the Army an increase in pay, for which the military authorities had been vainly pressing for several years. In 1798, during the brief French invasion of Ireland by troops under General Humbert, the only British soldiers who stood firm on the heights above Castleton were an artillery contingent, about a hundred men of the 6th Foot, and a small body of fencible dragoons. The French suffered heavily from a cannonade by eleven guns, and their Irish supporters took to their heels.

The Royal Horse Artillery's senior unit, Major Judgson's A Troop, later to be famous as the Chestnut Troop, had its baptism of fire in 1799 during the fruitless expedition to the Helder, aimed at the capture of the Dutch fleet. A Troop had an extraordinary mixed armament – three 6-pounders, two howitzers, and two 12-pounders. This was all the stranger because some 6-pounder battalion guns had been grouped into a battery, presenting the odd spectacle of the light artillery, designed for rapid movement, having guns considerably heavier than those used by what should have been the medium batteries. With its unsuitable armament, the troop, fighting gallantly, was overrun by Vandamme's cavalry, who sabred many artillerymen and carried off two or more of the guns, but these were recaptured by Lord Paget in a charge with the 15th Light Dragoons.

In the Mediterranean, the most important of the early ventures was the Egyptian campaign in support of the Turks against the French. Here the Ordnance Board became the target for bitter criticism by artillery officers responsible for the assembly and preparation of equipment.

From the isle of Houat on 24 June 1800, Major Cookson wrote pointing out 'how much the service is retarded for want of a clerk of stores who understands his duty. There is a man here who calls himself conductor of stores, but he is very far from being adequate to the situation, being, in the first place, *incapable of writing*. . . . On board the *John*, when in a hurry for completing the ammunition, we were much annoyed to find *12-pounder flannel cartridges* for the $5\frac{1}{2}$-inch howitzers, and other like mistakes; however, I *set the women* to work and got over that difficulty and many others. . . . All the camp equipage for the officers and men whom I brought out is deficient; do, pray, therefore send me out the camp equipage for my company.'

Great ingenuity was shown in the improvisation of special transport suitable for the sands of Egypt, as described in Brigadier-General Lawson's narrative on preparations at Marmorice Bay in Asia Minor. Carriages were made that would enable guns and ammunition to be hauled or carried by horses, mules, or camels. One of Lawson's ideas for helping gun carriages over soft sand was 'lengths of rope, about 30 feet each, with narrow netting between, to receive the wheels upon' – a device not unlike the steel matting used in the Western Desert and elsewhere in the Second World War.

After the landing in Egypt there was an acute shortage of draught animals, but the desert crossing was accomplished after weeks of effort. Alexandria was invested, French resistance collapsed, and the Royal Artillery won praise for 'the celerity with which the guns at the siege of Alexandria had been brought up . . . as they had to be carried over almost inaccessible rocks'. Artillerymen who served in this campaign were granted, as a personal non-regimental distinction, the right to wear a sphinx cap badge with the word 'Egypt'.

During the operations in Corsica some of the Royal Artillery had done duty with Nelson's seamen; in 1805, the year of Trafalgar, there were a number of artillerymen on board HMS *Victory* in the West Indies. The regiment was actively engaged in the operations resulting in the capture, or recapture, of St Lucia, San Domingo, Trinidad, Guadeloupe, Tobago and Curacoa.

The war in Europe was marked in 1806 by the almost forgotten British victory at Maida in Calabria, where the artillery was prominent. This success, with only slight loss, against seasoned French troops under General Regnier, had a considerable moral effect, both in England and on the Continent. At least 2,000 of Regnier's men were killed or wounded, the rest taking to the hills in some disorder. From about this time dates the build-up in southern Italy and Sicily of an artillery garrison which was retained for several years.

For the siege of Copenhagen in July, 1807, there was a sizeable Royal Artillery force, consisting of 989 gunners and 525 drivers, with 694 men of the King's German Legion artillery, all under Major-General Thomas Blomefield. Lieutenant-Colonel Harding wrote to London: 'No captain-commissary or veterinary surgeon has arrived. We are in great distress for horses. . . . We are distressed by so many different things being put in the store-ships; the things at bottom are required first, in many instances, and we half unload the ship to get at them.' Nevertheless, Copenhagen was bombarded, with extensive damage, and yielded on terms that included the surrender of the Danish fleet, the main object of the expedition.

A notable feat in the Caribbean in 1809 was the capture of Martinique, where day-and-night fire from forty-two pieces brought about the surrender of the French within five days, 'the British artillery being so well served that most of the fort guns were quickly dismantled'. Officers and men of No. 8 Company, 7th Battalion RA, were assembled by General Prevost to be consulted about what trophy should be bestowed on the company as a reward. At first a French gun, elegantly mounted, was proposed, but the officers, knowing that they were about to return to Halifax, Nova Scotia, that a new war with the Americans was likely, and that in such an event the company could hardly take the gun with it, chose instead an axe, to which a brass eagle was affixed, and a drum. The axe was to be carried by the tallest man in the company, who by virtue of his office would be permitted to grow a moustache. Ever since then this unit, and its successors, have borne the name of 'The Battle Axe Company'.

In the same year as Martinique, sixteen companies of the regiment, equipped with 144 guns and mortars, took part in the Walcheren expedition, which came to a dismal close, largely through failures in the supply services, with many deaths from sickness, after the reduction of the fortress of Flushing by a combined naval and military bombardment.

It was at the close of this campaign that General Macleod, as artillery commander, put forward the claim to the bells of Flushing, or compensation in cash to their value. The mayor and corporation replied, through the French commandant of the city, that they acknowledged with due respect a right established by custom immemorial, but hoped that consideration would be given to the already desperate plight of the citizens. To this Macleod said that, in view of the destruction suffered by Flushing, he had no wish to add to the misery of the inhabitants by demanding full compensation, but, on principle, he could not waive the ancient rights of the corps. Setting the value of the bells at £2,000, he would be prepared to accept £500.

The mayor answered with an indignantly worded letter in curious Dutch–French. It was unbelievable that such an exaction should be enforced, he wrote, and he was resolved to protest, if necessary, to the British Government, whose generous soul would ensure that justice was done, notwithstanding the claim of 'Messieurs les officiers de l'Artillerie'. In reply, Macleod said his claim had the full support of the commander-in-chief, but, as a final concession, he would be content with a token payment of one hundred guineas, 'to be disposed of in charity to the soldiers' wives and widows of the Royal Artillery, as may be thought proper hereafter'. But if the Flushingers persisted in their idea of an appeal to Parliament, then 'it is understood that the appeal is for the *whole* of the bells, or for the full amount of their value'.

A plea was in fact submitted to England, and legal opinion was taken at Doctors' Commons. The findings, as conveyed by Sir Charles Robinson in a letter to Lord Liverpool, the Prime Minister, were unfavourable to the artillery. Robinson wrote: 'With respect to the bells of the church, the demands of the artillery are, I conceive, altogether unsustainable. It is apparently not supported on the part of the prize commissioners, since they do not advert to that claim in their letter of 4 October. Anciently, there prevailed a law of pillage, which assigned to different corps and to different individuals a privileged claim to particular articles. Whether this was a privilege of the artillery under the ancient custom of England, as described in the petition, I am not informed; but in the modern usage of respecting property and public edifices, and more particularly those set apart for divine worship, such a demand cannot, I conceive, be sustained.' So ended an ancient custom.

At home, by this time the Royal Artillery had a headquarters staff of its own, to provide a link between the units and the Ordnance Board. The first brigade major was Captain John

Macleod, who became deputy adjutant-general in 1795. The regiment had been further increased by two battalions, and by 1806 eleven troops of horse artillery had been formed. When the question was raised of the RHA's claim to take the right of the line when parading with cavalry, the master-general had said in June 1804 that he 'considered the privilege so well established by practice, as well as opinion, that he is unwilling to suppose it can be disputed. They were encamped on the right of all the cavalry (of the Blues) at Windsor'. This precedence continued to be held as a matter of course until 1869, when it was ordered that the Household Cavalry, on occasions at which the sovereign was present, should have priority as a bodyguard, except when the RHA paraded with guns.

Presently the artillery was to be tested on a broader stage, and with more at stake, than ever before. The spring of 1808 had witnessed the rising of the Spanish people against Napoleon, who had placed his brother, Joseph, on the throne in Madrid. Under Sir Arthur Wellesley (later Lord Wellington), 9,000 British troops, subsequently increased to nearly 30,000, sailed for Portugal. In the Peninsula, after many tribulations, the gunners, and more especially the Royal Horse Artillery, were to come into their own.

IN THE PENINSULA

'It is always easy to begin a war, but very difficult to stop one.' – *Sallust*

When the British landed at Mondego Bay in July 1808, the dangers and precariousness of their situation were soon painfully clear. In Spain the regular troops of that country were totally unreliable as antagonists of Napoleon's marshals; the guerrillas were not yet the potent factor which they later became in harassing, tying down and gradually draining French strength; and the Portuguese were still an unknown element of doubtful value. On the fringe of a broad, arid and largely mountainous land with atrocious roads, the British faced not only the challenge of superior forces led by experienced French generals, but also a daunting array of supply problems, made worse by contradictory instructions, Ordnance Board errors, failure to obtain adequate information from those in charge in London, and ministerial objections to anything that involved the spending of more money.

At the start the expeditionary force had with it more artillery than available draught animals, and some guns had to be left on the beach for the time being. Colonel William Robe, the first of the British artillery commanders in the Peninsula, wrote from on board the transport *Kingston* that the horses supplied by the Irish commissariat were of pitiable quality – 'cast-offs from the cavalry', many of them being aged, lame, even blind.

A few days later he pointed out that the horses obtainable in Portugal were almost useless, as they were much too small and lightly built for artillery work. 'Three hundred good horses would have cost the country no more for transport than as many bad ones, and what we shall do for the brigade to be landed remains to be decided.' As regards stores, he added: 'Had I been made acquainted with what was to have been embarked, I should not have gone on board ship till the proper proportion had been furnished . . . I did at hazard request Mr Spencer to put on board one hundred sets of horse shoes and some nails, thinking them an addition to what would be provided for us. These are all I have had for the horses of three brigades; and had I not obtained some more from the commissary-general, belonging to the horses delivered to us, the horses must have taken the field *barefoot*.'

At first there was not one Royal Horse Artillery unit in Portugal. Within a few months three six-gun field brigades had been manned, but transport was still so scanty that in some cases the guns were drawn by oxen with a pair of horses in the lead. Somehow the artillery, or part of it, contrived to keep up with the rest of the Army, and at Vimiero it contributed largely to the decisive repulse of the French attack. Here Shrapnel's new shells proved most effective. From Torres Vedras, Robe sent a letter to the inventor, saying that the artillery had been 'complimented both by the French and our own general officers, in a way highly flattering to us. . . . It [the shell] is admirable to the whole Army, and its effect dreadful. I told Sir Arthur Wellesley I meant to write to you. His answer was: "You may say anything you please; you cannot say too much".'

Not long after Vimeiro came the singular Convention of Cintra, which provided for the evacuation of Portugal by the French, but on terms that disappointed the English. There were changes in command. Wellington returned to England in some disgust, perhaps justified, and Sir John Moore took over. The tragedy of Moore's retreat to Corunna, and of his death which robbed the Army of one of its most brilliant progressive-minded officers, is part of familiar history. In the long winter march through the snow, a heavy toll was exacted by hunger, toil and cold. Discipline was strained, sometimes to the breaking point. There were well over 2,000 men who 'strayed', but not a single straggler from the eleven brigades of guns was reported, and Moore himself wrote: 'The artillery consists of particularly well-behaved men.'

So great was the persistent shortage of draught animals that when some of the Royal Horse Artillery landed at Corunna the officers' mounts were taken – on repayment, but without the owners' consent – and they were left to provide themselves with such horses as could be found.

With the first unhappy phase of the war at an end, by April,

1809, Wellington had resumed command and a new campaign opened, aimed at clearing the French from Portugal once for all. The army of about 20,000 men now included four brigades of 6-pounders and 5½-inch howitzers and one of 3-pounders – a total of thirty guns in all, which was the maximum for which transport could be found. For the gunners, an unsettling influence lay in the repeated changes in the chief artillery command. Five officers in succession failed to give enough satisfaction to Wellington to hold the appointment for any considerable length of time, and there was no feeling of permanency until at last Alexander Dickson, a lieutenant-colonel in the Portuguese service but only a captain in the Royal Artillery, took over, still wearing his rather shabby Portuguese uniform, as a matter of tact to avoid offending his British senior officers, and steel-rimmed spectacles. This first-class officer – he was later to become Major-General Sir Alexander Dickson, Director-General of Artillery – held the post with marked success until the end of the war in the Peninsula.

The choice was an excellent one. Here it must be said, however, that Wellington, great soldier though he was, had little real sympathy or liking for the artillery as a corps and as an arm. Although repeatedly he accorded the gunners official words of praise – he could scarcely have avoided doing so – on many occasions he displayed an impatience almost amounting to open antipathy concerning artillerymen. His faith was in the bayonet, and brilliantly the foot soldiers fulfilled it; but more than once his grudging attitude towards the artillery had its consequences in battle, quite apart from the serious threat to morale. For some of his coolness, no doubt, he had reasonable grounds. Any commander-in-chief in his position would naturally have disliked the power wielded by the master-general of the ordnance under the absurd system of dual control over the artillery; and Wellington was by no means the only person in the Army who viewed with some disaste the apartness of the regiment, as a specialist body of men who looked not to the general in command but to the Ordnance Board for permanent advancement in their careers. Understandably, the duke was also frequently incensed about the undisciplined conduct of many junior officers, some of whom, he said, tended to regard written orders as 'amusing novels', to be lightly scanned and cast

5. John Churchill, first Duke of Marlborough, one of the great benefactors of the artillery. From a painting after Sir Godfrey Kneller (National Portrait Gallery)

6. Albert Borgard, the first Colonel of the Royal Artillery. From a painting in the R.A. Museum

7. Major-General Sir Alexander Dickson, who was Wellington's principal artillery officer in the Peninsula. From the painting by Salter, 1838, in the R.A. Mess, Woolwich

8. Lieutenant-Colonel Henry Shrapnel, inventor of the Shrapnel shell. From a painting by Arrowsmith in 1817 (R.A. Museum)

9. A sergeant of the Train of Artillery, 1710, equipped with hanger (short sword), powder horn, and linstock with burning slow-match (R.A. Museum)

10. An artillery driver, with smock and whip, about 1780 (R.A. Museum)

aside, rather than as binding commands. In fact, this seems to have applied less to the Royal Artillery than to some other regiments. Nevertheless, Wellington's disfavour remained, a fruitful source of possible trouble, and the actual cause of much deep resentment, as we shall see.

Meanwhile, the campaign made headway, the Douro was crossed, and combined British, Spanish and Portuguese forces moved on Madrid. At Talavera in July 1809, the thirty British guns, though opposed by a far stronger body of artillery, were admirably served. On the day after the battle, however, the approach of a French army on his left rear compelled Wellington to retire, and the winter was spent mainly in constructing the celebrated Lines of Torres Vedras in anticipation of a new French invasion of Portugal.

During the slow withdrawal in 1810 the Chestnut Troop, under Captain Hew Ross, distinguished itself at the Coa in covering the retirement of the infantry and breaking up the ranks of the enemy advancing on the same bridge, which became blocked with a mass of French dead and wounded, piled up almost to the height of the parapets.

The defence of the ridge of Busaco against Marshal Masséna's pressure was a success, but one which left some sharp criticism in its train. Duncan, the regimental historian, writes: 'Lord Wellington displayed an ignorance of artillery tactics, from the results of which he was happily saved by the intelligence and gallantry of the representatives of that arm. . . . Instead of massing his artillery in reserve until the attack should develop itself, the guns were placed, as a rule, in the easiest parts of the position, where it was supposed that the French *would* attack; and they were massed in these positions so as to form an excellent mark for the enemy's fire.'

Yet the French attack failed, Marchand's division losing so many of its men under a 'murderous cannonade' that Marshal Ney, who was present on the field, personally ordered a withdrawal. With good reason might Wellington report to Lord Liverpool, the Prime Minister: 'I am particularly indebted to Brigadier-General Howath and the artillery.' Sir H. D. Ross wrote later in his memoirs of the 'immense slaughter the enemy sustained from the shrapnel shells thrown from my brother's guns, and for a short time by those of Captain Bull's troop'.

At Fuentes d'Onoro in May 1811, two guns of Bull's troop, under the second captain, were cut off by French cavalry and given up as lost. Napier has described how they were saved: 'Presently a great commotion was observed among the French squadrons; men and officers closed in confusion towards one point, where a thick dust was rising, and where loud cries and the sparkling of blades and flashing of pistols indicated some extraordinary occurrence. . . . Suddenly the multitude became violently agitated; an English shout pealed high and clear, the mass was rent asunder, and Norman Ramsay burst forth, sword in hand, at the head of his troop, his horses, breathing fire, stretched like greyhounds along the plain; the guns bounded behind them like things of no weight, and the mounted gunners followed close, with heads bent low and pointed weapons, in desperate career.' Fuentes d'Onoro led to the evacuation of Portugal by Masséna, a tough old soldier who had risen from the ranks.

For the first full-scale siege against the border citadel of Badajoz in the spring of 1811, the artillery had to make shift with an almost farcical battering train of antiques from the Portuguese fortress of Elvas. The total comprised sixteen brass 24-pounders and eight 16-pounders, with two 10-inch howitzers and six 8-inch. The heavier pieces originated in the reigns of John IV and his son, Alfonso, bearing dates from 1646 to 1653; there were also some Spanish guns from the days of Philip III, the oldest dated 1620.

An engineer noted that 'in general there was room between the shot and the bore to put a man's finger in . . . so that the practice was necessarily vague and uncertain'. It had been intended to bombard the fortress at the rate of 120 rounds a gun per day, but it was soon discovered that the wretched old ordnance could not possibly stand this, and the daily quota was reduced to eighty rounds. Even with this, guns were repeatedly made unserviceable by the effects of their own fire.

Perhaps fortunately, this first attempt against Badajoz had to be abandoned, after assaults had failed, on the approach of a relieving force under Marshal Soult. It was Marshal Beresford, not Wellington, who commanded for the allies in the heroic and bloody combat of Albuera, where the French had more than

8,000 killed or wounded, and the Anglo-Portuguese Army nearly 7,000.

A few months later, when siege was laid to the frontier fortress of Ciudad Rodrigo, Wellington had a battering train of sixty-four pieces that included thirty-four 24-pounders and four 18-pounders. These, shipped from England, had been left lying on board ship in Lisbon harbour since March 1811, or earlier, as it was not considered prudent, in face of a superior enemy and with uncertain means of transport, to attempt to make use of them in the first attempt on Badajoz. When the siege train was moved at last, no fewer than 1,100 oxen were used for the guns alone, apart from artillery stores.

Bombardment was opened on 14 January 1812. On the night of the sixth day, when more than 9,000 rounds had been fired by the artillery, the breaches were declared practicable, and Wellington announced in orders that 'Ciudad Rodrigo *must* be stormed this evening'. It was done, not without cost.

The commander-in-chief was now able to turn his attention again to Badajoz, which still presented a formidable obstacle. For the new siege there were assembled sixteen 23-pounders, sixteen howitzers of comparable size, and twenty Russian-made 18-pounders that had been found in the Lisbon arsenal. With the guns were 862 men, all from field batteries, and two-thirds of them Portuguese. In an eight-day bombardment, 24,000 roundshot were needed to smash three gaps in the walls from a range of some 600 yards. The infantry then stormed the breaches, capturing the town after fierce hand-to-hand fighting with many casualties. In the siege operations as a whole the Army lost 5,000 men.

With Portugal secure as a base, the border fortresses in the hands of the allies (and Napoleon, on the other side of Europe, committed to the disastrous folly of the bid for Moscow), the tide began to turn against the French in the Peninsula, but for the British there was still much hard fighting ahead in Spain – the country where 'large armies starve and small armies are beaten'. At Salamanca in July 1812, after seeing one after another of their generals fall, and fighting at times confusedly for lack of orders, the French at last fled in utter rout. In this battle Wellington had fifty-nine guns compared with Marmont's seventy-four. During the enemy's final effort, against the village of Arapiles, shrapnel fired from howitzers did heavy execution on infantry, and one of the French batteries was put out of action by the same means.

The horse artillery was almost continuously at work with the cavalry division during the pursuit. In the next month Madrid was occupied. This, however, was followed by a failure – the siege of Burgos, in which the artillery available proved quite insufficient for its task. Only eight of the heavier guns were deployed, and ammunition was in such short supply that Colonel Dickson offered rewards for anyone who brought in spent shot that had been fired by the French. More than 1,400 rounds were collected in this way; it was found that the enemy's 16-pounder shot fitted the British 18-pounders well enough, while their 8-pounder ammunition could be fired by the 9-pounders of the British field brigades.

At length, on news of the approach of a strong French force, the siege was relinquished. Sir H. D. Ross, in a letter from Madrid, commented: 'Why he (Wellington) should have undertaken the siege of such a place which means so very inadequate appears very extraordinary, especially as there was little or no difficulty in augmenting it to any extent, either from the guns and ammunition found here, or the ships at St Andrew.'

During the siege of San Sebastian, in which four companies of the Royal Artillery were successfully engaged, there occurred the first recorded instance of British guns firing over the heads of infantry assault columns, lifting their fire only at the last moment. This feat, calling for a precision that was probably without parallel at the time, was accomplished by cannon, carronades and howitzers that prevented the defenders from making a stand on the ramparts just above the storming parties. It was the more remarkable because, according to Napier, the two new battering trains had been sent out from England, 'with characteristic negligence', with only enough shot and shell for one day's firing. Into the breach with the assault force went ten volunteers from the artillery, who did stout work by turning two of the enemy's guns upon the garrison, driving the defenders from the walls.

After San Sebastian the enemy were in full retreat towards the French border. Before this, at Vittoria (21 June 1813), their fate had already been sealed by a crushing defeat in which the whole of the French baggage, including a great amount of rich loot, fell into British hands. Colonel Dickson wrote later, with perhaps a slight, pardonable exaggeration: 'The French were generally obliged to retire 'ere the infantry could get at them.' At Vittoria he had finally been able to bring together a really powerful concentration of field artillery, some ninety guns; the French had an even greater number. There were frequent artillery duels before the headlong flight of the enemy's entire army. In a despatch Wellington remarked briefly: 'The artillery was most judiciously placed by Lieutenant-Colonel Dickson, and was well served. The Army is particularly indebted to that corps.'

Among the gunner officers who performed fine work at Vittoria was Norman Ramsay, central figure of the dramatic incident at Fuentes d'Onoro. Now he was to be involved in an episode of a very different kind, which has become famous in the annals of the regiment. On the day after the battle, Ramsay was given by Wellington a verbal order to take his troop for the night to a neighbouring village. The duke added that if there were any further orders he himself would send them; the exact wording of this is in dispute.

At six o'clock next morning an assistant quartermaster-general arrived upon the scene and told Ramsay to rejoin the brigade to which he belonged. The troop at once set out, but was soon overtaken by a rider with a written order from General Murray, Quartermaster-General of the Army, directing 'Captain Ramsay's troop to rejoin General Anson's brigade'. The troop halted, while Ramsay went forward to enquire about the route. At this point Wellington himself rode up and, after some exchanges with senior officers, ordered that Ramsay should be placed under arrest for disobedience, saying he had made it clear to the captain that he was not to move until he received the commander-in-chief's *personal* instructions. In point of fact, this was never said to Ramsay or understood by him, according to his own statement, and his account is confirmed by a sergeant and a corporal who were within earshot at the time of the duke's original order.

For some time, in spite of representations by officers of high rank, Norman Ramsay remained under arrest. Eventually, he was released, and after a time received a brevet promotion, but it appears that he was not mentioned in despatches for his service at Vittoria, as had been confidently expected. It must be borne in mind that Ramsay was not just a good average officer, but an outstanding one, liked and respected by all his comrades, and warmly admired by his men. He was regarded by all who knew him as the *beau ideal* of the Royal Horse Artillery, a hero who had brought honour upon the regiment. That such a person should be treated like a common defaulter for something that was, at the worst, no more than a misunderstanding created the worst possible impression. Rightly or wrongly, it rankled with many as a glaring instance of the duke's animosity and unfairness towards the artillery.

Ramsay himself took very much to heart the treatment he had received. Perhaps it is not too much to say that this unfortunate affair cast a lasting shadow over the brief remainder of this brave man's life.

In fairness, it should be mentioned that, on a more general matter about this time, Wellington did come to the aid of some artillery officers, though not without a dig (probably quite justified) at the Ordnance Board.

Slowness of promotion on the principle of seniority had long been a grievance in the Royal Artillery. Captain Hew Ross wrote: 'There has ever been a prejudice in the heads of our regiment against inferior officers obtaining brevet. Our senior officers, having grown grey themselves in the subaltern ranks, cannot endure the thought of their followers being more fortunate. After seventeen years in the service, I find myself seventy steps from a majority.'

Right down to 1813 a Board of Ordnance rule had forbidden the granting of brevet rank to second captains (seconds-in-command of batteries), even if they had been in actual command of their units for a year. Finally, a group of fourteen second captains serving in the Peninsula addressed to the Prince Regent, through Wellington, a petition seeking redress. Wellington told his artillery commander: 'Every word of this is perfectly just and true. I have already recommended some of these officers, but I suppose some damned ordnance trick has prevented their promotion; leave the papers with me and assure the second captains that I will do all I can for them.' The petition was granted.

On Shrapnel's new weapon, the duke, notwithstanding his compliment after Vimiero, said later that his faith in the shells had been 'much shaken'. He wrote: 'I have reason to believe that their effect is confined to wounds of a very trifling description. I saw General Simon [a brigade commander in Ney's corps, taken prisoner at Busaco], who was wounded by the balls of Shrapnel's shell, of which he had several in his face and head; but they were picked out of his face as duck shot would be out of the face of a person who had been hit by accident while out shooting.'

Three weeks later Wellington reported: 'They have been very destructive to the enemy in Badajoz when fired from 24-pounder carronades; and I have directed that some of them may be loaded with musket balls, in order to remedy what I have reason to believe is the material defect of these shells, viz., that the wounds which they inflict do not disable the person who receives them, even for the action in which they are received.'

The duke's reservations were in contrast with the enthusiasm of other senior officers, such as Sir Sidney Smith, famous as the defender of Acre. Smith thought so highly of the shells that he begged Shrapnel, in case the Ordnance Board did not provide enough of them, to let him know how he might obtain more at his own expense, and soon afterwards he placed a private order for a consignment of 200 rounds.

Wellington also showed some doubts concerning the new rocket weapons. These were tried twice in the Peninsula, largely, it seems, to please the Prince Regent, who was a friend of their designer, Major Congreve. The first trial, at Santarem in 1811, was unsuccessful, and the rockets were withdrawn from service. Later, in September 1813, the duke gave his consent to the return of a troop equipped with rockets, which, being more easily transportable than field guns, proved of value in the crossing of the Adour. After a time, however, Wellington, who was not alone in his scepticism about the accuracy of these projectiles, ordered the rocket troop to be rearmed with 6-pounders.

As the struggle in the Peninsula drew to a close in the crossing of the Pyrenees (with the gunners organizing their first mountain battery of the war, equipped with 3-pounders carried on mules), the artillery was able to forget minor irritants, for the time, in satisfaction at difficulties overcome and solid results achieved. This was almost entirely due to the hard, skilful work of the regimental officers and men in spite of the many imperfections of organization and supply. Not only had the Royal Horse Artlilery won its spurs magnificently; the general standard of the ordinary field batteries had also been substantially raised, though the need for still greater mobility was apparent.

Long before Wellington's victorious troops crossed on to French soil, units of the British Army, far away in America, were fighting another of the unhappy wars in which few of those engaged gathered any laurels. This war – almost completely forgotten in England today, though it is still a vivid memory in parts of the United States and eastern Canada – broke out in 1812 when the Americans, taking advantage of the European conflict, declared war on Britain and attempted an invasion of Canada. Most of the engagements were small in scale, though sometimes fierce; almost the only one of note, so far as the artillery is concerned, was the New Orleans expedition of 1814, and that accomplished nothing.

Once again the supply arrangements were chaotic. Colonel Dickson, who had come out by frigate to command the artillery, wrote home: 'With respect to our own ammunition and stores, great quantities of articles have been sent that are perfectly unnecessary and never have been demanded, whereas others greatly required have never been sent, although demanded in the most urgent manner.'

The British force under General Keane included 451 of the Royal Artillery, with some rocketeers among them, plus two officers and 246 men of the Driver Corps, which had been described by one RHA officer as 'a nest of infamy'. After a difficult approach through creeks and bayous, the troops had twelve guns ready for action against the Americans outside New Orleans. Dickson's first task was to deal with a fourteen-gun corvette lying in the Mississippi. The colonel, having 'a weakness for hot shot', bombarded this vessel with heated roundshot, and also shell, from guns on the levee. After 191 rounds he had the pleasure of seeing the corvette blow up, her crew having previously taken to the boats.

In the main effort against the outer defences of the city, on 1 January 1815, the British batteries were poorly constructed of sugar casks filled with unrammed earth; the gun platforms were uneven and unsteady, so that the carronades recoiled right off them each time they were fired, while the Americans' guns had strong emplacements made of cotton bales. After about three hours' firing most of the British artillery was idle for lack of ammunition.

A detached force, sent across to the west side of the Mississippi, made some headway, capturing enemy batteries containing sixteen guns and howitzers, one of which bore the inscription 'Taken at the surrender of Yorktown in 1781'. But elsewhere the attack lost impetus, Sir Edward Pakenham, who had taken over command, was killed, and the troops retreated.

Colonel Dickson was to have some consolation before long. Within five months he took part – not as chief artillery officer, but in a responsible post – in Wellington's first and last confrontation with Napoleon, at Waterloo.

THE WATERLOO MYSTERY

'It was a damned nice thing, the nearest run thing you ever saw in your life.' – *Wellington*

The traditional picture of the battle of Waterloo, the one that everybody knows, shows the unbreakable British squares, ably supported by the artillery, standing firm against every onslaught letting the French wear themselves out unavailingly, until the moment when the final culminating attack could be broken and hurled back, leaving the Prussians, joining in as night drew down on the field of slaughter, to complete the rout of Napoleon's shattered army. In view of the strange challenge which will be described a little later, it is relevant to say at once that – by and large, taking into account the fog of war and the difficulty in gaining a clear overall presentation of any battle – this familiar version, so far as it goes, is undoubtedly the true one, according to the bulk of all the available eye-witness evidence, which is voluminous in extent.

Waterloo was no masterpiece of the military art, but a 'hard pounding match' and a test of sheer fighting spirit and stamina. (Field-Marshal Montgomery, in his *History of Warfare*, dismisses the battle in a few lines as unworthy of serious study, because of the many errors committed by both commanders.) Wellington emerged the victor because his choice of position was sound, because he made the fewer mistakes, never for a moment losing his nerve, and because his trust in the British infantryman – 'that article', as he called him – was nobly justified.

In numbers there was no great disparity between the opposing armies on Sunday, 18 June 1815. The French strength was roughly 72,000, that of the allies about 68,000. Wellington had a mixed collection of British, Belgians, Dutch and Germans, including some formations of very doubtful quality. Against this, Napoleon was a sick man, past his best; he is believed to have been in severe pain on the crucial day, and exercised little direct control over the early stages of the battle, after having placed himself at a viewpoint from which it was impossible to see the whole of the field. In addition to the main body, the French had Grouchy's 33,000 men, but these were miles away, blindly chasing after Blucher's Prussians, who, having been beaten at Ligny on 16 June, had retreated towards Wavre, to the north-east, while part of the British force, which had been badly mauled at Quatre Bras, fell back northward towards the chosen position at Mont St Jean.

The British put into the field thirteen Royal Artillery troops or brigades, with seventy-eight guns; artillery of the King's German Legion and the Netherlanders brought the allied total up to 156. Blucher had 174 guns, Napoleon 366. In command of the allied artillery was Sir George Wood (of whom a gunner officer once disrespectfully remarked 'he is too fat'). Colonel Dickson, back from America, had been put in charge of three special brigades of 18-pounders. Six days before the battle no fewer than 1,000 drivers were lacking, partly through Wellington's insistence on the formation of the three heavy brigades, partly through the demands of small-arms ammunition transport.

It should be noted that the artillery, unlike a considerable part of the allied infantry, did not consist of raw units. Of the eight Royal Horse Artillery troops, five (Ross's, Gardiners', Webber Smith's, Beane's and Bull's) were made up of seasoned men from the Peninsula battles. Whinyates' rocket troop, which, as we have seen, had been ordered by Wellington to rearm with 6-pounders, had finally been allowed to bring a proportion of rockets with them, and had knocked out a French gun detachment in the retreat from Quatre Bras.

Wellington placed his divisions on the reverse slope of the low ridge where a country road crosses the Brussels highway before it dips into a broad shallow valley, on the southern side of which the French were drawn up. The allied position, giving some cover against artillery fire, was similar to several which the Duke had adopted with telling effect in the Peninsula. Marshal Soult, who had learnt his lesson through bitter experience, warned the emperor against making a frontal attack on Wellington in a position of his own choice. The marshal was snubbed for his pains.

After a preliminary cannonade by the French, the battle resolved itself into five acts. The first was the attempt by the enemy to seize Hougoumont, a large walled farmhouse in front of their left centre; for hours close-quarter fighting raged desperately here, Bull's troop firing shell with great accuracy over the heads of the British infantry. The second phase was the attack on the farm of La Haye Sainte, a few hundred yards in front of the allied left centre. Next came the famous series of charges by wave after wave of French heavy cavalry, who suffered terrible punishment from the guns deployed in front of the British squares. This was followed by Marshal Ney's dangerously successful attack on La Haye Sainte. Finally, in the great thrust at the allied centre by twelve battalions of the Imperial Guard, the head of the dense column was broken by the fire of Bolton's field battery *before* the British Guards and the 52nd Foot swept Napoleon's veterans in ruin down the slope.

A great deal of the day's confusion, and valour, can be seen through the eyes of one RHA officer, Captain Cavalié Mercer of D Troop, whose account of the Waterloo campaign appeared many years later, in 1870. Mercer, a general's son, commissioned at the age of sixteen, was thirty-two at the time of the battle. In private life he seems to have been a studious, reflective kind of man, with a taste for quiet country pursuits; he was an amateur artist of some talent. At Waterloo he was the senior second captain on the field, commanding a troop of six officers and 184 men, equipped with five 9-pounder guns and one $5\frac{1}{2}$-inch howitzer, with 220 horses. These were not the sorry nags of Peninsula days, but superb animals. When Blucher reviewed the Army on 29 May, he had said of this troop: 'Mein Gott! Dere is not von 'orse in diese batterie vich is not goot for Veldt-Marschal.' But, although it was to play such a notable part, Mercer's was not one of the more experienced units.

Throughout the whole of the day before the main battle, Captain Mercer had been busily involved in a fighting retreat. Arriving just too late to join in the action at Quatre Bras, he was given the task of covering the rearguard. While carrying out this duty he experienced (and was lucky enough to survive) an encounter with one of the real old hell-for-leather, neck-or-nothing military aristocrats – Lieutenant-General the Earl of Uxbridge, commander of the cavalry.

At one moment, when there was a danger of being outflanked by French cavalry, Uxbridge rode up, shouting: 'Here, follow me with two of your guns', and immediately led on into a narrow lane hemmed in by gardens. Mercer writes: 'What he intended doing, God knows, but I obeyed. The lane was very little broader than our carriages – there was no room for a horse to have passed them. His lordship and I were in front, the guns and mounted detachments following. What he meant to do I was at a loss to conceive; we could hardly come into action in a lane; to enter on the open was certain destruction.

'Thus we had arrived at about 50 yards from its termination when a body of chasseurs or hussars appeared there as if waiting for us. The whole transaction appears to me so wild and confused that at times I can hardly believe it to be more than a confused dream – the general-in-chief of the cavalry exposing himself amongst the skirmishers of his rearguard, and literally doing the duty of a cornet! "By God, we are all prisoners!" (or some such words), exclaimed Lord Uxbridge, dashing his horse at one of the garden banks, which he cleared, and away he went, leaving us to get out of the scrape the best way we could.'

The troop spent the night of 17 June in an orchard at La Haye Sainte. Soon after dawn a bombardier who had been sent for ammunition returned, bringing also some beef, biscuits, oatmeal and rum. The oatmeal was made into stirabout for the gunners' breakfast. Mercer and a fellow officer fared perhaps slightly better, sharing a scrawny chicken contributed by a German straggler who made his appearance through a hedge to share their camp-fire. Afterwards the captain gave a hand to some Guardsmen who were digging up potatoes in the kitchen garden of the farm. Then he set out to reconnoitre.

When the French cannonade opened, the troop, apparently forgotten by all, was still about a quarter of a mile in front of the allied line, completely exposed, almost in the middle of the battlefield. As Mercer began to move his guns towards the ridge he was met by an artillery officer who said that his brigade was being shot to pieces. Mercer promised to give covering fire; but soon he came upon his own major, who sharply reprimanded him for quitting his bivouac without orders. He was to go down the hill again, at once, and await further instructions. After some time an aide-de-camp brought orders to move. At the gallop, under fire, Mercer led the troop to a position in reserve, above Hougoumont and close to the 52nd Foot.

He was an onlooker when, in the middle of the charge by the Union Brigade of cavalry, Whinyates, the rocket specialist, seized his opportunity. (Earlier, when the commander-in-chief had been told that it would break this officer's heart to take away his rockets, he had replied: 'Be damned to his heart; let him obey my order', but apparently the duke relented.) Now, leaving behind the cumbersome bombardment frames, used for air shots with rockets, Whinyates galloped after the cavalry with his mounted detachment, carrying 12-pound rockets in holsters, sticks in quivers, and small triangular iron mountings for horizontal fire. Dismounting in the valley, the men found that the rye, not yet trampled down, was so high that they could not see through it, but they planted their triangles, let fly, and hoped for the best.

Their efforts did not make a favourable impression on Mercer, who wrote: 'Whilst our rocketeers kept shooting off rockets, none of them ever followed the course of the first; most of them, on arriving about the middle of the ascent, took a vertical direction, whilst some of them actually turned back upon ourselves – and one of them, following me like a squib until its shell exploded, actually put me in more danger than all the fire of the enemy throughout the day.'

After the first French cavalry charge Mercer was ordered up to the front line. He gave the word: 'At a gallop, march!'

From a distance Wellington noticed the troop and remarked: 'Ah, that's the way I like to see horse artillery move.'

Sir Augustus Frazer, the RHA Commander, rode up to the ridge with Mercer and passed on to him the duke's order: when attacked by cavalry, do not expose your men, but retire into the squares.

Shot was tearing gaps through the ranks of the Brunswick regiments as the troop came into position between two of their squares. Mercer gave the order: 'Form line for action. Case-shot.' Behind a low bank, with their muzzles only a few inches below its level, the guns were ready. The enemy's artillery fire ceased; then, out of the smoke, barely 100 yards ahead, with a glint of the sun on polished cuirasses, came Napoleon's troopers, riding at a sharp trot. The guns flashed and roared – and the ground in front of them was covered with a struggling mass of unhorsed, wounded men, while riders veered aside and others wheeled, trying to force their way back through the massed column of squadrons. Again the artillery fire, with every shot of the case striking home, until the rear ranks of the French opened and gave passage, and the attackers recoiled in failure down the slope.

Skirmishers now crept forward, sniping at the gunners, who had no muskets for self-defence. Mercer put his horse at the bank in front of the guns. Up and down he rode, encouraging his men. At 40 yards range several of the Frenchmen fired at him, but he was not hit.

Again and again the cavalry returned to the charge. Each time they fell in swathes, yet always a few pressed on, eddying round the squares, striving to find a weak point in the hedge of bayonets. Some, spurring their weary horses, rode right through the battery, others were killed within reach of the 9-pounder muzzles, while the gunners loaded and rammed and fired, and sponged and reloaded, like men caught up in an unreal and timeless nightmare.

Unlike other batteries, Mercer's troop, despite Wellington's order, did not take shelter inside the squares each time the cavalry surged upon them. He himself has given the reason: 'The Brunswickers were falling fast . . . these were the very boys whom I had but yesterday seen throwing away their arms and fleeing, panic-stricken, from the very sound of our horses' feet. Every moment I feared they would again throw down their arms and flee. . . . To have sought refuge amongst men in such a state were madness; the very moment our men ran from their guns, I was convinced, would be the signal for their disbanding. We had better, then, fall at our posts than in such a situation.' He therefore made his men stand to their guns until the cavalry were within a few feet.

Time passed. During a lull Sir George Wood, the artillery commander, rode up. 'Damn it, Mercer,' he said, 'you have hot work of it here.'

Now the troop was loading with the artillery's most lethal

weapon for ultra-short range work – case-shot on top of ball. Whole ranks of cavalry were swept away by the case-shot, while the roundshot cut deep into the columns. It was easier now to bring them down, for the French were balked by a mound of their own dead and wounded, piled high across the front of the troop position.

At last, hours after the guns had opened fire, the attacks died away. But the work of the troop was not yet ended. While its guns were joining in the disruption of the Imperial Guard, shot began to fall among the artillerymen from high ground far to the left, beyond the crossroads. This plunging fire caused havoc among the horses and limbers, which so far had received some protection below the ridge. Naturally assuming that a belated flank attack was being launched by the French, Mercer turned his two left guns and started to return the fire, 'but so few of the gunners were still on their feet, and these few were so exhausted, that they could not run the guns up into position after they recoiled, and at each round they fell back closer to each other, and to the limbers'.

Mercer dismounted and helped to serve a gun. Presently, out of the smoke and the gathering dusk appeared a furiously galloping horse, ridden by a tall man in an unfamiliar black uniform. Waving his arm, in broken English he called out to the troop commander: 'Vot you do? Dese are your friends, de Proosians!'

Mercer answered: 'The moment their fire ceases, so shall mine.' But the shooting continued. The remnants of the troop were saved only by some devil-may-care Belgian or Dutch gunners (Mercer thought they were drunk) who happened to be in a position from which they could enfilade the misguided Prussians and drive them off.

When he could snatch a moment, Mercer looked down the hill, across the valley now covered with dark confused masses of unidentifiable troops. The British cavalry and infantry had gone, the battle was won, and he and what was left of his troop were almost alone on the ridge, save for the dead and the wounded.

At that moment, as he sat wearily on a smashed gun-carriage, up rode an aide-de-camp, gesturing and crying: 'Forward, sir, forward!'

Mercer pointed towards the wreckage that lay all around him and asked: 'How, sir?' One hundred and forty of his splendid horses were down, the guns and limbers were in tangled heaps, and the men were almost incapable of stirring even to save their lives. Like most of the artillery, the troop was in no condition to join in the pursuit.

During the battle the artillery had fired 10,400 rounds, representing an overall average of roughly seventy per gun, though in fact not all of them were actually engaged. The British artillery and the King's German Legion gunners had a total of 332 casualties in dead, wounded and missing. Losses by the RHA and RA included four officers killed and twenty-one wounded. A total of at least 309 horses were lost or disabled.

In his despatch of 19 June, announcing the victory, the Duke of Wellington wrote: 'The artillery and engineer departments were conducted much to my satisfaction by Colonel Sir George Wood and Colonel Smyth.'

Senior officers gave unstinted praise for the conduct of the artillerymen under their command, naming a number of instances of gallantry and devotion. Brevet promotion was granted to nine regimental officers. The Prince Regent, on the recommendation of Wellington himself, appointed eight Royal Artillery colonels and one major as Companions of the Order of the Bath. Also at the duke's own request, five officers were given permission to receive from the Tsar of Russia the Order of St Anne, while Sir George Wood was authorized to accept a knighthood of the Order of Maria Theresa from the Emperor of Austria. The 'boon service' granted for the battle, and the Waterloo medal, were given to all artillerymen present, without exception.

After all this, one would have thought that the value of the artillery's services had been officially recognized and established beyond a shadow of a doubt. But a bombshell lay hidden, unknown to the Army in general and to the world, and not to make known its presence until more than half a century had passed. This explosive charge, of completely unexpected nature, was embodied in a letter from the Duke of Wellington to Lord Mulgrave, Master-General of the Ordnance. (Rather ironically, Wellington himself was master-general from 1818 to 1827.)

The letter was not written immediately after Waterloo, but

six months later, on 21 December 1815, and it was not published until 1872, when the second Duke of Wellington included it in a volume of supplementary despatches and correspondence by his father, who died in 1852. It had been sent in reply to a letter from Lord Mulgrave, seeking approval for his decision to refuse a request by certain field officers of the Royal Artillery for the grant of pensions similar to those that were given (to the disapproval of the duke) after Vittoria.

After saying that he thoroughly agreed with the master-general's action, Wellington wrote: 'To tell you the truth, I was not very well pleased with the artillery in the battle of Waterloo. The Army was formed in squares immediately on the slope of the rising ground, on the summit of which the artillery was placed, with orders not to engage with artillery, but to fire only when bodies of troops came under their fire. It was very difficult to get them to obey this order. The French cavalry charged, and were formed on the same ground with our artillery in general, within a few yards of our guns. We could not expect the artillery men to remain at their guns in such a case; but I had a right to expect that the officers and men of the artillery would do as I did, and as all the staff did, that is, to take shelter in the squares of the infantry till the French cavalry should be driven off the ground, either by our cavalry or infantry.

'But they did no such thing; they ran off the field entirely, taking with them limbers, ammunition and everything: and when, in a few minutes, we had driven off the French cavalry, and had regained our ground and our guns, and could have made good use of our artillery, we had no artillerymen to fire them; and, in point of fact, I should have had no artillery during the whole of the latter part of the action if I had not kept a reserve in the commencement.

'Mind, my dear lord, I do not mean to complain; but what I have above mentioned is a fact known to many; and it would not do to reward a corps under such circumstances. The artillery, like others, behaved most gallantly; but when a misfortune of this kind has occurred, a corps must not be rewarded. It is on account of these little stories, which must come out, that I object to all the propositions to write what is called a history of the battle of Waterloo.

'If it is to be a history, it must be the truth, and the whole truth, or it will do more harm than good, and will give as many false notions of what a battle is, as other romances of the same description have. But if a true history is written, what will become of the reputation of half of those who have acquired reputation, and who deserve it for their gallantry, but who, if their mistakes and casual misconduct were made public, would not be so well thought of? I am certain that if I were to enter into a critical discussion of everything that occurred from 14 to 19 June, I could show ample reasons for not entering deeply into these subjects.'

Wellington added: 'The fact is, that the army which gained the battle of Waterloo was an entirely new one, with the exception of some of the old Spanish troops. Their inexperience occasioned the mistakes they committed, the rumours they circulated that all was destroyed, because they themselves ran away, and the mischief which ensued; but they behaved gallantly, and I am convinced, if the thing was to be done again, they would show what it was to have the experience of even one battle.'

It is little wonder that the master-general expressed astonishment at this extraordinary letter. So far as concerns the main charge against the British artillery, amounting to cowardice in the face of the enemy, it can be said unhesitatingly that this accusation is wildly at variance with all known facts established both before and since Wellington wrote to Lord Mulgrave. The charge, and the manner in which it was made, were received with the deepest indignation in the Royal Artillery, where they were widely regarded (by many they still are) as a crowning example of the duke's prejudice against the regiment. If the allegations had been disclosed while the duke was still alive, one can imagine that some officers might have gone to the length of giving him the lie direct, even if it meant resigning their commissions, and challenging him to give satisfaction. (Wellington fought one duel, with Lord Winchilsea, over another matter.)

Fortunately, in 1872 there were still living some Waterloo veterans who could reply. One of them, General Cuppage, late of the Royal Artillery, in a letter to Duncan, the regimental historian, wrote: 'I never did hear, nor anyone else, of the artillery misbehaving at Waterloo. Sir Alexander Dickson took me with him into Brussels after the battle. We saw every officer who came in, and the action was in every part the constant theme of conversation, both in our private, as well as more general moments. Had anything bearing such a term taken place, it would certainly have been canvassed. I was in daily conversation with our wounded in the town. Surely I may say, but that the Duke of Wellington says it, it is as cruel as it is unjust.' Sir John Bloomfield, who spent three years in Paris with the headquarters staff, had never heard even a whisper on the subject.

The general tenor of the duke's remarks is entirely contrary to a long series of historians, military commentators and others. Of the accounts by artillerymen who were present, many (like Mercer's), though written long after the battle, appeared before the publication of Wellington's letter. They gain strength, therefore, as plain narratives of what men saw; they cannot be dismissed as simply making out a case for the regiment in reply to accusations. Nor does the case for the defence rest upon the artillery alone; there were many tributes from commanders of cavalry and infantry formations. As for the enemy, a French account says: 'The English artillery made dreadful havoc in our ranks. . . . The Imperial Guard made several charges, but was constantly repulsed by a terrible artillery, that each moment seemed to multiply.' An officer of HMS *Northumberland*, quoting a conversation with Napoleon on board that ship, writes: 'Bonaparte gives great credit to our infantry and artillery.'

Quite apart from its obscurities and a general looseness in wording, Wellington's letter is full of contradictions and inconsistencies. If the gunners 'ran off the field', how could they be said to have 'behaved most gallantly'? If they took away 'limbers, ammunition and everything', by what means, and by whom, were 10,400 rounds fired? By what kind of logic could the duke refer airily, in a later paragraph, to 'little stories' and 'mistakes'? How did he reconcile his present dissatisfaction with the awards and decorations which he had previously recommended? And if all this was 'known to many' (not one of whom is named), why was it necessary to impart this information to the master-general, after the fashion of one hinting, in a vague confused way, at dark secrets?

The allusion to the artillery reserve being brought up to save the situation is plainly inaccurate. This reserve (it consisted of

Ross's and Beane's RHA troops and Sinclair's field brigade) had in fact been in action from early in the day, and suffered heavy losses before 1.30 p.m. At the height of the battle no artillery reserve existed; all guns which could effectively be brought to bear were already engaged.

As regards disobedience of the order not to indulge in counter-battery fire, Mercer was certainly guilty. He himself wrote: 'Being impatient of standing idle, and annoyed by the batteries on the Nivelle road, I ventured to commit a folly, for which I should have paid dearly if our duke had chanced to be in our part of the field. I ventured to disobey orders, and open a slow, deliberate fire at his [the enemy's] battery, thinking with my 9-pounders soon to silence his 4-pounders.' In this Mercer was an exception, and also in his refusal to take shelter within the squares, for reasons already stated. On both counts his action was irregular, but far from dishonourable. He offended not by falling short in the execution of his duty, but by exceeding it.

A curious incidental point is that the French, in their attacks on other batteries, apparently never thought of trying to spike the guns, as they could have done while the artillerymen were inside the squares. A few specially detailed men in every squadron, each with a farrier's hammer and a few soft-iron nails, might have made a world of difference.

In general, what the duke had in mind may have been based, distortedly, on desertions or failures in duty that really did take place. Among those who fled, including one whole brigade of Netherlanders, there were a few foreign gunners, it appears, and possibly some of the Driver Corps: it should be remembered that the latter, though soldiers now, were not at this time members of the Royal Artillery.

Fortescue states that when the Netherlands brigade broke and ran, 'in their flight they carried away with them for the moment the gunners of Bigleveld's Dutch battery', which until then had stood to their guns well. In what seems to be a more general context, it is stated that 'the gunners, by or without orders, were leaving their guns to hurry to the rear'. A footnote adds that 'a sergeant of Rogers' battery actually spiked one of his guns at this time', but (rather uncharacteristically, one might think) no further facts are given by this historian, who was, in general, so meticulous in research and in detail. Fortescue writes that in the later stages of the battle one of the Dutch batteries, moving forward at a critical moment, did valuable work. He makes no direct reference to Wellington's accusations, though the duke's letter had been made public many years before the appearance, in 1920, of this particular volume of Fortescue's history.

Apart from the case of the Dutch gunners who ran, what may have given the impression of fading artillery support could in fact have been the effect of exhaustion and recoil on the gun detachments and their pieces. Colonel Frazer wrote that some guns 'by recoiling had retired so as to lose their original and just position. But in the stiff soil the fatigue of the horse artillerymen was great, and their best exertions were unable to move the guns again to the crest without horses; to employ horses was to ensure the loss of the animals.'

These points, however, fail to explain how the duke came to express 'much satisfaction' in his original official despatch. One possible theory might be that when he wrote the despatch he already had information, true or false, leading him to believe that the artillery had failed in its duty, but that, in the interests of the honour of the Army, he originated or connived at a move to cover up the unpleasant facts. This seems so improbable on the face of it, and so contrary to Wellington's previous actions in relation to the artillery, that it can almost certainly be dismissed. In any event, even if there had been an attempt at a conspiracy of silence, it would have stood little chance of success, assuming that there was anything to hide. As General Cuppage indicated, there were too many interested onlookers close at hand. Brussels was swarming not only with British officers, some of them with their families, but with unattached civilians, inquisitive journalists, and camp-followers of every description. If there had really been any large-scale flight by the gunners, some of these people would inevitably have seen it or heard about it. To suppress such a story in its entirety would surely have been impossible. Somehow the facts would have come out – with additions and embroideries, no doubt – and one might reasonably expect that there would have been official enquiries, courts martial and cashierings, perhaps even executions of some of the rank-and-file. It would have been the great public scandal of the hour, and the name of the Royal Artillery would have become a byword. Yet nothing of this kind happened.

One must assume, therefore, that on 19 June 1815, the duke was sincere in his official praise, so far as it went, and that at some time between then and 21 December, when he wrote his letter, further information from some undisclosed source led him to revise his opinion – though he left unchanged the open official record of good service by the artillery. His remarks to the master-general took the form of a personal communication which, almost certainly, Wellington assumed would never be made public. Nevertheless the letter contained charges of the gravest nature, addressed to the head of the Board of Ordnance, and must consequently be taken to represent, in however inexact and rambling a form, the commander-in-chief's considered opinion at the moment when he wrote.

The duke's comments on the undesirability of any history of the battle read very strangely indeed. Why did he feel so strongly that it might 'do more harm than good'? With or without justification, he hints at unsavoury matters of which he gives no details or proof whatever. Certainly there were many persons, in the Army as a whole, whose conduct at Waterloo fell a good way short of perfection. Was he indeed chivalrously shielding others, as he seems to suggest; or is it possible that there were aspects of his own leadership which he preferred should not be dragged into the full light of day? In view of his declared reluctance to have the facts about the troops' shortcomings exposed, one may wonder why he saw fit to put anything on paper at all, even in a private or semi-private letter – unless it was written in a fit of general pique or bad temper, perhaps over some unrelated matter, which would be equally discreditable in a nobleman and officer of the highest rank.

Wellington was a man who, like many others, hated to admit that he could have been wrong. In the years that followed the writing of his remarkable letter there was time to reflect, in the light of a mass of evidence, over what he had said. Either he held to his dying day the belief that the gunners had played him false in his hour of need, though he still allowed the accepted version of gallantry (which he had said was a false one) to be retained without modification for public consumption; or else, having changed his mind once, conceivably he changed it a second time, and at length became persuaded that he had wronged the artillery, that the laurels won at Waterloo were its rightful due. If so, as a man of honour, it would be his plain duty to see that the slur was removed, either by ensuring the destruction of his original letter, or by writing another to put right the supposedly secret record. No evidence that he ever did so is known to exist.

The resentment which Wellington had felt during the Peninsular War over the unsatisfactory system of dual control of the artillery could no longer have existed in the same personal sense after he himself had accepted appointment as master-general of the ordnance. In view of his earlier attitude, his position in this capacity was a curious one; it at least ensured that he had the fullest possible access to all relevant information, and every opportunity for further action regarding the role of the artillery in the battle, if he had considered it necessary or desirable.

Norman Ramsay, the officer whom Wellington once placed under arrest, was killed at Waterloo while in command of H Troop, RHA. On the morning of the battle, when the duke greeted him in passing, Ramsay had bowed his head low, almost to his horse's mane, without a word. It has been said that during the fighting he deliberately went where the enemy's fire was hottest. After he had fallen, during a lull in the action, Colonel Frazer saw to his burial on the battlefield. From the body he took a portrait of Ramsay's wife, which he had always carried next to his heart. About three weeks later, from Paris, the colonel wrote: 'I cannot get Ramsay out of my head; such generosity, such romantic self-devotion as his, are not common.'

Mercer, the captain who disobeyed, was not among those recommended for brevet promotion, and on his appointment by Lord Mulgrave to a vacant troop command he was deprived of the post by Wellington, who had the troop summarily disbanded in 1816. But time was on the captain's side. He lived to be a general, like his father before him, and today one of the British artillery's most modern units bears the title 'G Parachute Battery (Mercer's Troop), RHA'.

More than a century after Wellington's letter appeared, a gesture of reconciliation was made. At a Woolwich luncheon in January 1973, the present Duke of Wellington was a guest and presented to the master gunner a replica of one of the 9-pounders used at Waterloo.

DAYS OF FRUSTRATION

'We have retrograded fifty years since the Peninsular War.' –
Royal Artillery officer, 1827

During the occupation of France, in 1816, the Royal Artillery celebrated its hundredth birthday. From the original two companies of 1716 the regiment, now consisting of nine troops and 105 companies, had grown into a force whose equipment and skill had been admired, even envied, in the armies of Europe. General Foy, one of Napoleon's best artillery commanders, had written: 'The English gunners are distinguished from the other soldiers by their excellent spirit. In action their handling is skilful, their aim perfect and their courage supreme.'

This spirit was to be sorely tried. In the period after Waterloo there were, once again, drastic cuts in the Army, in the course of which the artillery suffered considerably. Many units disappeared completely, and those which remained were at minimum strength, most of the horse artillery troops that escaped disbandment being put on an establishment of only two guns apiece.

The Corps of Drivers was abolished in 1822, giving the Royal Artillery at last an opportunity to have its own transport, manned by soldiers belonging to the regiment. But there was a drawback; it was decided that all recruits should be enlisted as 'gunner and driver', the idea being that they should be trained to carry out both sets of duties, changing from one to the other as required. This was unrealistic, if for no other reason than that the gunners were too heavy and long in the leg to make suitable drivers. For the gunner-driver system the Duke of Wellington, as master-general, was mainly responsible.

In 1827, owing to a threatening attitude by Spain, Britain sent a military force to Portugal, but not a shot was fired. This was perhaps fortunate, as the artillery component (three four-gun brigades) was in a wretched state. Guns and wagons were under-horsed, the horse shoes and nails were defective, and the powder for over 1,000 musket, carbine and pistol cartridges was so bad that it had to be destroyed to prevent accidents. When Colonel Smith, the Artillery Commander, proposed certain changes in arrangements, Wellington, who had minutely examined all preparations for the expedition, recalled him and appointed another officer.

On 6 June 1827, a letter to *The Morning Herald*, signed 'RA, Lisbon', openly denounced the duke for having, from personal resentment, 'purposely rendered the British Artillery Corps in Portugal unfit for any service'. Some time later, when a regimental committee put forward several useful recommendations for improvements in equipment (including a flint lock for every gun, in addition to the existing means of ignition), Wellington refused to sign their report, and ultimately made it known that he was not to be approached on the subject.

It was decided in 1833 that artillery units should no longer bear individual battle honours. Instead, the regiment as a whole was granted by William IV the privilege of bearing the royal arms above a gun, with a scroll displaying the word *Ubique*, and the motto *Quo fas et gloria ducunt*.

In 1838 the Royal Artillery Institution, formed by a small group of officers, came into existence at Woolwich, using one end of a borrowed shed. Other arms at this time had no comparable society, and until the formation of the first School of Gunnery at Shoeburyness in 1859 (a forerunner of the Salisbury Plain training range and the School of Artillery at Larkhill), it was the only centre of its kind for the study of gunnery as a science and for much other activity.

The half century that followed Waterloo was a period, in Europe as a whole, of far-reaching development in weapons, though the British Army, which between 1815 and 1854 was involved in only a few minor campaigns, showed little radical change for the time being, so far as artillery equipment was concerned. Some of the features which were to transform continental armies by the end of the century had been foreshadowed long before, as in the early experiments with breech-loading, but their practical application had to await the scientific and technological advances after the industrial revolution. There had been, in fact, remarkably little alteration in the design and construction of guns themselves since the days of the Tudors, though ammunition had been greatly improved.

The nineteenth century witnessed the perfecting of rifled cannon firing, instead of roundshot, elongated projectiles which travelled farther and straighter and were less affected by wind. Breech-loading guns of fair efficiency were produced as early as the 1840s by Cavalli, a Sardinian officer, and Baron Wahrendorf of Sweden, but rifled field pieces did not receive their first test on a large scale until the American Civil War of 1860–64. Alfred Krupp was the first to make a successful all-steel gun, with the barrel drilled out of a single block of metal; a specimen exhibited in London in 1851 attracted much attention. Great strides were being made in the development of ammunition, cordite replacing the old black powder propellant, while inventors were busy on high-explosive bursting charges which would multiply the hitting power of artillery beyond the dreams of the medieval pioneers. Buffer and recuperator gear was being devised to take up recoil, ending the old laborious routine of running up the gun by hand after each round; better sighting apparatus was also on the way.

In Britain, however, almost the only important change in battery equipment since Waterloo was that Captain E. M. Boxer's time fuse was adopted about 1850, and friction tubes for firing the guns came into use in 1855. Slow-matches and portfires were still carried in case the newer devices failed. Artillery tactics remained practically unchanged, and no camp for exercises by troops of all arms had been held for forty-eight years up to 1853.

Although Britain might be at peace in Europe, there were always areas of tension, and sometimes war, far beyond the seas. Some missions in Central Asia, at a time when the extension of Russian influence was a cause of increasing concern, produced odd confrontations. At the siege of Herat in 1838 there were British military advisers on both sides. With the defenders was Lieutenant Eldred Pottinger, a political officer, late of the Bombay Horse Artillery, who had accepted on his own responsibility the post of adviser to Yar Mahomed, the Afghan vizier. With the Persian besiegers, who had the Russian ambassador as an observer in their camp, was Major D'Arcy Todd, a Bengal artillery officer seconded to the Shah's Army. The siege was raised after British pressure had been brought to bear in the form of an expedition to the Persian Gulf.

A small body of artillerymen were among those who perished in the Afghan war of 1840–42 – one of the most disastrous wars in which Britain ever engaged, and in many ways one of the most disgraceful. The so-called Army of Afghanistan had been kept woefully short of artillery from India, and the few units that were made available suffered from the almost incredible general mismanagement. Colin Mackenzie, who joined Brigadier-General Shelton's relief column, wrote: 'Shelton's gross want of arrangement and the unnecessary hardship he has exposed the men to, especially during their passage through the Khyber, have caused much discontent. Part of the horse artillery on one occasion mutinied and refused to mount their horses.' Outside Kabul, Lieutenant Vincent Eyre found that to defend an ill-sited camp with a perimeter of nearly two miles he had only six iron 9-pounders, four howitzers and three $5\frac{1}{4}$-inch mortars, manned by eighty Punjabis, 'very insufficiently instructed, and of doubtful fidelity'.

When it became necessary to drive Afghan attackers from a hill that commanded the cantonment, a single gun, in charge of Sergeant Mulhall, was taken out with the troops, despite a standing order in the East India Company's forces that in no circumstances should fewer than two pieces ever be sent into action. One practical reason for such an order became tragically apparent when, after an incessant fire of grape, the lone gun was so overheated that it could no longer be used, leaving no weapons save the old, worn muskets of the infantry, which were inferior in range and accuracy to the rifled jezails of the tribesmen.

The force that set out on the retreat from Kabul through the snow-covered mountain passes had about 4,500 armed men, of whom fewer than 700 were Europeans, and some 12,000 camp followers, including many women and children. Three mountain guns were with the advance guard, and four horse artillery pieces with the rearguard. In bitter cold, almost totally without food or shelter, the long straggling column was treacherously cut to pieces by the Afghans. Only one European, an army surgeon on a starving pony, reached Jalalabad, followed later by a few Indian sepoys and camp followers. Captain Nicholls of the horse artillery died gallantly after the last of his guns had been abandoned, useless.

Shortly before the Crimean War, the artillery in England still had smoothbore muzzle-loaders, the rate of fire from field guns being only about one round a minute, and the effective range not more than 500 to 800 yards. When it was eventually realized that the post-Waterloo cuts had been too severe, a number of units were re-formed, and by December 1853, there were seven troops of horse artillery and twelve battalions each consisting of eight companies, some of which were on garrison duty in various parts of the world. The RHA troops were armed with 6-pounder guns and 12-pounder howitzers, the field batteries having 9-pounders and 24-pounder howitzers; for garrison and siege purposes there were also heavier pieces of calibres ranging up to 10-inch.

There had been many changes in uniform, all keeping the emphasis on smartness rather than comfort. Elaborate hairdressing had been abandoned during the Napoleonic campaigns, but the men of the field batteries still went to war in tight blue coatees with high collars and stocks, and plumed shakoes. The horse artillery wore braided jackets; their helmets had now been replaced by the busby, whose name is so often misapplied to the tall bearskins of the Guards.

THE CRIMEA

'The first virtue in a soldier is endurance of fatigue; courage is only the second virtue.' *– Napoleon*

When Britain entered the war in the Crimea to check Russian expansion, she found herself aligned with the Turks as allies of the French, her traditional opponents, against the Tsar, whose country had been England's ally in the struggle with Napoleon. It was an unsettling change of partners; and one need not be too surprised that the commander-in-chief, Lord Raglan (who as Lord Fitzroy Somerset had been Wellington's military secretary) experienced a certain difficulty in remembering quite clearly at all times that the French were no longer the enemy.

The Crimean War is famous, or notorious, for the appalling confusion and incompetence which it revealed in the supply services – the scandalously primitive medical facilities, the soldiers without bedding or proper clothing, the ship (perhaps apocryphal, but typical) which arrived with a cargo of boots, all for the left foot. For much of this the Ordnance Board, as a principal supplier, must bear responsibility; but it is a point to its credit that, in spite of long peacetime stagnation, it did succeed in putting into the field, in an area about 3,000 miles by sea from England, a siege train, manned by nine artillery companies, which was eventually brought up to a peak strength of 183 heavy guns in action.

With Brigadier-General Thomas Fox-Strangways as artillery commander, eight field batteries and two troops of the Royal Horse Artillery completed disembarkation in the Crimea on 18 September 1854, the siege train being left on board ship for the time being. Next day the allied advance began, the British marching on the left, the Turks in the centre, and the French on the right. On 20 September the Army attacked the Russian positions on hills to the south of the Alma.

The British line, which had been pushed forward across the

river, met with a check and was drawn back, but there was a gap in the Russian centre, through which rode Lord Raglan, accompanied by his numerous staff, among whom was A. W. Kinglake, the war historian, and followed by C Troop, RHA, which took up a position, in support of the Light Division, from which it could command the Russian guns that were holding up the advance. E, G and B batteries also came into action. The Russian gunners were driven off, the British and French infantry moved on with support from other artillery, and before night the enemy were in full retreat.

By early October the allies had established themselves on the plateau and opened their entrenchments, in which were seventy-one British and forty-nine French guns for the siege of Sebastopol. The Russian defences had 118 cannon. On the 13th, although the Redan, the enemy's central work, was seriously damaged by heavy guns on land, manned by the Royal Navy and the Royal Artillery, a bombardment from warships met with no success, and siege operations were suspended. This gave the enemy a breathing space, of which excellent use was made by Todleben, their brilliant engineer.

The only firm link between the British Army's lines on the plateau and its base at Balaclava, 8 miles away, was by the Post Road. To defend this vital highway a series of redoubts had been set up, each having a British 12-pounder, served by Turks, with a British gunner in charge. On 25 October the Russian field army, now about 25,000 strong, gave battle. Although they were driven back before long, the redoubts on the Post Road were captured, the British artillerymen of W Battery spiking the guns before abandoning the works. Here Gunner David Jenkins won a French award of the Médaille Militaire. In one redoubt there were heavy casualties. The loss of the posts meant that in future all movement of ammunition, food, forage and stores from the base would have to be made over a rough farm track, which speedily became a quagmire.

Everyone knows at least something about that gallant but costly blunder, the charge of the Light Brigade at Balaclava. Comparatively few, probably, have ever heard of the charge of Scarlett's Heavy Brigade on the same day, which was almost equally heroic, and a success – but which might have ended in failure had it not been for covering fire given by the Royal

Artillery. In this action, attacking up a slope, the Heavy Brigade – the Greys, Inniskillings and 4th Dragoon Guards, supported by the 93rd Highlanders – drove from the field a body of Russian cavalry which outnumbered them by four to one, for a loss by the British of seventy-eight killed or wounded.

Unaccountably, the Russian squadrons had halted about 500 yards from the British, offering an opportunity too good to be missed. Brigadier-General Scarlett, with his trumpeter and staff officers, riding about fifty yards ahead of the first line of the brigade, made straight for the Russians. A moment later the three leading squadrons crashed headlong into the stationary mass of the enemy. The Russian cavalry swayed but did not break, and their wings began to swerve inward as though to engulf the British. While this move was still uncompleted, the rest of the Heavy Brigade struck a series of quick successive blows from the flanks, which threw the Russians, numbering more than 3,000, into utter disorder.

It was at this stage that the artillery came into play. Captain John Brandling, of C Troop, RHA, had just returned from the dawn parade at Inkerman when a call for reinforcements reached the plateau. At top speed he and his troop made for the Col. When they arrived there, some French chasseurs were about to descend the slope, but they made way for the guns, and the troop, with somewhat jaded horses, reached Scarlett's right just as his brigade was advancing for the charge. As soon as the Russians began to retreat, C Troop opened up on them at a range of about 700 yards, frustrating all attempts to rally.

Colonel Frank Foster, who was with the 4th Dragoon Guards, wrote years later: 'If there are any officers alive who were in John Brandling's troop of horse artillery at Balaclava, they would tell you how his opportune arrival with his guns, after the Heavy Brigade charge, saved them from a fresh attack from a very strong force of Russian cavalry.'

The next action of note, the fighting on the ridge of Inkerman on 5 November, is memorable as the 'soldiers' battle', though in fact a great deal was done by the regimental officers, and the main responsibility rested with Brigadier-General Pennefather, the 'swearing general'. Townsend's battery on the plateau was overrun in the first Russian onrush, but the guns were recovered later. As the enemy pressed on, driving British piquets before

11. On parade and off parade; Woolwich cadets of the eighteenth century (R.A. Museum)

12. Artillery at the battle of the Boyne in 1690. From a print in the R.A. Museum

13. Captain Norman Ramsay, at the head of his men, breaks through the encircling French at Fuentes d'Onoro in the Peninsula. From the painting by Captain J. R. L. French, R.F.A., in the R.A. Museum

them, they became exposed to three guns of Turner's battery. These, however, were unable to fire until the infantry, who were keeping up a running fight as best they could, were induced to lie down. A few rounds fired over the heads of the piquets then sufficed to turn back to the foremost Russians, those behind wavered, and the British infantry chased them back to Shell Hill.

But more battalions were brought up by the enemy, and a series of desperate hand-to-hand combats developed, fought in dense fog among ravines, scrub, and boulder-strewn slopes. Two batteries attached to the 2nd Division had been silenced by heavier Russian guns. A couple of 18-pounders from the siege train, which Raglan had ordered to be hauled up, at last arrived, dragged by 150 gunners, and were placed behind an embankment. With the fog now lifting, the artillerymen quickly found the range, and in reply the Russian batteries immediately concentrated their full force against the siege guns. In the first fifteen minutes seventeen British gunners were killed or disabled. Then the 18-pounders began to gain the upper hand, and finally they overwhelmed the opposing batteries. A Russian despatch after the battle bore witness to the fact that it was the 'murderous fire' of Lieutenant-Colonel Collingwood Dickson's heavy guns that forced the tsar's troops to withdraw from their stronghold on Shell Hill.

But for hours fighting continued, more and more reserves being thrown in by the Russians until, as night closed in, they fell back within the shelter of Sebastopol fortress. Out of their 60,000 men engaged, nearly 12,000 were casualties. In the British force of about 16,000, with fifty-nine guns, 2,573 men were killed or wounded.

Among the fallen was General Fox-Strangways, the artillery commander, mortally wounded by a bursting shell while at the side of Lord Raglan. Forty-one years earlier, as a subaltern at the battle of Leipzig in 1813, he had taken over the Royal Artillery rocket detachment when its commander, Captain R. Bogue, was killed. At Leipzig he received the personal thanks of the allied sovereigns for his work, and the Emperor of Russia, taking from his own breast the Order of St Anne, pinned it on the coat of the young lieutenant.

During the battle of Inkerman, Colour Sergeant Andrew

Henry of G Field Battery earned the VC for defending the guns of his battery against a swarm of Russian infantrymen, after all the rest of the British detachment were dead. He killed several of the enemy with a handspike before collapsing with twelve bayonet wounds. Henry recovered from his wounds, transferred later to the new Land Transport Corps, in which he was given a commission, and rose to the rank of captain. His was one of the earliest awards of the new decoration institututed by the Queen 'For Valour'. The first VC of all was won by Charles Davis Lucas, a mate in HMS *Hecla*, who picked up and threw over the side a Russian shell which had fallen on board, with fuse burning, during the bombardment of Bomarsun fortress in the Baltic on 21 June 1854.

Another artillery VC was won at Inkerman by Lieutenant F. Miller of P Battery, three of whose guns had been overrun. Through the mist Miller rode to his commanding officer, Major Townsend, who spoke to some of the infantry officers, and soon, headed by Miller, a mixed party of gunners, Connaught Rangers and the 49th Foot made for the spot where the guns had been left. Two of them were soon recovered, and the lieutenant, following the tracks of the wheels, presently found the third, with his own cap still lying on the ground beside it, and one of his men stretched out dead across the trail. The Russians had 'spiked' two guns after a fashion with pieces of twig, but had not tampered with the other. Soon the limbers were brought, but the guns could not be removed before a body of Russian infantry had been fought off.

Kinglake writes: 'As though bewildered by the novelty of the challenge and the sudden necessity of having to encounter a horseman, these men (the Russians) for a moment stopped short in their onset, and then there followed a conflict of a singular kind between, on the one hand, a great weight of advancing infantry, and on the other a few score of artillerymen, finding vent for some part of their rage in curses and shouts of defiance, but wildly trying besides to beat back the throng from their beloved guns with swords, with rammers, with sponge staves, nay even, one may say, with clenched fist – for the story of the mighty Clitheroe bruiser felling man after man with his blows, and then standing for a while unmolested and seemingly admired by the enemy, is not altogether a fable.'

The action in which Miller figured so bravely was to be one of the last of its kind for some time, for the season was far advanced. As winter closed its grip on the Crimea, the broad peninsula jutting out into the Black Sea became a wilderness of dreary, back-breaking toil and searing misery. From early in November rain fell constantly, reducing trenches to water-logged ditches and roads to treacherous channels of sticky mud in which pack horses slipped and foundered and stores were lost or ruined. Transport and artillery draught animals, worn out by exposure, starvation, or sheer exhaustion, collapsed in their hundreds, some of them falling dead after gnawing in their hunger at the spokes of the wheels.

The troops had received no issue of fresh clothing since they landed at the assembly areas in Bulgaria. Some of the gunners had to trudge to the batteries in their socks, or barefoot, even when there was snow on the ground. One artillery officer who, like others, had been compelled to leave most of his kit on board ship when the troops disembarked, found to his dismay that it had been sent back to England; he did not receive it until the summer of 1855.

Soldiers in threadbare, ragged uniforms, with perhaps an improvised blanket cape if they were lucky, sickened and died of dysentery or cholera. Sickness was aggravated by a staple diet of salt pork (sometimes eaten raw for lack of cooking vessels or fuel) and ration biscuits; Lieutenant Garnet Wolseley, later to be a field-marshal, contrived with a fellow officer to concoct a semblance of a Christmas pudding out of pounded biscuit, old dried figs, and a few oddments, set to boil in a large fragment of a Russian shell, but eaten half-cooked owing to the exigencies of the service.

In the great gale of 14 November twenty-one ships were sunk or damaged in the inadequate, overcrowded harbour. Among the vessels that went down were one full of stores and warm clothing, another carrying 10 million rounds of ammunition, and others with a month's supply of forage for the horses. Some degree of readiness was still maintained in the siege batteries, but the breaking point was perilously near on 1 February 1855, when the number of men sick equalled the number of those parading for duty.

More guns and mortars began to arrive in December. As the

few wagons that the siege train possessed were not suitable for heavy loads of shot, store limber wagons were adapted as a makeshift, enabling a team of ten horses to haul six 13-inch shells. The transport of a hundred such shells from Balaclava to the siege parks was considered a very good day's work, as Colonel Jocelyn records in his artillery history of the Crimea period.

Troop detachment horses were also utilized as pack animals. Pairs of canvas bags, joined by stout bands, were made on board ship and these containers, with a 32-pounder shot in each bag, were slung across the horses' backs. They moved three abreast, the centre horse being ridden by a gunner. Men, too, were used as beasts of burden; every day one thousand were detailed, each of whom carried one 32-pounder or 24-pounder shot, in a sandbag slung over his back, from Balaclava to the Col depot, from which they were taken on to the siege parks by detachments of Turks. At one time it was proposed to use the latter on the Col road, and hook them into trench carts with man harness; but as most of the Turks on the first occasion lay down exhausted before they had gone a mile, and several died where they lay, the experiment was not repeated.

With the coming of spring it was possible to muster sufficient strength to start the bombardment of Sebastopol in earnest. Five hundred heavy guns now faced the fortress. The British batteries, however, were still in an incomplete state, owing to the physical impossibility of moving all the bigger guns with the means at hand and in the conditions that prevailed. At first light on 9 April fire was opened by artillerymen and bluejackets standing ankle deep in mud and water, and drenched to the skin by rain. One face of the Redan had been laid in ruins before the guns ceased fire at dusk; even later the men with the mortars kept up their work, playing havoc among the enemy's working parties, who laboured all night long to repair the damage.

Marshal Canrobert, the French commander, dissatisfied with the rate of progress, sent to Raglan message after message, remonstrating over the fact that the most advanced British battery facing the Redan was still not armed. On the night of 10 April a great effort was made to haul into position six 32-pounders, each weighing nearly three tons, but the muscle-power of 300 men failed to drag them through the deep mud, and the Russians knocked out one of the guns with a direct hit on the muzzle. Eventually four were brought in, and they opened fire on the 13th.

The battery in which they stood was exposed to converging fire from at least twenty guns of large calibre in five different enemy positions, all on commanding ground, in addition to the Russian sharpshooters who from rifle pits on the space in front of the besiegers sent streams of bullets into the embrasures. In spite of this, the artillery officer in charge kept his guns in action for five hours, by which time three of them were disabled. He continued firing with the last remaining piece until ordered to withdraw; forty-four out of the sixty-five men with him had fallen.

Bombardment with other guns was maintained for ten days. The gunners spent an hour making their way to the batteries, eight hours with the guns, and another hour returning to quarters, which meant that they were on their feet for at least ten hours a day.

At one stage, after a Russian raid on our batteries had been repulsed, a local truce for burial of the dead was arranged. During the truce soldiers from both sides fraternized. Some of them went so far as to organize a 'sporting match' between two opposing pieces of ordnance; on this official accounts are reticent, but General Sir D. Lysons, who was present as a young staff officer, has given the following version:

'While the flag of truce was flying, a Russian artillery officer enquired if General Dacres was on the ground, but he did not happen to be there. General Airey, however, who was present, asked what he could do for him. "Your 68-pounder gun," said the Russian, "that your people call 'Jenny', is a beautiful gun; but we think we have as good a one in that embrasure" (pointing up at the Mamelon), "and we should like to have a fair duel with her." Airey took up the challenge at once, and everything was arranged for noon next day. All the batteries on both sides ceased firing, and a large number of officers, French and English, assembled at the lookout station behind the Twenty-One Gun Battery to look on.

'Our 68-pounder was manned by a crew of sailors, who mounted the parapet and took off their hats in salute to the

Russians, who returned the compliment. The English gun, as "senior gun", was given the first shot, which struck the side of the Russian embrasure, and a good shot was returned; the third shot from 'Jenny' went clean through the Russian embrasure, and up went two gabions; the bluejackets mounted their parapets and cheered; but out came the Russian gun again, and in a little 'Jenny' got a nasty thump; but it did her no harm, for at the seventeenth round she knocked the Russian gun clean over. The Russians mounted their parapets, took off their caps in acknowledgment of defeat, and dropped the mantlet. Then all the batteries resumed their fire.'

Dacres was a senior officer of the Royal Artillery; Airey was quartermaster-general to Lord Raglan. The commander-in-chief's personal views on this unusual duel are not recorded, but doubtless he would have approved of its outcome.

Presently infantry assaults on the fortifications were tried. Little was gained in the first two attacks, but on 6 July the French stormed the Mamelon, and the British took possession of the ground immediately in front of the Redan. A further bombardment was followed by more assaults, all of which were beaten off with heavy losses.

Early in September, when the allies were ready for the final bombardment, the French had 620 guns in position, and the British 183; about 600 pieces are believed to have been manned by the defenders of Sebastopol. The British cannon ranged from 24-pounders to 68-pounders, with many 13-inch mortars. A newcomer among the artillery weapons was the Lancaster gun; this was not a rifled piece in the accepted sense of the term, but it had a specially designed bore which imparted a certain amount of spin to the shell. It fired an oval elongated projectile, some of which, though made of cast iron with an explosive charge of ordinary black powder, proved extremely destructive. The heavier specimens of the Lancaster, however, were inaccurate and unreliable; three 8-inch pieces and two 24-pounders burst, two men being killed in one battery, and four wounded.

In the infantry assaults in September, those on the Flagstaff Bastion and the Redan fell short of complete success, the British losing 2,000 men but the French fought their way into the Malakoff. This, and the effect of the previous bombardments, proved decisive. During the night the Russians evacuated

Sebastopol, leaving city and fortifications a heap of ruins, and the end of the war was in sight. The British had fired in the course of the siege 252,872 rounds from a total of 401 guns and mortars.

In addition to those already mentioned, seven members of the Royal Artillery won the VC in this campaign. Among them were Colonel Collingwood Dickson (son of Alexander Dickson of Peninsula fame) and Captain M. C. Dixon, both for gallantry during the siege operations. Dixon was the officer who kept his one remaining gun in action until sunset, after a shellburst in the magazine had devastated the battery on 17 April 1855. He retired in 1869 with the honorary rank of major-general, and died in 1905 at the age of eighty-four. The others who won the VC were Captain G. Davis, Bombardier D. Cambridge, and Driver T. Arthur at Sebastopol, Sergeant G. Symons at Inkerman and Lieutenant C. C. Teesdale at Kars in Asia Minor.

Lord Raglan, the last of a long continuous line of masters-general of the ordnance, died on 28 June 1855. His health had already been undermined before the failure of the assault on 18 June, and this disappointment hastened the end. Although far from being a great general, he had been burdened with a heartbreaking task, and many people now think that much of the criticism of which he became the butt could more justly have been levelled at politicians and bureaucrats in England.

About a month before Raglan's death, the ancient powers of the Board of Ordnance, which had been in existence for some four hundred years, were abolished, largely as a result of the storm of indignation and horror aroused over the state of affairs disclosed in war correspondents' despatches on inefficiency in the supply services. At last, the Royal Artillery, like the Royal Engineers, came under the commander-in-chief and the secretary of state for war, in common with the rest of the Army.

Lack of transport in the Crimea, which brought the artillery dangerously near to disaster, and which for a time practically immobilized the field batteries, was mainly the fault of the Ordnance Board. Before the war the lamentable state of unpreparedness had been pointed out, but the warnings were ignored, and for this senior military officers on the board must take their share of the blame, together with the politicians whose niggardliness made thorough provision in advance so difficult.

There was an acute shortage not only of horses, and food for them, but of artillerymen who could ride and drive. As regards equipment, the armament of the field batteries stood the test well, and most of the siege guns proved satisfactory in general, though there were a number of premature bursts, some trouble was experienced with mountings, and fuses of the latest type were not available at the start of the campaign. There was, however, a strong feeling among officers of the siege train that the numbers of their men were much too small for the work entailed, and that this did not receive sufficient consideration at artillery headquarters. In this respect the Royal Artillery batteries compared unfavourably with those of the Royal Navy, which were more amply manned, and in which the naval system of duty watches functioned well, giving the men a better chance of adequate rest periods. During the latter part of the siege Florence Nightingale drew the attention of Lord Panmure, Secretary of State for War, to the high incidence of pulmonary disease in the siege train, and the need to give the gunners more assistance in their severe labours.

Old jealousies and outdated exclusiveness die hard, and some artillery officers in the Crimea were not without their share of these. Lieutenant Markham (later to be General Sir Edwin Markham) received a severe reprimand during the war from a Royal Artillery lieutenant-colonel for having described and shown to a staff officer, serving as chief divisional representative of the quartermaster-general, various types of projectiles and fuses. Markham was informed that he was divulging secret scientific information that should be known only to artillery officers.

MUTINY IN INDIA

'There is many a boy . . . who looks on war as all glory, but, boys, it is all hell.' – *General Sherman*

Little more than a year after the Crimean War, mutiny among the Bengal sepoys at Meerut, in May, 1857, made urgently necessary the dispatch from England of troops, including artillery, to aid the forces of the East India Company in stamping out the revolt. The gunners' part in this task, which offered little scope for brilliant large-scale actions on orthodox lines, was carried out with great devotion under conditions which for British soldiers could hardly have been more exacting or more repugnant.

All the artillery in India at the outbreak of the mutiny belonged to the Bengal, Madras or Bombay Armies of the Company. As in Britain, the gunners were organized into horse artillery troops and artillery battalions, companies from the latter being formed into field batteries as required. Altogether there were seventeen 'European' and six 'native' horse artillery troops, the 'native' units having British officers and a few British NCOS. There were thirteen European and six Indian battalions, of which about half were equipped as field batteries. Equipment was much the same as in the British Army, except that friction tubes were not used, guns being primed with powder in paper tubes or quills.

The performance of the European units (for whose formation a dozen companies from the Royal Artillery had been transferred a century earlier to the service of the Company) had always been of a high standard. The bulk of the Indian artillery remained loyal, only two troops and eight companies joining the mutineers; but they managed by some means (through administrative negligence, according to Fortescue) to lay hands on large numbers of cannon, some of them of such calibre that the gunners of the relief forces, armed mainly with lighter pieces often found themselves at a grave disadvantage.

Four RHA troops and twenty-five artillery companies were sent out to India. They were none too many. Within a month of the Meerut outburst the North-West Provinces had been lost and, save for a few beleaguered garrisons, British authority from the Nerbudda to the Jumna had been swept away. Delhi had been seized by rebels proclaiming the rebirth of the Mogul empire; Sir Henry Lawrence with 3,000 combatants and civilians was besieged in the Residency at Lucknow; and a garrison of 400, with 600 women and children, were holding out inside a feeble entrenchment at Cawnpore.

Here the defenders had one heavy howitzer and two field guns. All of the fifty-nine artillerymen were killed or wounded during the first week. Before the end all the rest, with the exception of four, died at their guns, which were fired to the last round, the 9-pounders having eventually been compelled to make shift with 6-pounder ammunition. After three weeks, the garrison was forced by lack of food and ammunition to capitulate on terms that seemed acceptable. Having laid down their arms, all the surviving men, except three, were shot or drowned in the Ganges, while the women and children, after being held prisoners under barbarous conditions, were all massacred on the approach of the relief column under General Havelock.

When the rebels moved on Delhi in May, Lieutenant G. D. Willoughby, Commissary of Ordnance, Bengal Artillery, had been in charge of the arsenal. He prepared to hold out as long as possible, and then to blow up the magazine. After a call to surrender, which was ignored, the mutineers advanced in force, and for some hours Willoughby with eight Europeans, six of whom were artillerymen, defended the magazine with guns and musketry. When the defences had been penetrated, Willoughby gave the order to explode the magazine. Conductor Scully of the Bengal Artillery set light to the powder train with a portfire, causing an explosion in which hundreds of the rebels were blown to pieces, together with five of the heroic nine. The survivors were all recommended for the VC, but Willoughby was killed by rebels before his nomination had been approved.

One of the first tasks facing the British was to recapture

Delhi with troops based on the Punjab. Lord Canning, the Governor-General, wrote to Sir George Anson, Commander-in-Chief: 'Your force of artillery will enable you to dispose of Delhi with certainty.' It was not so simple. To attack with 10,000 men (only 3,000 of whom were Europeans) a strongly fortified city held by 30,000 rebels was a hazardous affair. At the outset the artillery of the British force consisted of only three horse batteries, one field battery, and about 150 gunners, mostly recruits, with a rudimentary siege train. This comprised eight 18-pounders and sixteen mortars, the largest of 8-inch calibre.

In heat that reached 120 degrees, the troops marched on Delhi in their shirt sleeves, wearing on their forage caps white covers and neck shields that gave only poor protection against the sun. Outside the city they occupied a ridge that lay right across the line of communications with the Punjab. As soon as the batteries had taken up position the rebels moved guns to enfilade them. Before long it was evident that the British and their Indian loyalists were the besieged rather than the besiegers on the ridge, where they were to remain for twelve weeks, during which they fought thirty actions, both offensive and defensive.

Early in June, when the mutineers opened a cannonade from the walls, it was found not only that the British guns could not silence those of the enemy, owing to superior range, but that stocks of ammunition were falling dangerously low. The commanding officer, like Dickson at Burgos in the Peninsula, offered a reward for shot fired by the mutineers that was recovered and brought to the artillery park.

Meanwhile the insurgents were able to pass, more or less as they pleased, to and from the city. During a cavalry raid by the rebels, a Bengal Horse Artillery troop under Lieutenant Hills (later Lieutenant-General Sir J. Hills-Johnes) was charged by more than a hundred troopers. To give his men time to unlimber and load, Hills galloped at the enemy alone. When he was unhorsed, after killing two of them, he fought on foot with sword and fist, but was struck down just as a fellow officer, Major Tombs, came up to his aid. Together they fought their way out; both were awarded the VC.

In September the main siege train at last arrived, with thirty-two pieces, making up the heavy artillery to a total of fifteen

24-pounders, twenty 18-pounders, and twenty-five howitzers and mortars. To keep these in action every available soldier was on almost continual duty, even the lancers and carabineers being called upon to find men for the gun lines. Casualties were heavy; Tombs's battery lost twenty-seven men out of forty-eight, and Campbell's in similar proportion; but after a few days of bombardment the Kashmir and Water bastions had been hammered to pieces. The assault was launched on 14 September, and six days later Delhi was again in British hands after bloody fighting, in the course of which Lieutenant Renny, Bengal Horse Artillery, won the VC by climbing the wall of the citadel and throwing shells with lighted fuses among the rebels inside.

A week later, with 3,000 men and about twenty guns, Havelock fought his way through the enemy before Lucknow. On 26 September he joined hands with the garrison in the Residency, now in desperate straits through casualties and disease. The gun detachments in particular had suffered heavily, every officer but one being dead or wounded. During Havelock's operations Captain F. C. Maude, RA, and Captain W. Olpherts, Bengal Artillery, were awarded the VC. The rebels were still in great numbers, but the defenders, with the reinforcements they now had, were able to hold out until a much larger relief force, with a siege train, finally captured the enemy positions in March, 1858.

About this time three field forces were organized to clear central India, which of necessity had been left in almost complete chaos while efforts were concentrated on Delhi, Cawnpore and Lucknow. A number of widely separated rebel groups had to be rounded up and driven northward in the direction of the main British force. The artillery played its part in these operations, which entailed many engagements, with the occasional breaching of a walled city or fort, and much arduous marching. The Chestnut Troop once covered 78 miles in twenty-four hours, according to Brigadier-General Graham, the regimental historian.

One fortress which had to be reduced was that of the Ranee of Jhansi, a redoubtable chieftainess whose stronghold was protected on one face by steep and almost inaccessible rock walls. Sir Hugh Rose, in command of a Bombay column, advanced despite stiff opposition as far as Jhansi town, to which he laid siege. The British guns were successful in disabling most of the enemy's cannon, and when the ranee's men tried to build a stockade, to close a breach which had been opened, the timbers were set on fire, in the old style, with red-hot shot. Bombardier J. Brennan, attached to the Hyderabad contingent, won a VC.

Just as the breach was judged to be practicable, a large rebel force made a thrust to raise the siege, but Rose with his guns and only 1,500 men defeated 22,000. Two days later the town was taken by storm. The ranee, once described as 'the best soldier of them all' on the rebel side, escaped, but was mortally wounded later while riding into battle.

Soon afterwards Rose resumed his advance and, after four engagements, entered Kalpi, rounding off a brilliant campaign by the capture of Gwalior in June, but scattered bands of rebels continued to give trouble until the spring of 1859.

Among Bengal Artillery officers who won the Victoria Cross during earlier operations was a future field-marshal, Lieutenant F. S. Roberts, who saved a comrade's life and recaptured a standard from two mutineers near Khodagunze, between Cawnpore and Delhi. Forty-two years later his son also won the VC, in a famous artillery action of the South African War.

After the mutiny the Crown took over from the East India Company, and it was decided that all its European regiments should be absorbed into the British Army. This process was carried out gradually; by 1862 the amalgamation of the British artillery with those of the Bengal, Madras and Bombay provinces was complete. The only 'native' artillery that was allowed to remain in existence in the Punjab Frontier Force were two mountain trains, three lighter field batteries, and one garrison artillery battery.

A reorganization of the Royal Artillery itself also took place in 1859. The term 'battalion' lapsed, being replaced for administrative purposes by 'brigades'. The five horse artillery brigades consisted of two batteries each, and the fourteen field and Royal Garrison Artillery brigades about eight batteries each. For the RHA and the RA there were now two separate depots. Another change was the discontinuance of the unsatisfactory gunner-driver system, and the introduction of separate establishments for gunners and for drivers. Artillerymen in the sixties were given rifles and bayonets as personal arms.

The Royal Artillery's deputy adjutant-general during this reorganization was Sir Hugh Ross, who had commanded the Chestnut Troop throughout the Peninsular War and at Waterloo, and who in 1867 was the first artilleryman to attain the rank of field-marshal. At the time of his death he had seventy-four years' service; officially, of course, a field-marshal never retires, but always remains on the active list.

It should be noted that in the period after the great mutiny, owing to the new responsibilities assumed with regard to the Indian Empire, the peacetime strength of the Army at home, in artillery as in other arms, was governed mainly by the requirements of Indian and colonial service, rather than any plans for readiness for possible hostilities in Europe. This raised a host of problems – the provision of normal reliefs for units overseas was in itself a major undertaking – but in India it had the advantage of maintaining at a high level of general efficiency (though in some respects perhaps ill-adapted to action against a first-class enemy with modern arms) large numbers of trained soldiers, with many experienced officers.

Until the end of the century, in fact, the plains and hills of India were to be the Army's greatest school for war. This continued a process that had begun long before, in the campaigns against the French and their Indian auxiliaries, as well as the hard fighting with the Mahrattas, the Sultans of Mysore, and others. In some of these wars, often raging over vast extents of arduous terrain, considerable numbers of British troops were engaged. For the drive against the Pindaris in 1817, Lord Moira, as Governor-General, had assembled an army of 113,000 men with more than 300 guns – the largest British force seen in India up to that date.

After the rule of the Empress Victoria had been firmly established over all the more settled regions and main centres in the sub-continent, for many years one perennial danger zone remained – the North-West Frontier. Here, in the debatable land of jagged hills and parched, stony valleys winding up to and beyond the Khyber Pass, the Indian Army was pitted, time after time, against tough, wily and elusive foes, Afridis, Pathans and Baluchis, men knowing every inch of the ground, crack shots from boyhood, adepts in the arts of ambush and the use of cover. It was a country in which basic skill at arms was only the groundwork; a soldier, indeed any human being, had to be quick, enduring and resourceful if he hoped to survive.

Scarcely a year went by without the planning, fitting out and despatch of some punitive expedition into tribal territory, and almost all of them had artillery support. In many cases they were operating over roadless country in which any kind of wheeled transport was out of the question, but there were always the pack-mule guns, the old 7-pounders followed by the 2·5-inch jointed pieces (Kipling's 'screw-guns') of the Indian mountain trains, which eventually became the nineteen Royal Artillery mountain batteries of the Indian Army. Where foothold could be found for a mule or a man, there the guns went, usually in small numbers, but often with great effect. So highly did the enemy think of them that in a certain tribal feud one side applied for the services of a couple of the guns, offering to feed the men and animals and pay for all ammunition expended, and even to raise money for their hire if the Government desired this.

The mountain batteries were made up of British officers and Indian other ranks. To handle the loads the gunners had to be big men, and many of the Sikh and Punjabi Moslem artillerymen were tall fellows of fine physique. It is on record that at Maizar in 1897, when the pack mules had been killed by enemy fire and the guns were in danger of capture, two Indian under-officers and three gunners carried a gun and its mounting for a hundred yards into cover.

Between 1847 and 1913 there were no fewer than sixty-six punitive expeditions. Not all of them were affairs of a small mobile column; for the biggest, the Tirah campaign of 1897, practically the whole of an army corps was mobilized. The long association between British gunners and Indian troops was of real benefit to the Royal Artillery; but it was far from being the only training ground for war in which the regiment was engaged during the last forty years of the nineteenth century.

THE 'LITTLE WARS'

'You may hide in the caves, they'll be only your graves, but you can't get away from the guns!' – *Kipling*

Between 1859 and 1899 the British Army was involved in two fair-sized enterprises (in Egypt and the Sudan) and more than a dozen Asian and African expeditions of the kind that are usually lumped together, somewhat disparagingly, under the heading of 'little wars', though the majority of them were quite big enough, and strenuous enough, for those serving in them, who often found themselves, in the wildest and most desolate of environments, fighting actions of the most desperate and uncertain nature.

In 1860 an Anglo-French force was sent to north China with the object of compelling the Chinese to observe the terms of the treaties granting extraterritorial rights and privileges to westerners. With the artillery of Sir Hope Grant's contingent were two batteries of Armstrong 12-pounders, breech-loading rifled guns representing the latest development in ordnance.

The rifled guns were used, for the first time in the history of the regiment, for the bombardment of the Taku forts, which were barring an advance towards Peking along the Peiho river. Lieutenant-Colonel Wolseley wrote: 'Whilst the storming parties were struggling across the ditches, our Armstrong guns were making admirable practice a few feet over our heads, actually throwing the wall about so that portions of it fell upon our men's heads.' The armament of the forts included two British 32-pounders, recovered by the Chinese from gunboats sunk during an abortive naval attack in 1859. As soon as the infantry had gained a footing, these guns were taken over by a dozen artillerymen, who had carried 32-pounder ammunition with them, and the guns were turned against the works that still held out. This proved decisive.

Lieutenant-Colonel John Pawson, who enlisted as a trumpeter

in 1849 and died in 1933 at the age of ninety-six, claimed to have fired the first of these Armstrong guns. Pawson was Riding Master at Woolwich in the eighties.

An Armstrong battery was also included in the extremely thorough preparations for Sir Robert Napier's expedition of 1868 into Abyssinia, a land which was then still all but unknown to the outside world. In the event the overthrow of the Emperor Theodore (who shot himself) was accomplished with little armed opposition, but only after terrible natural obstacles had been surmounted in the movement of the artillery and stores from the base at Zula on the Red Sea for a distance of some 400 miles, much of it over rugged mountains, to the fortress of Magdala, lying nearly 10,000 feet above sea level.

Napier had four mountain batteries and two heavy mortars in addition to the Armstrong guns, which relied partly on elephant transport. The task of the few artillerymen with the Armstrongs was to load their guns and carriages on to the elephants when it was impossible for horses to draw them, and to offload when the road could take wheeled transport. The 8-inch mortars weighed 8¼ hundredweight, their beds 7½ hundredweight, and each had a travelling frame weighing 1½ hundredweight. All this fitted into a cradle, which in turn rested upon a pad on the elephant's back, so that the load of a 'mortar elephant' was well over 15 hundredweight. The men had an almost intolerable struggle. Sometimes the elephants threw off their burdens, and on a particularly steep, slimy incline one beast slipped back for fifty yards, threatening destruction to soldiers and animals behind it. On the return journey to the coast there were only twenty-six men to cope with twenty-nine elephants, and as the normal drill provided for eighteen men to load and unload one elephant, the gunners were almost completely worn out. When they reached Zula, after the last stage, they had marched 177 miles over the mountains in thirteen days without any but the briefest halts, and had not had a real night's rest for six days. On the artillery's part in this campaign, Fortescue writes: 'The Royal Regiment has never done finer service than this.'

In country of a very different kind, C Battery, 4th Brigade, RA, served Armstrong guns during the New Zealand campaigns of the sixties against the Maoris, a brave and skilful enemy. The battery's main work was in the destruction of Maori stockades, ingenious in design and often so tough that shot rebounded from the elasticity of the palisades, made with interlaced vines and huge bundles of bracken bound with flax; but the artillerymen also had to give a hand with roadmaking and general transport duties. Later the battery was converted into a mounted squadron, though still manning the guns when necessary, and on one occasion the gunners were called on to act as infantry in the assault on an entrenched position at Rangiriri. For gallantry in this action Lieutenant A. F. Pickard was awarded the Victoria Cross. Assistant Surgeon W. G. N. Manley won the VC with the gunners at Tauranga in 1864.

'New-fangled' ideas such as the Armstrong guns, and the experiments with different systems of rifling, were viewed with misgivings by some in the regiment. One distinguished veteran of the Kaffir and Crimean wars and the Mutiny used to grumble: 'First of all they insisted on having a lot of grooves in the bore of the gun. Now they are only going to have three grooves in the bore of the gun. Please goodness, they will next have no grooves at all, and we shall get back to the good old smoothbore which did all that was necessary to beat the Russians and to smash the Mutiny.' In the 1870s there was a change back to muzzle-loading, largely on the grounds of simplicity and lower cost, but this reversion did not last many years.

On the North-West Frontier of India, after a number of punitive expeditions in which mountain batteries were used, a larger and more varied contingent from the regiment was required in the Afghan War of 1878–80. This was notable as the first campaign after the adoption of rifled guns in which the enemy had any artillery worthy of consideration. It was also the last war in which elephants were used by both sides for artillery transport; during the early stages two RHA batteries were given elephants, and similar lumbering beasts dragged 40-pounder guns.

The campaign opened with a successful advance from the Khyber towards Kabul by the force under Major-General Roberts, VC, while a southern column occupied Kandahar, and by July 1879, the Amir of Afghanistan agreed to British terms, one of which was the acceptance in his capital of a British envoy, with escort. When operations seemed over, the treacherous murder of the envoy led to a renewal of the war, and the occupation of Kabul after a hostile force had been defeated with heavy losses by Roberts at Charasia. Two mountain batteries of the Punjab Frontier Force, with F/A Battery RHA, and G/3 RA, formed part of Roberts's army, which included one infantry division and a cavalry brigade.

The British troops established themselves for the winter in an entrenched cantonment at Sherpur, near Kabul, from which, after several engagements, a mass assault by about 60,000 Afghans was beaten off. Throughout the next few months our communications were perpetually harassed. In April a division was sent from southern Afghanistan by way of Ghazni as reinforcement. This force had with it A/B Battery RHA, and G/4 RA, both armed with 9-pounder rifled muzzle-loaders; II/II RA with 7-pounder mountain guns; and 6/11 RA, with 40-pounders and 6·3-inch howitzers, using elephant transport. In a hot fight near Ahmed Khel the artillery won praise from the general in command.

A rising in the south later threatened the British position at Kandahar, and on 27 July 1880, a small column, including E/B Battery RHA, and an improvised battery of captured smoothbores, moved out to seize Maiwand before the enemy could reach that point. An Afghan force, outnumbering the British by seven to one, was encountered while on its way to invest Kandahar, and was attacked, with disastrous results. Despite a stubborn resistance, the column was overwhelmed. In the RHA battery, Major Blackwood, one subaltern, and many of the gunners were killed, and another officer wounded. Two guns had to be abandoned; the others were brought out by a captain, after being limbered up in a hail of bullets, with some of the Afghans inside the battery position. For conspicuous bravery in this action Sergeant P. Mullane and Gunner J. Colliss were awarded the VC.

After Maiwand the remnants of the column retreated to Kandahar, which was at once besieged, and relief measures were urgently planned. In his famous march from Kabul to Kandahar, Roberts successfully moved an army 10,000 strong a distance of 300 miles over wretched tracks through hostile territory, without any secure base or communications. As no wheeled transport was used, the artillery at the outset was limited to three mountain batteries, but two guns of C/2 Battery

RA were taken on from Khalat-i-Ghilzai with the garrison of the fort there. After the defeat of the Afghans, and the relief of Kandahar, this unhappy war ended with a new amir installed on the throne.

One incident in the battle of Maiwand had a sequel fifteen years later, when the VC awarded to Gunner Colliss was declared forfeit – one of the very few cases in which such action has ever been taken. Colliss was deprived of the decoration, under Royal Warrant dated 18 November 1895, after being convicted of bigamy. Forfeiture has now been discontinued in practice, though the sovereign still has the right, under the terms of the Victoria Cross rules, to erase from the list the name of any man convicted of 'treason, cowardice, felony, or any infamous crime'.

The end of the Afghan War did not by any means mark the coming of lasting peace on the Indian frontier. Mountain artillery was in action again on many occasions in the North-West, and also in the conquest of Burma; occasionally, when the terrain was favourable, the greater firepower of field batteries was brought into play. During the ascent of the Irrawaddy in 1885, in a campaign which added 140,000 square miles of territory to the British Empire, artillery was mounted in barges, with guns in the bows and howitzers on the broadside, behind iron shields. A great number of cannon, ranging from 1-pounder to 60-pounders, were captured by the troops, including some of ancient European make, and one complete battery of 9-pounders inlaid with gold.

In African expeditions, such as the Ashanti campaign in which Wolseley's force captured and burned Kumasi, light guns frequently had to be carried by blacks, owing to the lack of adequate roads and prevalence of animal diseases. A normal allocation was eleven carriers for each 7-pounder, with the same number of men as reliefs, but in emergency there were times when one African alone took a gun across a log bridge on his head.

During the Zulu war of 1879–80, Royal Artillery units manned 9-pounders, 7-pounders and rockets. They also had with them the Gatling, one of the earliest types of machine-gun to take the field. Guns of this type, with multiple revolving barrels, had already been used in America; General Custer's failure to take with him the Gatling guns which were available probably sealed the fate of his 7th Cavalry, wiped out in the famous 'last stand' on the Little Bighorn in the Dakota Territory on 26 June 1876.

Two artillery units – N/5 Field Battery and the Rocket Battery – shared in the tragedy of Isandhlwana, where part of Lord Chelmsford's force was attacked in its encampment and almost totally destroyed by Cetewayo's impis, with 800 European casualties. The rocket detachment was taken by surprise and wiped out while in action on a small knoll in front of the camp. One of the survivors of N/5, Lieutenant H. T. Curling, told in a letter how he escaped.

'When we got the order to retire we limbered up, but were hardly in time as the Zulus were on us at once, and one man was killed (stabbed) as he was mounting on a seat on the gun carriage. Most of the gunners were on foot, as there was not time to mount them on the guns. We trotted off to the camp, thinking to take up another position there, but found it in possession of the enemy, who were killing the men as they came out of their tents. We went right through them, and out the other side, losing nearly all our gunners in doing so, and one of the two sergeants. The road to Rorke's Drift that we hoped to retreat by was full of the enemy, so, no way being open, we followed a crowd of natives and camp followers, who were running down a ravine. The Zulus were all among them, stabbing men as they ran.

'In a moment the Zulus closed in and the drivers who now alone remained were pulled off their horses and killed. I did not see Major Smith [in command of the battery] at this moment, but was with him a minute before. The guns could not be spiked, there was no time to think of anything, and we hoped to save the guns up to the last moment. As soon as the guns were taken I galloped off and made off with the crowd. How any of us escaped I don't know; the Zulus were all among us, and I saw men falling all round. We rode for about 5 miles, hotly pursued by the Zulus, when we came to a cliff overhanging a river. We had to climb down the face of this cliff and not more than half of those who started from the top got to the bottom. Many fell right down, among others Major Smith, and the Zulus caught us up here and shot us as we climbed down.

'I got down safely, and came to the river, which was very deep and swift. Numbers were being swept away as they tried to cross, and others were shot from above. My horse fortunately swam straight across, although I had three or four men hanging on to his tail, stirrup-leathers, etc. After crossing the river we were in comparative safety, though many were killed afterwards who were on foot and unable to keep up. It seems to me like a dream. I cannot realize it at all. The whole affair did not last an hour from beginning to end.'

Some gunners who had been left in camp managed to escape on spare horses, but the battery lost sixty-two men and twenty-four horses. N/5, or what was left of it, took part five months later in the victory at Ulundi, which shattered the power of the Zulus. The same battery also saw action in the defence of Potchefstroom in 1881, during the first war against the burghers in South Africa. After the Boers cut off the garrison's water supply, a competition in well-sinking was organized, and was won by the artillerymen. Another contribution was in the improvisation of a Union Jack to be flown on the fort. This flag was put together in the gun pits from the linings of the officers' and sergeants' cloaks (white and red respectively) and some blue serge from the infantry. When the garrison was forced to surrender, through shortage of food, the troops marched out with the honours of war, and the battery was allowed to keep the flag, which was presented later to the Royal Artillery Institution.

The first of Britain's bigger wars in the northern half of the African continent broke out in 1882, after an armed rising and the massacre of Europeans in Alexandria. Operations in Egypt led up to a night march across the desert, followed by a dawn attack on the enemy's entrenched position, resulting in complete victory at the battle of Tel-el-Kebir. In the approach march the field artillery was stationed between the two infantry divisions, and the horse artillery with the cavalry on the right flank.

During the battle N/2 Battery, RA (later to become the 71st Anti-Tank Battery) distinguished itself by crossing the entrenchments in column of route at the gallop, and unlimbering for action level with the first line of infantry. On the entrenchments the leading gun checked, tottered, and dropped back from the parapet into the ditch, smashing a wheel, while the five other guns got clean over. From this time on N/2 was known as the 'Broken Wheel Battery'.

Lord Denbigh, who was a subaltern in the battery, said in a letter: 'All of a sudden the smoke lifted like a curtain and we found ourselves close to a long line of entrenchments. . . . We at once went on, and Major Brancker found an angle in the line just in front where the ditch was not so deep, so the right gun galloped straight at it. It went with a bump into the ditch, and stuck fast in the face of the parapet, with most of the horses over; but a lot of the 42nd rushed to our help, and we lifted and shoved the gun over; but found one of the wheels smashed to pieces.'

Less than two years after Tel-el-Kebir, Britain was fitting out for the south an expeditionary force of all arms, under Sir Garnet Wolseley, to rescue General Gordon, besieged in Khartoum, with hopelessly inferior resources in troops and arms, by many thousand fanatical adherents of the rebel Mahdi. After the long slow passage by boat up the Nile, a detached portion of Wolseley's Army, including three 7-pounder screw-guns, was marching over the desert, to cut across a loop of the great river, when it was heavily attacked at Abu Klea. Troops formed square, with infantry at the sides, the scanty artillery at the angles, and the transport camels, horses and mules in the centre. By weight of numbers the Sudanese broke the square, but after a desperate struggle all who had hacked their way in were killed or hurled out, and the square re-formed. The attackers were then driven off, the screw-guns inflicting heavy casualties.

Gunner Albert Smith won the VC for saving from the enemy Lieutenant Guthrie, but this officer died later of wounds.

Wolseley's expedition arrived too late to save Gordon, and Anglo-Egyptian troops evacuated the Sudan. Twelve years later, after the Egyptian Army had been raised to greater efficiency under General Sir Herbert Kitchener, a powerful force was organized to stamp out lawlessness in the Sudan. Planning was careful and thorough, and decisive victory was gained on 2 September 1898, at Omdurman. Here a combined British and Egyptian Army, in which were two Royal Artillery field batteries, as well as Egyptian gunners commanded by British officers, routed the entire dervish host of 40,000 men. Brigadier-General Graham writes: 'The destructive effect of lyddite shell was first observed on service from the fire of the howitzers of the 37th Field Battery on the fort at Omdurman.' It was also the battle in which young Winston Churchill, in the dual role of cavalryman and war correspondent, charged with the 21st Lancers.

Most of the campaigns which have been briefly outlined were waged against enemies possessing little or no artillery. They therefore demanded from the British only the simplest of fire tactics; but in Europe the sweeping victories of the Prussians, culminating in the French debacle of 1870, had prompted some drastic rethinking on the handling of guns in battle. The methods of Wellington's day, when guns came into action in front of or in line with the infantry, and a battery was more or less pinned to its position from the start (thus making necessary an artillery reserve under the control of the general in command) would no longer suffice, so far as continental warfare was concerned.

Now that rifling and elongated projectiles had made possible greater range and accuracy, batteries normally took up positions to the rear of the infantry. An inactive reserve was no longer justified; the accepted rule was for all available guns at the start of a battle to join in attempting to overwhelm the enemy's artillery. Afterwards, fire was switched to the opposing infantry, while some batteries would assist the attack by moving forward in close support. Direct laying was still the general practice, and batteries usually came into action, where possible, on the crest of rising ground; but the introduction of cordite in the nineties enabled guns to open fire without disclosing their location by clouds of smoke, and this led to the more frequent use of concealed positions. Heavy artillery was not yet sufficiently mobile for general use in the field.

Advances in metallurgical technique produced notable improvements in equipment. Cast-iron guns were followed by other applications of iron and steel, the wire-wound process being perfected before 1890. Steel ousted wood for gun carriages, making them less cumbrous, so that a more powerful weapon could be provided without increasing the weight behind the team. About 1883 a 12-pounder breech-loader was issued to the horse and field artillery. Before long, some of the field batteries were firing 15-pound shells. Quick-firers had made their appearance on fixed mountings, but not yet on mobile carriages.

By about 1886 common shell was being made of forged steel, and after 1895 lyddite high explosive as a filling was in fairly general use. The shrapnel shell had been adapted for rifled guns by Colonel Boxer. With this ammunition the Boxer wooden time fuse was used for many years, until superseded by a time-and-percussion fuse made of metal.

In the coastal artillery, large rifled muzzle-loaders were added to the defences. At a time when relations with Russia were strained, four 17·72-inch guns of 100 tons each were produced, two for mounting at Gibraltar, and two for Malta. Coast artillery was at its zenith, in armament at any rate; Gibraltar had 700 pieces, manned by a whole brigade of artillerymen.

Developments in coast defence eventually led to the division of the regiment into two separate corps – the Royal Horse and Royal Field Artillery, and the Royal Garrison Artillery. In the nineties many new batteries and companies were added, until at the end of the century there were twenty-one RHA batteries, ninety-five RFA batteries, ten mountain units, ninety-one companies of the RGA, and no fewer than eight depots. To bring officers' promotion up to a level with that in other arms, the first captains in charge of batteries became majors in 1872. This change was an offshoot of the Cardwell reforms. Rather ironically, these innovations, which did so much good for the Army in general, had threatened at first to have an adverse effect on the Royal Artillery because, with the abolition of the purchase system, many suitable young men, who in earlier days would certainly have looked to the regiment, would now have a greater opportunity of obtaining commissions in other branches of the service.

During the seventies long-service engagements were reduced, with the object of providing a larger reserve on mobilization. This also had the effect of improving the soldier's chances of promotion. He benefited further by a free issue of bread and meat rations, calculated to save him fourpence halfpenny a day, and later an allowance for groceries was also given. The basic rate of pay was a shilling a day – 'bloomin' good pay', as Kipling's soldiers chorused ironically; but anyone who cares to delve into the dark impenetrable mysteries of army pay and allowances may find that, if one takes into account changes in prices, it did not really compare so unfavourably with the two shillings a day that was drawn by thousands of men who joined up in 1939.

All ranks of gunners at home still wore the traditional dark blue, but khaki was on the way. Clothing of this colour, first adapted in India as an improvisation, was now generally worn by troops serving in India and the colonies. The *British Grenadiers* was officially recognized as the regimental quick march in 1882, after having been in actual use for many years.

In 1895 the Duke of Cambridge, who had been colonel of the Royal Regiment of Artillery since 1861, became its first colonel-in-chief.

FIGHTING THE BOERS

'Soldiers ought more to fear their general than their enemy.' –
Montaigne

The South African War of 1899–1902 is perhaps the classic example of a contest in which the British military machine, hampered by poor generalship at the start, underwent a succession of humiliating reverses, not through any real lack of available manpower or arms, but mainly because of its unimaginative stiffness and sluggishness in the face of hardy opponents who fought their own kind of battle resolutely and well, impelled by an intense nationalist pride, and exploiting to the full their superior knowledge of a vast and rugged country.

It was scarcely to be wondered at that the infantry, trained in the school of close-order drill and set manœuvres according to the book of rules, should so often have been a comparatively easy prey, among the kopjes and on the veldt, for the Boer commandos, consisting of expert marksmen who could chose their moment to strike from cover, then mount their ponies and speed away into the blue distance long before the British columns had laboured up to their firing positions. A further shock to British military pride – perhaps a greater one, and more surprising even today – was that the Boers' artillery, in the early stages at any rate, was often more formidable than the British Army's own.

Before long it was evident that the embattled burghers were using mobile guns of larger calibre and longer range than had been thought possible. This was due in part to the Boers' shrewd contacts with European suppliers of arms. Their best pieces, such as the high-velocity Krupp 12-pounders and 14-pounder Creusots, were more up-to-date than any of the British standard equipment before the war. The Creusot 155-millimetre gun was the largest yet seen in the field. The Staats Artillerie, it should be noted, was not composed of citizen militia or guerrilla fighters, as in the commandos, but of trained soldiers, in whose ranks were to be found some German gunners lent from the Kaiser's Army. Luckily for their opponents, the Boer artillerymen, though quick and active enough on occasion, seem to have shown at times some lack of accuracy, and certainly of initiative. More could have been achieved, particularly in the sieges, with the material they had. Nevertheless, the disparity was a real one. It was cancelled out before the end, but for many months, on the British side, the artillery effort was one of makeshift and improvisation, scraping together every gun, old or new, that could be found, from the Navy or from odd corners in South Africa itself, to supplement the Army's own ordnance.

One gap was filled through the alertness of General Sir Henry Brackenbury, Director-General of Ordnance, after the French Army manœuvres of 1900, with the debut of the famous 'seventy-fives', had proved that true quick-firing guns, far in advance of anything previously known, were being produced on the Continent. Among the foreign establishments visited by Sir Henry's agents was a Düsseldorf firm, Rheinische Metalwaren und Maschinenfabrik, hitherto unknown as gunmakers. Their engineer, Herr Ehrhardt, exhibited a 15-pounder quick-firer in which the whole of the recoil was taken up by a top carriage, so that the undercarriage itself remained absolutely steady when the gun was fired. An order was placed with this firm for the equipment of eighteen batteries.

As public opinion in Germany would certainly have been adverse, the whole transaction was carried out with the utmost secrecy. The guns for each battery were despatched, as soon as ready, to Hamburg for shipment, consigned as 'machinery and explosives'. It was arranged with the Customs that the cases should be delivered without examination, their contents being known only to a few officials directly concerned. One day, before the secret had been revealed, a foreman at the Royal Gun Factory rushed excitedly into the office, saying that 'one of those packing cases on the quay has broken open, and there is a gun inside!'. The superintendent, who was equally in the dark, hastened to the War Office to report the 'discovery' and enquire what it meant.

When war broke out in October 1899, most of the few scattered British units were forced by superior numbers to shut themselves up in garrison towns which were invested by the Boers, as at Ladysmith and Kimberley. To relieve these garrisons became the primary objective as soon as reinforcements arrived from England, India, the dominions and colonies.

In Natal, the defenders of Ladysmith, which was invested in December, numbered about 13,000, including six field batteries and some naval detachments with guns on locally built carriages. An attempt by General Sir Redvers Buller's relief force to cross the Tugela River at Colenso led to an artillery action which has become famous in the regiment. Like another episode, to be described later, it was an example not of brilliant offensive action but of artillery extricating itself, with unsurpassable gallantry, after being caught at disadvantage in a situation of the deadliest danger.

At Colenso on 15 December 1899, two field batteries, the 14th and 66th, were under the command of Colonel Long, who had enhanced a reputation as a dashing officer by his handling of the Egyptian artillery at Atbara in April, 1898. Owing to his eagerness, it appears, the 14th and 66th outstripped the infantry on the flanks, and also the slow ox-drawn guns from HMS *Terrible*. The two batteries came into action in the open, despite the fact that the foremost Boer trenches were only 500 to 700 yards away. Men and horses fell, 'but the gunners continued to fire the guns as though firing a salute at a ceremonial parade'.

Soon the casualties inflicted by the Boers' rifles and quick-firers were so many that the position became untenable. One gun alone was still being served, by four men who refused to leave, and who were all killed. The body of one gunner was found later with sixty-four wounds. The survivors sheltered in a small rocky hollow; there Major William Babtie, RAMC, tended the wounded.

General Buller, who had come forward with members of his staff, now called for volunteers to save the guns. Among those who responded were his three ADCs, one of whom was Lieutenant F. H. S. Roberts, King's Royal Rifle Corps, the only son of Field-Marshal Lord Roberts, VC. Corporal George Nurse, RFA, and six gunners went with the ADCs. Through a storm of shells and bullets they galloped two limbers, and succeeded in bringing back two guns. Roberts was mortally wounded. Captain Hamilton Reed, of the 7th Field Battery, then led three teams from his own battery in a vain attempt to save more guns. Of the twenty-three horses that his men took out, thirteen, including his own mount, were killed before they had reached halfway.

Awards of the VC were made to three artillerymen, Hamilton Reed, Nurse, and Captain H. N. Schofield, as well as to Major Babtie, Lieutenant Roberts, Captain Congreve of the Rifle Brigade, and Private C. Ravenhill, Royal Scots Fusiliers. Nineteen men received the Distinguished Conduct Medal. The gun which Roberts had died to save was afterwards presented by the War Office to his father, Lord Roberts. On it, fourteen years later, the coffin was borne at the funeral of the field-marshal, who had won his own VC during the Mutiny in 1857.

Although the heroism displayed at Colenso was outstanding, the fact remained that ten guns had been lost. For this Colonel Long was blamed, and was replaced; but General Botha, the Boer commander, said later that Long had 'saved the British Army' on that day, as his action in pushing the guns so far forward had disrupted his opponents' plane.

Before the Ladysmith relief force achieved its objective there was further severe fighting, the enemy having to be driven out of successive positions by outflanking movements combined with concentrated shelling of his trenches. At Pieters Hill on 27 February 1900, the British supported their attack with seventy guns, including twelve from the Royal Navy. The high-explosive shell fired by the field howitzers and a 5-inch battery manned by the Royal Garrison Artillery were particularly effective. Operating to a well-arranged fire plan of several stages, the attack met with complete success, and the handling of the artillery on this occasion is cited as the first instance of the method of fire control by a CRA (Commander, Royal Artillery), which became standard practice subsequently.

The action cleared the way to Ladysmith, which was relieved the following day. Its garrison were in good heart, though short of rations; some of the horses had been eaten.

A force pushing north-eastward through Cape Colony to relieve Kimberley had also encountered stiff resistance, in which the strength of the Boers' artillery emphasized the British need for heavier guns. One answer to the problem was the arming of more batteries with 4·7-inch and 5-inch guns, drawn by oxen, and a fuse with a longer time of burning was also issued to the field artillery. After careful preparation by Lord Roberts, who had now taken over command with Kitchener as his Chief of Staff, General French moved his cavalry division, which included seven RHA units, round the Boers' left, and at the end of three days' hard riding Kimberley was relieved in February. Roberts's main army captured Cronje, the Boer leader, and 4,000 of his men a few days later at Paardeburg, and on 13 March 1900, Bloemfontein was entered without resistance.

Before the advance on Pretoria there was a period of refitment, during which harassment of the British communication lines grew in intensity. On 31 March a cavalry column to which Q and U Batteries, RHA, were attached was ambushed by a commando led by Christiaan de Wet while crossing the Korn Spruit drift near Sannah's Post. U Battery, which was in the lead, entangled with a mass of refugee wagons, was surrounded, losing five of its guns and almost all its men, the majority of whom were rounded up before they could make a fight.

The other battery, fortunately, was still two or three hundred yards from the ford when the alarm was given. Major Edmund Phipps-Hornby of Q Battery, having got most of his guns clear, unlimbered and went into action, but they were still dangerously far forward and under heavy fire. Colonel Rochfort, the brigade commander, had been shot while pulling up a limber so as to have the ammunition closer to hand. When the order to retire came, only the major and ten other men, several of them wounded, were still on their feet. With scratch teams from the limbers four of the guns were saved, but two were lost, and almost every man in the battery was either killed or wounded.

Four VCs were awarded to Q Battery for bravery in this engagement. The commander-in-chief decided to treat the case as one of collective gallantry under Rule 13 of the VC Warrant, and directed that one officer, one NCO, and two gunners or drivers should be selected by their comrades. Major Phipps-Hornby was named, as senior officer; Sergeant Charles Parker was chosen by the NCOs, and Gunner Isaac Lodge and Driver Horace Glascock by the other ranks.

Another VC went to Lieutenant Francis Aylmer Maxwell, Indian Staff Corps, attached to Roberts's Light Horse, who five separate times went out to help in bringing in two guns and three limbers, one of which he and Captain Humphreys of Q Battery dragged in by hand. After this Maxwell went out again with Humphreys and another officer in an effort, which had to be abandoned, to retrieve the last gun. Maxwell, after a distinguished career in the Indian Army, was killed in action as a brigadier-general near Ypres in September 1917.

Six weeks after Korn Spruit, from a small beleaguered town on the Cape–Rhodesia railway, far to the north and close to the Transvaal border, came news that caused public rejoicing in the streets of London, and for at least a decade or so added a new word to the English language. Mafeking, 'the Place of Stones', had been relieved. Here for 217 days a small force of the Protectorate Regiment, Bechuanaland Rifles, British South Africa Police and civilian volunteers had held out against large numbers of Boers armed with vastly superior artillery.

In his account of the siege, *Mafeking*, Duncan Grinnell-Milne writes that 'the garrison's artillery consisted at the start of two broken-down museum-pieces – muzzle-loading 7-pounders dating almost incredibly from 1820 – that had been abandoned in the fort fifteen years earlier by General Warren. . . . For a day or two much excitement had followed the receipt of a coded telegram from the Cape announcing the despatch by rail of two modern 5·7-inch howitzers. Troops crowded the station when the train pulled in. Disappointment. No guns. At length someone peered into the guard's van – and discovered two more muzzle-loading 7-pounders. "Why!" exclaimed a veteran from Rhodesia. "There's old 'Crooked-tail Sal'. Know her from Matabeleland. Can't fire a shot straight." The Cape, it seemed, had made a trifling error in coding.'

With regard to light weapons the outlook was not quite so dismal. Colonel Baden-Powell had managed to lay hands on some invaluable ·303 Maxim machine-guns and two small but fairly modern quick-firers, a 1-pounder Hotchkiss and (second-hand from naval stores) a 2-inch Nordenfeldt firing a three-quarter-pound shell. Not one of the four 7-pounders, however, was serviceable; fittings were worn, carriages in disrepair, metalwork rusty, wood rotted – and there were no spare parts. With grave misgivings, the local wagon builder and his assistant took charge of the ruinous collection and set to work to provide

14. A mountain battery in the Peninsula. This painting is one of a series by G. B. Campion, drawing master at the Royal Military Academy, 1841–1870 (R.A. Museum)

15. *The Bengal Army on the March*, about 1817. This picture, one of a series in the museum at Woolwich, was painted by an artillery officer on the long voyage home after service with the Honourable East India Company's forces

16. The mortar battery at Woolwich, about 1847 (R.A. Museum)

17. *A Heavy Day in the Batteries*, during the siege of Delhi in the India Mutiny. From a print in the R.A. Museum

18. Action before Kassassin, in the Egyptian campaign of 1882. An *Illustrated London News* picture in the R.A. Museum

19. The last gun in action at Colenso, South African War, 15 December, 1899. From a picture in the R.A. Museum

20. Saving the guns after the Boer ambush at the Korn Spruit (Sannah's Post), 31 March, 1900 (R.A. Museum)

21. Moving a 60-pdr. with a 12-horse team, aided by men on drag-ropes; Bezentin-le-Petit, October 1916 (Imperial War Museum)

new carriages. As soon as the guns could stand on their wheels and fire, however inaccurately, Major Panzera, an officer of skill and incurable optimism, took over the 'battery of popguns', whose maximum effective range was well under 2,000 yards.

Against this pitiable array, the Boers, who had eight modern guns with plenty of ammunition, might have been expected speedily to inflict damage and losses so heavy that the garrison must have surrendered or been wiped out, but the enemy bombardment, though at times destructive, was spasmodic and often ill-directed, wasting itself on targets of little military significance. By dint of sheer bluff – use of decoy positions and dummy minefields – together with boldly aggressive raiding tactics up to the limit of their meagre resources, for week after week the defenders contrived to hold off the Boers. The triumphs of improvisation accomplished by the little garrison are the more remarkable when it is remembered that not one of them was a serving regular artilleryman, though the rickety 7-pounders owed much to the handling of Kenneth Murchison, a retired officer of the Royal Artillery, whose patience had coaxed them into action so well that from every engagement in which they had been used the enemy were forced to retire.

While out riding one morning, Major Alexander Godley of the Protectorate Regiment (who later became a general) noticed at a farm that one of the gate posts, half buried and almost hidden by a thorn bush, was in fact an old cannon. He had it dug up and taken to the railway workshops, where, on being cleaned, it proved to be a bronze 16-pounder, dated 1770 on the barrel – evidently a ship's gun, but without the naval crown and cipher, so that it probably came from some privateer. It was believed that the gun had been brought to the coast more than a century earlier, then left there, perhaps after a wreck, until it was carried north by members of a tribe migrating into Bechuanaland, who eventually abandoned it for lack of powder. Cleaning revealed on the breech the letters 'B.P.', but spiteful gossip to the effect that Baden-Powell had had these added as a piece of self-advertisement was apparently quite unfounded; later research showed that they were the initials of the eighteenth-century makers, Bailey and Pegg of Brierley Foundry in Staffordshire.

After the old cannon, given the name of Lord Nelson, had

been furbished up and mounted on a carriage, it was taken to the Malmani road, aimed at a Boer laager about three thousand yards away, and fired. The first roundshot curved high in the air, dropped just in front of the laager, and bounced through it, raising clouds of dust and causing the Boers to move back for three miles.

By the end of January the defenders of Mafeking had only enough powder left for about fifty rounds per gun. Scouring the town, Major Panzera unearthed in various stores large numbers of shotgun cartridges and a considerable quantity of blasting powder. In an isolated shed he carried out a series of highly dangerous experiments to find a correct blend of these materials, producing enough reasonably satisfactory powder to keep the guns firing.

His next project was more ambitious – nothing less than the manufacture of a gun to answer the challenge of the Boers' biggest piece, called Gritje by them, but known to the garrison as Creechy. From an unexploded round it was known that this fired a 94-pound shell measuring six inches across the base. At Kimberley, in reply to a Creusot 'Long Tom', a big gun named 'Long Cecil', in honour of Cecil Rhodes, had been successfully built and fired, but the workshop facilities at Mafeking were much more restricted. However, the job was tackled, and by 25 February a 5-inch howitzer was ready for use. For the barrel, a steel tube that had been a steam pipe was strengthened by a jacket made of iron railings bent into rings and shrunk on. The breech and trunnions were of bronze cast at the railway foundry, the carriage was improvised from the chassis of a thrashing machine with wide track and bronze-tyred iron wheels. Scrap metal was collected from the town's soda-water factory, from unexploded projectiles and discarded horse shoes, to be melted down and cast into spherical shells.

The first test of the 18-pound shells, when three or four were fired in the direction of Game Tree Hill, was a resounding success. It was found that the maximum effective range was no less than 4,000 yards, and the gun was immediately put into active service. It was given the title of the Wolf, after the Africans' name for Baden-Powell – 'Impeesa', the Wolf Who Never Sleeps. Later this gun found a resting place at the Royal United Services Institute in Whitehall.

Before the siege ended, more than 20,000 shells had been fired upon the town and its outskirts. Taking into account the 1,500 rounds contributed by Creechy, the total weight of metal dropped by the Boer guns amounted to slightly over 150 tons, yet, thanks to shelters and other safety measures, fewer than a dozen white non-combatants were killed or wounded by artillery. Casualties among the fighting men were much higher in proportion, naturally, and also among the Africans, largely owing to their neglect of precautions.

When relief forces at last drew near, Colonel Mahon's column of 1,100 men had a 12-pounder battery of the Royal Horse Artillery and fifty-two supply wagons, with ten mules to a wagon, that had advanced over arid land at an average rate of nearly 20 miles a day. Both men and animals suffered acutely from shortage of water. Colonel Plumer, who had been ordered to make a junction with Mahon at Massibi, received reinforcements that included a battery of the Royal Canadian Field Artillery with some new 12-pounders, but when he arrived with 450 men (all for whom mounts could be found) they had with them only eight guns, two of which were 7-pounder muzzle-loaders. After some sharp fighting the Boers withdrew, and in the ceremonial entry of the relief column into the town the march-past was headed, amidst great jubilation, by M Battery, RHA, 'spick-and-span despite long service', followed by the Canadian gunners.

In the same month of May, the main British Army pressed north, and Pretoria was entered after one or two engagements. Within a few weeks the Natal forces, which by this time had been re-equipped, linked up with Roberts's right flank. The main force of the enemy was beaten, but it had not been destroyed, and for nearly two years, long after the war had seemed at an end, a harassing guerrilla struggle was maintained by Boer raiding parties, foremost among whose leaders was the elusive De Wet – the 'will o' the wisp', as a *Punch* cartoon depicted him. For some time the British troops, despite their numbers, could do little to check the hit-and-run thrusts by well-mounted irregulars, free from the impedimenta of heavy equipment and fixed lines of communication, and able to choose their targets at widely separated points.

To deal with this, Kitchener, who had become commander-in-chief on Roberts's return to England, organized a system of blockhouses connected by wire entanglements along roads and railways, enclosing areas in which mobile detachments could execute sweeping movements to round up the Boers. But even after the expansion of the Yeomanry, and the arrival of thousands of volunteers from the dominions, there was still a shortage of the mounted men required, and eventually many artillery units, returning their guns into store for the time being, were converted to mounted rifles. Gunners seldom take kindly to being parted from their own traditional weapons, and it may be imagined that grumbling was rife, but at least the change showed practical results. In their new role the artillerymen won high praise for good horsemanship in trying conditions, and for the skill attained in mounted infantry duties.

But the work of the artillery as such was by no means finished. It distinguished itself at Noirtgedacht on 13 December 1900, when one of our columns was attacked by Delarey's commando. A British position was captured, and the troops who had held it fell back to a new one on Yeomanry Hill. The artillery – P Battery RHA, 8th Battery RFA, one 4·7-inch gun of No. 5 Company, Eastern Division, RGA, and a pompom – retired section by section or gun by gun, by different routes, under intense rifle fire. One of the RHA guns had its whole detachment shot down, and was brought out with the aid of some Marines, and the 4·7 had to be dragged out by hand, but all were saved. The general in command reported that the conduct of the artillery was 'beyond all praise'.

Shoeing Smith Alfred Ernest Ind, RHA, won the VC on 20 December 1901, at Tafelkop while serving in a pompom section. (The pompoms were 37-millimetre Vickers-Maxim guns, belt-fed with 1-pounder shells.) When all the other men had been killed or wounded, Ind stayed at his post and continued to fire on the advancing Boers until the last possible moment. The section commander, who was wounded, then galloped the limbers away to prevent the enemy from removing the guns, which were recaptured shortly afterwards. Ind, who was promoted to corporal, was wounded and mentioned in dispatches on three other occasions.

At Tweebosch in March 1902, when a British column was

overwhelmed by Delarey's raiders, a section of the 38th Battery, RFA, remained in action until every man had been hit. Lieutenant Nesham was then called upon to surrender. On refusing to do so he was shot by the Boers. A section of the 4th Battery, RFA and a pompom detachment also held out until all the gunners had fallen. Lieutenant Venning, the section commander and last survivor, was shot while serving a gun.

In an action at Itala in Zululand, Driver F. H. Bradley of the 69th Battery, RFA, earned the VC for bringing up ammunition under heavy fire. Four men who helped him received the DCM.

As a result of the war, which ended in May 1902 with the submission of the Boers, far-reaching changes were introduced in the British armed forces. One of the most important was the reorganization of the Yeomanry and Volunteers into a Territorial Army, which was to prove its worth in 1914–18. The old militia artillery was incorporated in a Special Reserve in 1908. A quick-firing field gun with a shield (the 18-pounder Mark I) was produced, and the 4·5-inch QF replaced the 5-inch breech-loading howitzer. Shields had been impossible with the older armament, owing to the necessity for the detachment to stand clear of the recoil when the gun was fired.

Heavier batteries with longer range, yet sufficiently mobile for use in the field, made their appearance, including 60-pounders drawn by teams of eight horses. The horse artillery man's sword was discarded, improved patterns of rifles, bayonets, and small-arms ammunition came into use, and all batteries were issued with a proportion of rifles for local protection.

An important part was played by members of the Royal Garrison Artillery in manning the new heavy batteries, and also in other ways before long. There had been a tendency among many in the Royal Artillery's mounted branches to look down on the static role of the RGA, with its coast defences and siege batteries, as something of a repository for the less able and energetic officers; but they also included a good many who were more interested in the technique of gunnery than most of the RHA and RFA men, and officers of this stamp were to be very largely responsible for pressing through the conversion of the field artillery to up-to-date scientific methods during the First World War.

Modernization after the Boer War still met with criticism. When the adoption of shields was first proposed, there was some unfavourable comment on the ground that the men would take cover behind them instead of 'standing up and working their guns'. Similarly, when guns were painted khaki, before manœuvres in India in 1891, commentators in the press deplored this attempt to 'hide' the guns as out of keeping with the traditions of the RHA, and certain to have a deleterious effect on morale.

Firing from behind cover, where possible, was now regarded as the normal procedure, and the dial sight was introduced. As a result of the use of forward observation officers in South Africa a higher standard of signalling became necessary for contact with the gun position officers, and before long field telephones were provided. These made possible closer control of his batteries by the lieutenant-colonel. Divisional artillery units carried out training with their cavalry or infantry formations after the annual practice camps. One of the eternal problems in training was that of obtaining a satisfactory degree of tactical realism without sacrificing technical skill in gunnery.

By 1901 the RHA batteries had been grouped in 'brigade divisions' of two batteries each, and the old RGA divisions were done away with, all the companies being numbered consecutively. Two years later the term 'brigade' was substituted for 'brigade division' in the RHA and RFA. Khaki service dress had come into general wear in 1902 (uniforms of the same colour had been worn in India about the time of the Mutiny, some of the first specimens being 'dyed' with mud from a river to tone down the conspicuous whiteness of tropical drill clothing).

In 1904 the ancient post of master-general of the ordnance, abolished during the Crimean War, was revived as the designation for the fourth member of the Army Council. (The appointment was again discontinued in 1938, but was revived in 1959.) King George V consented to become colonel-in-chief of the Royal Artillery on 5 June 1910.

During the years before 1914, while European rivalries mounted towards the cataclysmic end of an era, British troops fought in several minor wars in Asia and Africa. A feature of the Malakand expedition on the North-West Frontier in 1895 was the handling of three mountain batteries as a brigade by the senior battery commander. Their concentrated fire was a revelation to those whose experience had been limited to single batteries acting independently. New 18-pounder field guns were used in action for the first time against the Mohmands in 1908 in one of the brilliant little campaigns waged by Major-General Sir James Willcocks, and described by *Punch* as 'Willcocks' weekend wars'.

Three artillery units – B Battery RHA, 12th Battery RFA, and No. 4 Company, Hongkong-Singapore Battalion, RA – formed part of the international force which was sent to China when the Boxer Rebellion, a fanatical anti-foreign movement with some encouragement from extremists in high places, led to the murder of the German minister and the siege of the Legation Quarter in Peking, where diplomatic envoys with their staffs, as well as missionaries and hundreds of Chinese Christians, had taken refuge.

Peking was entered in August 1900. Among the reinforcements which arrived, too late to be utilized there, was the siege train from South Africa, with some 9·45-inch Skoda howitzers. Those had been bought in Europe, shipped from Trieste to the Cape, taken to railhead at Roodeval, then dragged by a great team of oxen to Pretoria, but the Boer capital surrendered before the 9·45s were called upon. After their further long voyage to China, it was ironical that they were again deprived of a chance to show what they could do. The story of the purchase of the howitzers is a remarkable one. In November 1899 Sir Henry Brackenbury, the vigilant director-general, learnt that Skoda of Pilsen had four 9·45s for which German agents were negotiating, their ultimate destination, presumably, being the Transvaal for use by the Boers. A deal was effected by the British, and a steamer set out with the howitzers, bound 'direct for Shanghai', but she put into Gibraltar, where the cargo was unloaded into a freighter despatched from England, another ship having to be found to carry the ammunition.

Four years after the operations in China, British guns were taken to Lhasa, the 'forbidden city', in Sir Francis Younghusband's expedition which brought about the signing of an Anglo-Tibetan treaty. The artillery consisted of one section of a mountain battery and two little 7-pounders manned, by the 8th Gurkhas and known to the troops as 'Bubble and Squeak'.

During the march over the mountain passes, ranging in height from 14,000 to 17,000 feet, the mountain guns went into action at an altitude far exceeding that of the summit of Mont Blanc.

MEN OF 1914

'They stood, and earth's foundations stay.' – *A. E. Housman*

By many of the older generation in Britain the dark years of 1914–18 are remembered, perhaps above all, as the war of the guns – the long, deadly, strength-draining conflict in which the artillery was methodically built up to a peak of destructive power incomparably greater and more terrible than anything witnessed in any previous struggle known to man. It was the war in which, while the enduring infantry held on, with ghastly losses, through month after month in the deadlock of the trenches, whole sections of British industry were geared to munitions production, working day and night to supply and arm the ever-increasing numbers of field, medium and heavy artillery whose storm of steel reduced hundreds of square miles of fertile land, stretching in a great arc across the face of France and Belgium, into torn and ravaged wildernesses of mud and debris, where a few splintered stumps rose where forests once had been, and mounds of pulverized brickwork marked the sites of populous villages.

Largely by this deluge of fire, and by no other means so obviously, was it at last made possible, not through great generalship or any masterpiece of strategy but through sheer weight of metal, to batter a breach sufficient for the infantry, aided by the new armoured weapon, the tank, to advance to victory over the huge and highly efficient German Army.

But in August 1914 all this lay far ahead, beyond conjecture. There were no massed batteries of heavies, no overwhelming barrages to crush enemy defences. The artillery of the 'Old

Contemptibles' consisted of 486 guns and howitzers (scarcely more than were mustered for the Crimean War), and of these only twenty-four were of medium calibre. In those desperate days the task was to preserve all that could be saved of the British Expeditionary Force as its five divisions, outnumbered by more than three to one, fell back in a fighting retreat while the Kaiser's war machine wheeled through Belgium and on into France for the death blow at Paris. The original BEF – in quality, morale and skill at arms almost certainly the finest army of its size that Britain has ever sent overseas – was ground down to fragments, but enough survived to fight again, to provide a stiffening and a nucleus for the men who came after. This was due to the discipline and fighting spirit of the regular infantry, and to a series of artillery rearguard actions which have won a place of honour in the annals of the regiment.

On 24 August the 119th Battery, RFA formed part of a flank guard, holding in check far stronger German forces which were attempting to envelop II Corps near Elouges. After coming under the concentrated fire of three enemy batteries, the guns were enfiladed by yet another battery. When the order came to retire, only the British battery commander, Major Ernest Alexander, and three gunners were left. To withdraw the guns, Alexander was aided by volunteers from among troopers of the 9th Lancers, who had suffered heavily a short time earlier in a charge against a large body of unbroken German infantry, and who had been rallied behind a railway embankment near the battery. Although the lancers' officer, Captain Francis Grenfell, had been hit twice, he called for volunteers, and his men, with the gunners who survived, manhandled the guns out, one by one, to a place where the drivers could gallop their limbers up and remove them. Both Alexander and Grenfell received the VC. Grenfell was killed in May 1915; Alexander rose to the rank of major-general.

Two days after Elouges, as part of a battle on a larger scale at Le Cateau on 26 August (the anniversary of Crécy), the artillery fought an action which is famous not only for the heroism displayed, but also as an example of something that was to be increasingly rare – the deployment of guns well forward in the open, within full view of the enemy.

In nine hours of slaughter during the retreat from Mons,

II Corps, halted on a ridge, fought to a temporary standstill a German force of four times its size, lavishly equipped with artillery and machine-guns. The intention of General Smith-Dorrien, the corps commander, was merely to hold up the enemy for long enough to give a breathing space to some of his almost exhausted battalions, and then disengage to continue the retreat; but the orders as they reached Brigadier-General John Headlam, CRA 5th Division, or as interpreted by him, were different. He took it that there must be a 'fight to the finish', and he therefore intervened, ordering batteries which had already taken up positions under cover to move forward, and come into action in the front line.

This ran counter to one of the most bitterly learnt lessons of the Boer war: that against resolute troops, armed with modern rifles, it was suicidal for guns to be deployed in the open within rifle range, particularly if the enemy also had artillery support. There can be no doubt that this was perfectly well known to Headlam (who later became a colonel commandant, and one of the historians of the regiment), and that he acted as he did quite deliberately as a gesture and an example in a moment of dire emergency. Whether he was right or wrong must be left for the experts to debate: it can be said that the gesture was a gallant one, and that the manner in which the artillery order was carried out was superb. The infantry, seeing the gunners share the same risks as themselves, received a boost to their morale. But the cost was high.

On the left of the line the artillery of the 3rd and 4th Divisions had fair cover. With few casualties they were able to silence German batteries which deployed in the open, and shrapnel cut down hundreds of the enemy's infantry and dismounted cavalry. 'They went down,' it has been said, 'like a target at practice camp when the rope is cut.' Over on the other flank, however, the 5th Division's artillery was immediately in grave trouble, not only from close-range machine-gun fire but also from the German artillery, which was a keen attacking arm with good light howitzers and many of the famous 5·9s (150-millimetre), firing mainly high-explosive shell. The 37th Howitzer Battery was dangerously exposed, and the 28th RFA, supporting the 13th Infantry Brigade, was little better situated. Seven of the twelve field batteries on the British right were silenced, and in the end twenty-six of the forty-two exposed guns were left in enemy hands; but it took six hours to wear the gunners down, and through the self-sacrifice of officers and men sixteen guns were saved.

When the order to withdraw reached the 37th Battery, Douglas Reynolds, the battery captain, called for volunteers to save two of his guns. This meant bringing up teams from the limber lines under heavy fire. It must be remembered that at this time a six-gun field battery was absolutely dependent for its mobility on eighteen six-horse teams (one team for each gun, and two for its ammunition wagons), making a total, with mounts for officers, of well over a hundred horses for each battery.

With two subalterns, a sergeant, and a trumpeter aged fifteen, Reynolds led two limbers to the guns. By this time Germans were inside the battery position, rather aimlessly milling around, evidently in the belief that the fight was over. Not until the guns were limbered up and away did these men fire, bringing down one team. Reynolds got back with one gun. He and the two drivers of the surviving team, Frederick Luke and Job Drain, were awarded the VC, and the 37th Battery was given the right to include in its name the honour title 'Le Cateau'.

Later, at Pysloop on 9 September, while making a forward reconnaissance. Reynolds spotted a German battery which was harassing the British, and gave information enabling our guns to deal with it. During the battle of the Aisne on 15 September he was severely wounded by shrapnel in the chest. Three months later he was gassed, and he died in February 1916, having insisted on staying with his battery to the end.

Another unit which had distinguished itself at Mons and in the rearguard actions which followed was L Battery, Royal Horse Artillery. On the morning of 1 September 1914, troops of the 1st Cavalry Brigade, to which the battery was attached, were bivouacked in the village of Néry. Under the cover of thick mist, a German force of six cavalry regiments, with considerable artillery, succeeded in approaching to within a short distance before being seen. The British guns had already been limbered up, and the teams hooked in (but with the poles down), when at 5 a.m. heavy fire from rifles and artillery was suddenly opened on them from a range of a few hundred yards. Many casualties occurred, and owing to the broken nature of the ground only three guns could be brought to bear, but these were quickly in action in an apple orchard. Dismounted troopers of the Queen's Bays and the 11th Hussars gave what covering fire they could, but the battery was under such deadly attack that within a short time only one 13-pounder remained in action, manned by E. K. Bradbury, the Battery Captain, Lieutenant Mundy, and Sergeant D. Nelson.

Although the German batteries all concentrated against this solitary gun, they could not silence it. When Mundy was severely wounded, Battery Sergeant-Major G. T. Dorrell came forward to take his place. Soon afterwards Captain Bradbury, while fetching ammunition from a wagon, had a leg torn off by a shell-burst. He propped himself up, tried to conceal his terrible wound from the men still serving the gun, and continued to direct fire until he died. All the officers now being dead or wounded, Sergeant-Major Dorrell took charge, with the support of Sergeant Nelson, who refused to leave him although badly wounded. Together they loaded, aimed and fired their gun until the last of the ammunition was gone. The two men, and the brigade, were saved by the arrival from Compiègne of the 4th Cavalry Brigade, whose troopers dismounted and, with some infantry, poured a steady fire into the Germans' flank, forcing them to give ground, abandoning eight field pieces and a machine-gun. Only three men of L Battery were unwounded, but their last gun was still in action when the enemy withdrew, under heavy fire from I Battery, RHA.

For this action three VCs were awarded, to Captain Bradbury, B. S. M. Dorrell and Sergeant Nelson, and L Battery was officially granted the honour title 'Néry'. Dorrell, the last survivor of the Néry VCs, died on 7 January 1971, in his ninety-first year, after having attained the rank of lieutenant-colonel.

After the allied victory in the 'miracle of the Marne', the advance against the German right wing group of armies was held up by strong enemy positions along the Aisne. Then followed the 'race to the sea', each side in succession lengthening its front in the attempt to overlap the other, while the Germans made repeated and determined efforts to smash their way through the weak formations that were clinging to a widely extended line. During the first battle of Ypres a stubborn defence by the 41st Brigade, RFA (the 9th, 16th and 17th Batteries) held up a dangerous thrust at the Nonne Boschen wood on 11 November 1914. An intense bombardment by the enemy was followed by infantry attacks with large numbers of fresh troops, until the British, who for three weeks had been under incessant strain, were near the breaking point.

At one moment the Germans' 1st Guards Brigade pierced the thin line which was being supported by the 41st Brigade's artillery. There were no reserves; all that stood between the enemy and a complete breakthrough was the line of field guns. Cooks, batmen and orderlies from brigade headquarters were hastily formed into a rifle screen, while the guns fired at point-blank range. After a short, sharp fight the attack slowed down, the allied position was reorganized, and the advance of the enemy towards the Channel ports came to a standstill.

In the official phrase, the front was stabilized – meaning that the allies and the Germans, dug into intricate systems of entrenchments stretching 400 miles from the sea to the Swiss frontier, faced each other across No Man's Land in a deadlock that neither could break. The lethal effect of modern small arms and machine-guns, in the hands of troops entrenched behind deep belts of barbed-wire entanglements, and backed by powerful artillery, was sufficient to make any advance across the open impossible, save at the price of almost insupportable losses. For a long time generals (and others, too) hoped, or believed as an act of faith, that somehow, somewhere, the enemy line would be pierced, that the infantry, with artillery support, would widen and exploit the breach, and that the cavalry would go through. This never happened. Not until 1916, with the advent of the tank – adding 'fire *with* movement' to the old military principle of 'fire *and* movement' – did the wit of man devise a possible battle-winning solution, and then, by using the first armoured fighting vehicles piecemeal, in small numbers on the Somme, the British all but nullified the value of their carefully guarded secret. So the deadlock was unbroken, and for three years, except for limited offensives in which small areas of ground, usually of little tactical value, were sometimes wrested from the enemy at heavy cost, the line remained with little material change.

This was a situation which neither side had foreseen. In the light of hindsight, it is now fairly generally held that tactical doctrine in both the British and the French artillery in 1914 had unduly emphasized mobility, to the detriment of firepower. On the British side this was perhaps not unnatural, in view of the Army's experiences in South Africa. Now mobility virtually disappeared, and there was urgent need for many more guns, and heavier ones, than were to be found in the divisional groups of batteries.

For counter-battery work and the reduction of enemy strong-points long-range guns and heavy howitzers were required. These were organized as corps and army artillery. Among them were the 6-inch howitzer and 60-pounder gun, which became classified as medium artillery, and the 4·5-inch howitzer. The 60-pounder had a range of about 16,000 yards. Weapons of bigger calibre, the 'heavies', such as the 8-inch and 9·2-inch howitzers, each with a range of 10,000 yards, were manned by the Royal Garrison Artillery. Super-heavy batteries of 12-inch and 14-inch calibre, on railway mountings – rivals, after a fashion, of the Germans' Big Berthas, one of which bombarded Paris from a distance of 76 miles – were used to shell enemy communication centres and headquarters far behind the front line.

Some of the British monsters, produced to the designs of Admiral Bacon, a retired naval officer who had become general manager of the ordnance factory at Coventry, were 15-inch howitzers that could be transported by road. The first, though not ordered until after the fall of Namur in August 1914, were fired in the battle of Neuve Chapelle. The eight enormous caterpillar tractors that were used to carry each howitzer, in sections, together with its firing platform and ammunition, aroused keen interest, and played some part in leading to the series of experiments which eventually produced the tank.

For the field batteries of the divisional artillery, deployed in most cases within a few hundred yards of the infantry, the standard weapon, which served throughout the war with credit, was the 18-pounder. This had a range of 6,500 yards with shrapnel, ultimately extended to 9,500 yards using high-explosive shell. The field guns, which at the start of the war had shrapnel only, were issued with high explosives in addition before the battle of Loos in September 1915, to give increased power in smashing defences. With the heavier pieces high explosives were used almost exclusively; later came smoke and gas shells. Accurate large-scale maps and regular meteorological reports, together with flash-spotting and sound-ranging units, now made it possible to lay down sudden fire without registration – that is, shooting for immediate effect, cutting out the older preliminaries of feeling towards a target by trial-and-error bracketing.

As an early step towards making good the deficiencies in the numbers of field artillery, Lord Kitchener, Secretary of State for War, approved the despatch from India of thirty-one regular batteries, to be replaced by Territorial units from England. While the build-up gained momentum, with the arrival of more and more artillery from the Territorials, the New Army, and the dominions, the gunners were called on to deal with new and unfamiliar targets, from the deep recesses of enemy trenches to the skies above the battlefield. In the front line with the infantry, some of them manned trench mortars, which could lob a projectile effectively, and which had the advantage of being simpler and cheaper to make than conventional artillery weapons. To meet the growing challenge of military aircraft, 13-pounder and 3-inch guns adapted for high-angle work were placed on special mountings, but in the absence of adequate fire control systems their effect was extremely limited. Their detachments, making the best of what they had, blazed away optimistically at the firmament.

Before long the work of the artillery on a typical sector of the western front began to assume a form and scope very like that of a large-scale and highly organized non-stop industry – an industry whose output was havoc and the violent extinction of life, and which was carried on in conditions that varied from ordinary hard work and discomfort to unremitting toil amidst hideous filth and squalor, under the constant threat of death or mutilation. In close support of the infantry, the divisional artillery manned their pieces, ready at all times to join in neutralization of centres of special activity on the enemy front, to engage targets of opportunity (transport, or movements of troops from the rear), or to answer appeals from the trenches to counteract bursts of aggressiveness from German artillery, mortars and machine-guns.

Indirect fire was now the almost invariable rule; few gunners, in the long period of static warfare, ever saw the target at which they shot. The eyes of the artillery were the forward observation officers who, from whatever points of vantage they could find, scanned the muddy wastes of the battle area and sent back to the batteries, by field telephone and later by wireless telegraphy (not yet known as 'radio') map-reference data which could be converted into terms of bearing, elevation and fuse setting for the guns. These subalterns, with their signallers, sometimes installed themselves in church steeples, if any were still standing. These gave a good field of view, but were dangerously tempting targets for the enemy; a safer method, where possible, was the construction of a concrete tower, hidden within the shell of some wrecked building. Balloons, moored behind British lines, were another form of observation post, whose occupants often had to make a hasty descent (if warned in time) on the approach of the Fokkers, which sent down many of them in flames. Limited use was also made of information from Royal Flying Corps aircraft.

Artillery liaison officers were posted with the infantry, always before a planned attack and sometimes on other occasions, sharing some corner of a dugout, cellar or tunnel among battalion staffs with their orderlies and runners, in a cramped stuffy clutter of web equipment, telephones, tea mugs and message forms. Linking the liaison officers with the divisional artillery commanders, and with the corps and army headquarters at whose word the mediums and heavies could add their weight, was a communications network of growing complexity, which had to be maintained despite every enemy action, and all of which would probably have to be laid out afresh after any readjustment of front. Among the signallers, liable at any moment of the day or night to be sent out, often under shellfire, to trace and repair breaks in the line, there must have been many unknown heroes whose names have been lost for ever. The same may be said of the drivers who, as part of inexorable routine, brought up the ammunition lorries along shell-swept tracks, where many a crossroads was a target for accurate fixed-line fire by German long-range guns. And always, in 'quiet' times or in spells of frenzied activity, for the gun detachments there were the daily tasks of digging in, cleaning, maintenance, and ammunition carrying. It was a routine which justified, as perhaps never before, the unheroic definition of war as 'long periods of intense boredom punctuated by short periods of intense fear' – only this time the boredom was more abysmal, and the interludes of terror more devastating.

Ammunition requirements had been gravely underestimated. The British reserve had been calculated on a basis of a probable expenditure of seven rounds a gun by the heaviest mobile artillery of the day, but the actual daily consumption by some field batteries rose occasionally to 500 rounds or more. Fire for cutting the enemy's wire before an attack, and for silencing machine-guns, used up shell at a rate never anticipated. During the first battle of Ypres in 1914, towards the end of October a form of rationing had to be imposed on gun ammunition, and a quarter of the divisional artillery was withdrawn because it had nothing to fire. Even the guns that remained were limited, on an average, to one round every half hour. After some months the original deficiency in stocks was made good, but one attack involving several divisions on a limited front could mean scarcity conditions in many other sectors. This, when taken in conjunction with the disquieting number of shells that, through faults in manufacture, failed to explode, and the inevitable proportion of 'fall-shorts', was not calculated to inspire confidence, or to improve relations between the infantry and the gunners.

A former infantry officer, Guy Chapman, has described how one day in 1915, when his men were suffering acutely from 'whizz-bangs' and minenwerfers, he ran to company headquarters, where he was told that an appeal for fire support had already been telephoned to the artillery. He and the company commander waited.

'We heard an English shell pass overhead. "Dud," I said. A second burst in our wire. A third – "Dud". We waited a minute. "Any more?" Smith cocked his head to listen. "No; that's the lot."

'"We can't help you," the FOO explained later in the day. "Every bloody shell is going up to Loos. Our teams have been taking our spare stuff there for the past week. We haven't got any shells. Three a day is our allowance, and you've had it this morning."'

This incident occurred a few months before the final abandonment of an allied attempt to divert German resources from the west, and end the stalemate, by an effort in a distant theatre – Gallipoli. Hopes of a knockout blow to the kaiser's Turkish ally, by the forcing of the Dardanelles, were frustrated for many reasons, probably the greatest being the lack of wholehearted commitment to the enterprise by many of those in high military and political office; but it is clear that lack of guns and ammunition played a significant part in the failure, which occasioned the departure from the Admiralty of Winston Churchill, who as First Lord had been an ardent advocate of the Dardanelles project.

In his book *The World Crisis, 1911–1918*, Churchill has told how Major-General Simpson-Baikie, who commanded the British artillery at Gallipoli, reported that in June and July, 1915, the total number of rounds of 18-pounder ammunition at Cape Helles never reached 25,000. Before an attack it was brought up to its maximum, about 19,000 to 23,000. The total available was therefore limited, to about 12,000 rounds, as it was necessary to keep in reserve 6,000 to 10,000 rounds to guard against Turkish counter-attacks. As there was no high-explosive shell for the 18-pounders (except 640 rounds expended on 4 June), the gunners could fire only shrapnel, which was of little use against trenches. On 13 July only 5,000 rounds of field artillery ammunition remained at Helles, and all active operations had to be suspended.

General Simpson-Baikie, in a statement appended to General Sir Ian Hamilton's *Gallipoli Diary*, set out his problem in terms which, if one takes into account changes in equipment, recall in a striking manner some of the anguished complaints sent to England by sufferers from Ordnance Board errors well over a century earlier. He wrote: 'The whole story of the artillery at Helles may be summed up in the following sentences: insufficiency of guns of every nature; insufficiency of ammunition of every nature, especially of high explosives: insufficient provision made by the home authorities for spare guns, spare carriages, spare parts, adequate repairing workshops, or for a regular daily, weekly or monthly supply of ammunition; guns provided often of an obsolete pattern and so badly worn by previous use as to be most inaccurate; lack of aeroplanes, trained observers and of all the requisites for air observation; total failure to produce the trench mortars and bombs to which the closeness of the opposing lines at Helles would have lent themselves well – in short, total lack of organization at home to provide even the most rudimentary and indispensable artillery requisites for daily consumption; not to speak of downright carelessness which resulted in wrong shells being sent to the wrong guns, and new types of fuses being sent without fuse keys and new types of howitzer shells without range tables.

'These serious faults provoked their own penalties in the shape of the heavy losses suffered by our infantry and artillery, which might have been to a great measure averted if sufficient forethought and attention had been devoted to the "side show" at the Dardanelles.'

In the Suvla Bay landings, an opportunity was lost through the failure of the IX Corps commander to push ahead immediately the troops were ashore, and before the arrival of fresh Turkish forces. As a result, nearly 8,000 men were killed or wounded on May 9 and 10 in taking positions which might have been occupied on the previous day with little or no resistance. Colonel Aspinall, staff officer to General Hamilton, the Commander-in-Chief, has described how, while he was making a tour of investigation, the commander of the 11th Division's artillery came up to him on the beach and 'asked whether I came from General Headquarters. On my reply in the affirmative he begged me to do everything in my power to "get a move on". He was convinced that it was essential to press on at once, but nothing was being done and apparently nothing was going to be done.'

Some troops and items of equipment which might otherwise have been utilized in France were diverted for the Dardanelles, in spite of bitter opposition by the western front school of thought, but they were too few to exercise any decisive influence. The weight of field gun ammunition available to prepare and support the British assaults in the Gallipoli peninsula never exceeded 150 tons, compared with more than 1,300 tons fired during the first two days of the battle of Loos, and upwards of 25,000 tons in a number of two-day periods of the August offensive in 1915.

The end of the Dardanelles campaign brought to a close the second main period of the war. Now that the Central Powers had successfully defended their southern flank, the front stretched not only from the sea to the Alps, but across the Balkans, through Palestine, across the lands between the Tigris and the Euphrates. All hope of a decisive blow elsewhere than in the west was set aside, and the struggle resolved itself into the 'war of exhaustion', with repeated frontal attacks in which, despite artillery support on an unprecedented scale, allied casualties almost invariably exceeded by far those inflicted on the Germans.

In October 1915 there was fierce fighting around Béthune, in which Acting Sergeant John Raynes, of A Battery, 71st Brigade, RFA, won the VC. The battery, at Fosse 7 de Béthune, was being heavily bombarded with armour-piercing and gas shells. Raynes went to the assistance of Sergeant Ayres, who was lying wounded forty yards away; he bandaged him, and returned to his gun. Soon afterwards, when the battery had been forced to cease fire owing to the intensity of the shelling, Raynes carried Ayres to a dugout with the help of two gunners, both of whom were killed a little later. When gas shelling was resumed, Raynes put his own respirator on Ayres and then, though himself suffering from the effects of gas, staggered back to the gun. He survived, but next day was buried under the wreckage of a house which collapsed when hit by a heavy shell. As soon as he was extricated he had two wounds dressed, and immediately reported for duty with his battery, which was again under intensive fire.

Among the many thousands of gunners and ex-gunners who died in 1916 was that fine old soldier, Field-Marshal Lord Roberts. Now holder of the ancient office of master gunner of St James's Park, he was on a visit to the troops in France when he died of pneumonia at St Omer at the age of eighty-two, nearly sixty years after he won his VC in the Indian Mutiny.

On 26 May 1916, General Sir Douglas Haig, Commander-in-Chief of the British armies in France, wrote in a special Order of the Day: 'This day two hundred years ago the first permanent organization was given to the artillery by a Royal Warrant. . . . The commander-in-chief knows that the other arms will join with him in congratulating the Royal Artillery on this occasion and in recognizing the efficiency with which it has supported the other arms in every action in which it has been engaged. The discipline and devotion to duty displayed by the officers, NCOS and men of the artillery throughout this campaign have been in accord with the highest traditions of their regiment.'

It was a well-deserved tribute, at a time when any word of praise or encouragement was welcome; but a long road of travail still lay ahead.

STORM OF STEEL

'The monstrous anger of the guns.' – *Wilfred Owen*

The ammunition shortage was eventually overcome, though not without upheaval and recrimination in England, and for months during the spring and early summer of 1916 preparations were made for an offensive on the Somme. For this vast quantities of shell and stores of all kinds had to be accumulated within easy reach of the front. All available roads were improved, many new ones were made, miles of rail track and trench tramways were laid, as well as trenches for communication lines, and numerous gun emplacements and observation posts.

The preliminary bombardment lasted for a week, and the manner in which it was laid down indicated the extent of the gains at which the commander-in-chief aimed. Instead of being concentrated mainly on the enemy's front line, it was dispersed over the support trenches and on many strongpoints far to the rear, in the hope that these might be reached in the first day or two of fighting. British and French cavalry stood ready close at hand.

Although it did not make possible the longed-for break-through, the effect of this tempest of high explosive was cataclysmic. The war diary of the Germans' 27th Division, one of their best formations, which defended Guillemont, says: 'The enemy's fire never ceased for an hour. It fell day and night on the front line and tore fearful gaps in the ranks of the defenders; it fell on the approaches to the front line and made all movement towards the front hell; it fell on the rearward trenches and the battery positions and smashed up men and material in a manner never seen before or since; it repeatedly reached even the resting battalions far behind the front and there occasioned exceptionally painful losses, and our artillery was powerless against it.'

But the German position was one of immense strength. As Haig himself said: 'The first and second systems each consisted of several lines of deep trenches, well provided with bomb-proof shelters and with numerous communication trenches connecting them. The front of the trenches in each system was protected by wire entanglements, many of them in two belts 40 yards broad, built of iron stakes interlaced with barbed wire, often almost as thick as a man's finger. The numerous woods and villages in and between these systems of defence had been turned into veritable fortresses. The deep cellars usually to be found in the villages, and the numerous pits and quarries common to a chalk country, were used to provide cover for machine-guns and trench mortars. . . . The salients in the enemy's line, from which he could bring enfilade fire across his front, were made into self-contained forts, and often protected by minefields.'

At 7 a.m. on 1 July, when fourteen British and five French divisions advanced across No Man's Land on a front of about 25 miles, they were met with intense machine-gun fire from Germans who emerged from their deep dugouts to shoot with deadly effect through the lanes which the artillery had torn in their wire, or to harass the attackers even when the first wave had already passed over the front-line trenches. Though the enemy's front was crossed at every point, no deep penetration was made except on the right. Before night fell the British had lost in dead, wounded and prisoners nearly 60,000 men – the greatest carnage suffered in a single day in the entire history of the Army.

Day after day, week after week, on a gradually decreasing scale but with flareups now and again to the dimensions of a major operation, the bitter struggle continued. By the end of July an advance of about 2½ miles had been made on a front which at this depth did not exceed 2 miles. For this 171,000 British had been killed or wounded; 11,400 Germans had been captured, but more than twice that number of British prisoners and wounded had fallen into enemy hands. Churchill, who was deeply sceptical about a strategy of attrition, has declared that 'the campaign of 1916 on the western front was from beginning to end a welter of slaughter, which after the issue was determined left the British and French armies weaker in relation to the Germans than when it opened, while the actual battle fronts were not appreciably altered'. Against this must be set the fact, which he himself admitted, that the effects on enemy morale were lasting. Never again, after the ground they had yielded and the losses they had suffered, did the mass of the German rank and file fight as they had done in the summer and autumn of 1916.

The blood bath of the Somme did not end the use of enormous and prolonged artillery concentrations before attacks. Such were the methods for Arras and Messines (April–July 1917) and the third battle of Ypres. On a number of occasions thousands of tons of ammunition were fired daily during an operation on a front of a few miles, the preliminary bombardments often lasting four or five days, sometimes longer. Yet still, after this vast expenditure of effort, cost and blood, the power of the defence still held the upper hand; still, after their front line had been saturated with high explosive, German infantrymen survived, in concrete pillboxes impervious to anything less than direct hits by heavy shells, to take toll of the allied battalions until the bayonet, the grenade, the flame-thrower, or the machine-guns of the tanks did their work.

For close support of the infantry assault a new artillery technique was developed – the 'rolling' or 'creeping' barrage, a curtain of fire behind which the helmeted and burdened infantry struggled forward across the corpse-strewn wastes of No Man's Land. Only at the last possible moment did the barrage lift, leaving before the attackers the last few deadly yards in front of the enemy trenches. The demands that this made upon the discipline of the infantry, and the leadership of their junior officers in the most appalling conditions, could scarcely have been more exacting or more nerve-racking. It was impressed upon the men that at all costs they must keep as closely as possible behind the barrage, failing which, at the moment, when the rain of shells ceased, they would find themselves exposed and unsupported in front of the barbed-wire entanglements. The danger of casualties among our own troops was accepted as a calculated risk. Undoubtedly an unknown but fairly considerable number of British soldiers lost their lives in this way. For the gunners it was a grim duty performed, like others, in accordance with orders.

In addition to the failure to achieve complete obliteration of front-line defences, the massive preliminary bombardments had two grave defects. By their very nature they entirely sacrificed any element of surprise, giving the Germans warning of attack in ample time for counter-preparations to be put into effect; and the effect of prolonged heavy shellfire on the battlefield terrain was such that forward movement became almost impossible.

Under the storm of steel, ground which in some cases had been fought over repeatedly was riven and churned into a tortured waste of almost bottomless clinging mud, pock-marked with the broad water-logged craters left by the heavies. Any kind of wheeled transport was completely ruled out, in some large areas near the front, as a result of enemy fire. Between the trenches, a man labouring onward under the weight of rifle, ammunition, respirator, entrenching tool and other equipment could, if he took an unwary step, be clutched beyond rescue in the grip of the morass, and sink to death from suffocation in the stinking mire. Men fought in a landscape, hitherto unimaginable, like the surface of a doomed planet or a Gustav Doré illustration of something out of Dante's *Inferno*.

During the battle of Messines in 1917 a great artillery belt, 4,000 yards deep, was built up along the narrow arc from Ypres to Armentières by way of Kemmel. In eight days, with 2,374 guns firing on a front of 17,000 yards (an average of about one gun to every 7 yards), the British artillery used 92,264 tons of ammunition. The preliminary bombardment before the Ypres offensive in this year completed the ruin of the intricate system of dykes on which the drainage of the area depended. Conditions at Passchendaele are described in the official war history as follows: 'The shelled areas near the front became a barrier of swamp. . . . The margins of the overflowing streams were transformed into long stretches of bog, passable only by a few well defined tracks which became targets for the enemy's artillery; and to leave the tracks was to risk death by drowning.'

As it was impossible to get supplies to the field and medium batteries at any distance from the sole remaining road, they were massed in line alongside it. No concealment could be provided there, with the result that German counter-battery fire caused very heavy losses in men and guns, and killed nearly all the artillery horses.

The self-defeating aspect of long preliminary bombardments was brought home more unmistakably after the advent of the tanks, which had their first, and successful, large-scale opportunity at Cambrai in November–December 1917. Obviously it made no military sense to shower down wholesale destruction if in the process the going was rendered so hopeless that the tanks were in danger of being unable to advance at all, or of being bogged down in large numbers. In later battles a shorter, all-out 'hurricane' bombardment was adopted.

By this time the Germans in the west, though formidable and still unbroken, were on the defensive; behind the war zones, the superior industrial might of the allies (with American help) was beginning to tell. Haig, in a despatch written later, said: 'As regards material, it was not until midsummer, 1916, that the artillery situation became even approximately equal to the conduct of major operations. Throughout the Somme battle the expenditure of artillery ammunition had to be watched with the greatest care. During the battles of 1917 ammunition was plentiful, but the gun situation was a source of constant anxiety. Only in 1918 was it possible to conduct artillery operations independently of any limiting consideration other than that of transport.'

Production for the artillery rose, with some setbacks, from zero level in 1914 to a peak of 1,750 pieces (guns without carriages) and 1,275 carriages in May, 1918. In October 1917 the French had about 10,000 guns to the British Army's 6,000, but those of the British were, on the whole, bigger and newer. Against this allied total of roughly 16,000, the Germans had 12,432 on the western front, 5,176 on the Russian front, and 808 in the Balkans and Italy, a total of 18,416, according to War Office information obtained in 1917; in a book published in 1924 by General von Wrisberg of the Prussian War Ministry, the figure was given as 17,966 – remarkably close to the British wartime estimate. In the west, therefore, the allies now had superiority in artillery numbers; but in weight of metal the enemy still held the lead. If one deducts from each side the field guns, of which the British possessed by far the greater number, the figures for heavier weapons were: Franco-British 6,654, German 7,568.

Through the weary years, while the machines bore down and the relentless pressure was applied, the triumph of human fortitude and of the unconquerable spirit shone out amidst the gloom and the drab horrors in deeds of selfless bravery. One of these was at Francilly, where Major Frederick Lumsden, DSO, of the Royal Marine Artillery, won the VC on 3 April 1917, at the age of forty-five. Six enemy field guns had been captured but, as they had to be left in their dug-in positions, 300 yards in front of the British troops, they were kept under heavy fire by other German artillery. Lumsden undertook to bring them in to the British lines. To do so he led four artillery teams and a party of infantrymen through the enemy barrage, in the face of rifle and machine-gun fire as well. He himself made three trips, and remained directing operations until the last gun had been brought in. During later actions Lumsden won three bars to his DSO. He was a brigadier-general when, in June 1918, he was shot through the head and killed instantly.

No fewer than seven VCs were won by British soldiers on 30 November 1917. Among them was Sergeant Cyril Gourley of D Battery, 27th (West Lancashire) Brigade, RFA, at Little Priel Farm east of Epehy. Although enemy infantry, advancing in force, had reached to within a few hundred yards of him, both in front and on the flanks, Gourley managed to keep one of his howitzers in action. When the Germans pressed on further he engaged a machine-gun at 500 yards and knocked it out with a direct hit. All day he held the enemy in check, firing over open sights, thereby saving the remainder of his battery and enabling the howitzers to be withdrawn at nightfall. Gourley had previously been awarded the DCM.

In the spring of 1918 came the Germans' last great offensive effort, which made dangerous gains, but which may finally have sealed their fate, even before its palpable failure, through the terrible casualties that were incurred. During the attack many British batteries were overrun, but remained in action long after machine-guns and riflemen had been overwhelmed and the guns were practically surrounded.

Near Messines on 10 April, as a result of an early morning

attack, A Battery, 88th Brigade, RFA, found Germans in occupation of a farm just in front of the battery, and British infantry falling back towards the guns. Captain Eric Dougall, MC, a special reserve officer, maintained his guns in action despite a fierce concentration of high-explosive and gas shell. Seeing that his fire could not clear a crest, owing to the withdrawal of the line, he had two guns run up to the top of the ridge to fire over open sights. By this time the infantry had been pressed right back, level with the battery. Dougall rallied and reorganized the men, handed out Lewis guns, and armed with rifles as many artillerymen as he could spare. With these a defensive line was formed in front of the battery, which was pumping rapid fire into the advancing enemy.

Erect among the shells and bullets, Dougall walked about, giving orders and words of encouragement. He told the infantry: 'As long as you stick to your trenches, I will keep my guns here.' Throughout the day the line was held, delaying the enemy's entry into Messines for more than twelve hours. In the evening, having used up all its ammunition, the battery received orders to withdraw. This was accomplished by manhandling the guns over half a mile of shell-cratered land under severe fire from machine-guns.

Dougall was awarded the VC, but did not live to receive it. He was killed four days later at Mount Kemmel while directing the fire of his battery.

One of many fine examples of the work of the battery signallers was that of Gunner Kirby of the 12th Siege Battery, RGA. This man, who had already received the Military Medal during the Flanders fighting in 1917, was on duty as a telephonist in March 1918 when the tunnel serving as a forward post was blown in by a shell. Kirby was buried by the fall of earth, but managed to make himself heard. On being rescued he immediately went out into the open, under heavy fire, to take back information to his battery. He then obtained fresh wire and instruments, laid out a new line under fire, established contact from another observation post, and continued all day to send back information. Kirby was awarded the Distinguished Conduct Medal.

An honour of a unique kind was won by the 5th Battery, 45th Brigade, RFA, to which, as a unit, the Croix de Guerre was awarded by the French military authorities. With IX Corps on the Aisne, at Pontavert on 27 May 1918, the men of the battery fought their guns to the last round. Surrounded by the enemy, the surviving gunners were then assembled by their officers, who led them in a counter-attack with rifles and Lewis guns on the German infantry, in conjunction with the 2nd Battalion, Devonshire Regiment. Few of the gunners came through alive. The Devons were cited by the French in an Order of the Day, directing that their colour should be decorated with the Croix de Guerre, and a similar distinction was conferred on the battery.

During 1918 the allied war effort mounted to a crescendo. Early in March, about a fortnight before the German offensive, it had been calculated, as a rough estimate, that of the total military effort in manpower and material the artillery represented as much as 40 per cent, with the infantry accounting for a similar proportion, while all other arms – air, cavalry, machine-guns, tanks and gas – together amounted to 20 per cent. By the reorganization of plants under the Ministry of Munitions, the factories, absorbing the labours of nearly 2½ million men and women, were at last turning out all the guns and shells that the artillery could use. Demands were enormous, but Churchill, who in July 1917 became minister of munitions in the Lloyd George administration, had close at hand a friend with the needs of the gunners at heart – General Furse, Master-General of the Ordnance, who was specially appointed as a member of the Munitions Council.

Suggestions had been made in March that the limit of what could be achieved by gun power had almost been reached, and that it was time to consider whether, if the war continued into 1919, some men and equipment should be relinquished by the artillery to reinforce other arms. But on 9 September 1918, after the tide had definitely turned, though the German armies were still resisting doggedly, Churchill, during a visit to France, wrote to the prime minister, saying that, so far from seeing any prospect of reduced expenditure of artillery ammunition in the new conditions of more open warfare, there was every likelihood of an increased demand. He said: 'In each of the last two weeks of open fighting on the wide battle front they have fired over 70,000 tons, and they are now asking for a daily intake of over

9,000 tons against 5,000, 6,000 and 7,000 with which we have been able to satisfy them to date.

'It appears that although the prolonged bombardments, like Messines, etc. have been given up, the firing is now maintained by all the guns of the Army over practically the whole front at once. The old limiting factor, namely, the fatigue of the gunners, which imposed a certain limitation on the concentrated local operations of last year, is no longer present when all, or almost all, the batteries of the Army are able to fire over the whole front. It would, of course, be quite impossible to continue to supply ammunition at the present rate indefinitely, and I do not think that will be demanded of us.'

This proved true, for German resistance was beginning to crack. For fifteen successive days the British expenditure of ammunition exceeded 10,000 tons a day. A captured German document, containing an order by General Ludendorff, stated that in a single month more than 13 per cent of the German artillery in the west had been destroyed by counter-battery fire. In a note drawing the Cabinet's attention to this, Churchill added these comments: 'As this method is comparatively little used by the French, the main credit of this astonishing achievement falls to the British artillery. A superior artillery supplied with ample ammunition and working in combination with a superior and highly trained air force is thus producing an immense effect, not only in destroying the enemy's power of resistance but in saving our own men.

'If the destruction of German artillery could be maintained at the rate stated by General Ludendorff, it would become practically necessary to replace the whole of the German artillery, apart altogether from the wear of guns, twice in the course of a year. This would be quite impossible. We are therefore in this field of effort also within measurable distance of decisive and final results. It would be disastrous if, for any reason, we were compelled to stint our gunners in ammunition at the very time when the results of all the immense efforts which have been made to increase the power and perfect the combination of our artillery and air services is coming to hand. Rather than do that we ought to be ready to make very great sacrifices indeed in every direction.'

On Armistice Day, 11 November 1918, Germany, in fact

though not in words, admitted defeat. After four years and three months the guns were silent. At terrible cost, the British artillery had established and proved its dominance; though it never amounted to overwhelming superiority, it was enough. From a total on 4 August 1914, of 557 units in all theatres of war, in India, and at home, with 4,083 officers and 88,837 other ranks (92,920 all told), the Royal Artillery had expanded by the end of the war to 1,796 units, having a strength of 29,990 officers and 518,790 others – an almost sixfold multiplication in numbers of men.

By the armistice the British Army, which at the start of the war had 486 pieces of artillery, had 6,437 guns and howitzers, in addition to the anti-aircraft artillery and trench mortars. The gunners had fired, in France and Belgium, 170,385,295 rounds of ammunition of all types. (During the siege of Sebastopol 252,872 rounds had been fired from 401 guns and mortars.)

Eighteen VCs had been awarded to men serving with the Royal Artillery. The soldiers who won them, in addition to those already mentioned, were: 1914 – Bombardier E. G. Harlock, 113rd Battery RFA (Vendresse, France); 1915 – Captain G. N. Walford (Sedd-el-Bahr, V Beach, Gallipoli); 1916 – Captain W. B. Allen, RAMC, attached 246th (West Riding) Brigade RFA (near Mesnil); 1917 – Sergeant W. Gosling, 3rd (Wessex) Brigade RFA (near Arras), Second Lieutenant T. H. B. Maufe, 124th Siege Battery RGA (Feuchy), Lieutenant S. T. D. Wallace, C. Battery, 63rd Brigade RFA (Gonnelieu); 1918 – Gunner C. E. Stone, MM, C Battery, 83rd Brigade RFA (Caponne Farm, France), Lieutenant R. V. Gorle, A Battery, 50th Brigade RFA (Ledeghem, Belgium). The DCM was awarded to 2,602 members of the regiment. A total of 49,076 artillerymen died.

Although the western front took by far the greatest part of the forces, gunners also fought in many other areas of the world. Italy, Macedonia, Mesopotamia, Egypt and Palestine, Arabia, Persia, East and West Africa – these names, and others, can be found on the base of the artillery memorial at Hyde Park Corner. For the central feature of this work the sculptor, Charles Jagger, broke with tradition. He chose to portray in stone not some allegorical or symbolic figure, but the squat, purposeful bulk of a 9·2-inch howitzer. There it stands, in massive dignity, pointing out over London, within a hundred yards or so of the windows of Apsley House, the mansion bought for the Duke of Wellington, the general who did not love the gunners.

THE YEARS BETWEEN

'Our God and soldier we alike adore, when on the brink of ruin, not before.' *– Francis Quarles*

The struggle of 1914–18 had been the 'war to end wars'; so people had been told, and for a long time they believed this, so far as most of them thought of such matters at all. Revulsion from the drab regimentation of the war years, and the need to recover from the drain on national resources, combined to push the armed services and everything connected with them into the background. With luck, it was hoped, they would never be needed in a brave new world under the beneficent aegis of the League of Nations. Disarmament was the watchword; disillusionment came afterwards, dangerously belated.

In the period that followed the armistice, the artillery equipment of seventy British divisions, amassed with infinite effort and huge expense, was melted down for scrap, according to figures given by Brigadier R. F. Johnson in his history of the Honourable Artillery Company in the Second World War. The Americans, perhaps more prudent on this point, kept many of their guns, stored away in grease, in case of need. The long process of demobilizing millions of men took its course. Some, including gunners, were required for service with the army of occupation in Germany; there were more of the perennial flurries on the Indian frontier, another Afghan War (the third), and various disorders in distant corners of the Empire. Apart from these, the likelihood of any war appeared remote. The

Territorial Army was stripped to its peacetime skeleton, many regular units were disbanded, and others reduced to cadres.

So far as the artillery was concerned, it was a period mainly of internal reorganization. There were few radical new departures in gun design or production, though a combined gun-howitzer was on the drawing board in the thirties, and an anti-tank gun was introduced. The greatest change was the completion of mechanization in the transport.

Up to the end of the war there was still a good deal of horse-drawn artillery in France, but many of the medium batteries, and all the heavies, had mechanical transport with RASC drivers – a form of divided control recalling the old Driver Corps of more than a century earlier. By 1927, however, the heavy draught horse had been discarded, all medium guns were tractor-drawn, and all their personnel were artillerymen, the 'driver in charge' having made his appearance. In the same year two field brigades were mechanized; at first battery staffs were mounted, and the guns were towed by 'dragons' which also carried the detachments. Each year more brigades were converted; the 'dragons' became more efficient, but eventually were superseded by six-wheeled vehicles, to which tracks could be fitted if necessary; rubber tyres were introduced. By 1938, for home-based artillery the transformation was complete, save for a few batteries on foreign service, and one RHA unit in London (the King's Troop), which retained its horses, together with the old-style blue jackets and busbies, for ceremonial duties.

Mountain artillery was an exception, the mule being still without a rival for this particular work. The former British-manned mountain batteries, however, were converted into units of other categories; those serving on the North-West Frontier were manned by Indians under British officers. In their armament the 3·7-inch howitzer marked a definite advance.

Soldiers tend to be sentimental fellows, as well as being conservative in their ways, and the departure of the horse, which had served the artillery so well, was a source of real grief among many in the regiment. It was felt with particular keenness in the old RHA units, whose fame was so inseparably linked with the dash and spirit of carefully matched teams, the jingle of harness and the gleam of meticulously groomed horses as the guns swept into action. All this must go, and the horse artillery must

22. Anti-aircraft gun (13-pdr. 9 cwt.) mounted on a motor lorry; St Jean (battle of Broodseinde), 5 October, 1917 (Imperial War Museum)

23. Getting a field gun into action alongside a ruined cottage near St Floris, 2 May, 1918 (Imperial War Museum)

24. Pulling an 18-pdr. up the slope of a cutting across the Canal du Nord in September, 1918. About this time gun teams had been reduced from six horses to four, so that horses could be supplied to the United States Army (Imperial War Museum)

now adapt themselves to machines, though with the basic role fundamentally unchanged, in common with their comrades of the cavalry who were changing over to the tanks and armoured cars. It was not easy, in a corps with a tradition of good horsemanship and horse management; one may recall that in the early days of the Royal Artillery one inducement that led many young officers to join was the prospect of a ready supply of mounts, which, for men with little money, would otherwise have been beyond their means. But the change was made, and efficiently, despite a certain amount of vocal indignation among a few diehards.

Mechanization, while it brought many fresh problems – new trades to learn, new techniques to master – also did away with some worries and uncertainties. Time after time in the past the artillery had been harassed, and often gravely hampered, by the lack of an adequate number of draught animals, and the difficulty of feeding them and organizing a system of replacements. Even during the First World War this must have occupied a vast amount of effort behind the lines. Shipments to the western front in 1914–18 included over 750,000 horses (a large proportion being for the artillery), and no less than 4 million tons of fodder. Though no definite figure can be given, certainly many thousands of these animals perished in the battle areas; some instances of the terrible losses of horses under fire have already been mentioned. While one may sympathize with the gunners who mourned the disappearance of their friend the horse, when one considers these losses it is surely some cause for satisfaction that, so far as can possibly be foreseen, this particular slaughter is one of the horrors of war that has vanished for ever.

To eke out the scanty numbers of the artillery, a number of Yeomanry and Territorial infantry units were converted. In 1924 the formal distinction that divided the horse, field and garrison branches was abolished (though the RHA batteries still kept with pride the letters that distinguished them), and the Royal Artillery became one corps, which included the gunners of the Territorial Army. In 1938 two broadly distinct functional branches were given official recognition, the field artillery, of whatever calibre, forming one, and anti-aircraft, anti-tank, and coast defence the other; the Territorial artillery was not affected by the latter change. All the reserve brigades and depots had been amalgamated into one Royal Artillery depot at Woolwich, comprising two training brigades and a depot unit.

There were frequent rearrangements, involving the redesignation of many batteries. The term 'brigade' was dropped in favour of 'regiment', which by 1938 consisted in the field artillery of two twelve-gun batteries of three troops each, instead of four six-gun batteries. Full-dress uniform was, in general, now a thing of the past, and the khaki service dress of 1914–18 in its turn gave way to the drably utilitarian but moderately comfortable 'battle dress', but more than a few artillerymen, including Territorials, took the trouble to equip themselves, for walking-out purposes and usually at their own expense, with the somewhat smarter old-style tunics, complete with sets of brass buttons bearing the gun insignia.

The School of Artillery had been founded in 1920 at Larkhill on Salisbury Plain. Here courses of instruction were given, latest ideas in equipment and tactics could be studied and assessed, and demonstrations of new devices and methods were staged by picked batteries for the benefit of regimental and staff officers. To qualify as an instructor in gunnery at Larkhill was a coveted distinction. The wearers of the 'IG' brassards were not always greeted with warmth by the men at practice camps, where they were regarded, inevitably, rather in the light of prying know-alls, always on the lookout for faults, but undoubtedly they did much to maintain and raise standards of gunnery.

The development of military aircraft, and the great strides made in bomber and fighter strength by all the main powers, led to large increases in anti-aircraft artillery, both regular and Territorial. In the case of regular formations the searchlights were also a Royal Artillery responsibility; in the Territorials, however, searchlight companies were Royal Engineers units until within a few months of the outbreak of the next great war.

The AA artillery faced a role that bristled with complexities and unknown factors, in a sphere where theory, which was constantly changing, had not yet been put to the test of combat on any extensive scale in the new conditions of war from the air that had sprung into existence since 1918. Not only must mobile protection be provided against air attack on troops in any continental campaign; in Britain, defence must also be given to vital points such as ports, military installations, and industrial centres, and (most vividly present in the minds of all) the vast, sprawling cities with their millions of inhabitants. Luckily there was some good equipment, though many of the best (and most exacting) refinements produced by the back-room boys of science and technology were not ready for use until after war had come.

For mobile anti-aircraft work, either with the Army in the field or in home defence, there were the general purpose 3·7-inch gun and, as the pre-eminent light quick-firing weapon, the 40-millimetre Bofors, originally produced in Sweden, and capable of sending a 2-pound projectile to a maximum height of 3 miles at a rate of 122 rounds a minute. For static defence against bomber attacks, on a ring of sites encircling London the ordnance artificers began to supervise the installation of the 4·5-inch guns of the Heavy Anti-Aircraft Regiments, mounted within concrete emplacements on armour-shielded turntables, very similar to some naval artillery, and linked electronically with their predictors in sand-bagged command posts at the centre of the sites. It was to the anti-aircraft units that a considerable number of volunteers found their way when their country seemed on the brink of war in the 'Munich crisis' of September 1938. Some of these men dropped out, unfortunately, when the clouds rolled by for the moment; but there was a new call before long, and many of them returned.

It may be judged that, in the years between the wars, a respectable amount of progress had been made by the artillery in many ways, though always within rigorous limitations imposed by restraints on manpower and expenditure. Of the 3·7 guns, fewer than fifty were available for the defence of London in September 1938. Useful work had been accomplished; but it was little enough in comparison with the leeway that still had to be made good when, on 3 September 1939, Britain again found herself at war with Germany, impelled this time by forces darker and more sinister than the Prussian militarism of 1914, and under the ruthless leadership of a fanatical megalomaniac who had functioned as a minor cog in the kaiser's war machine as Corporal Hitler.

DUNKIRK AND AFTER

'We shall defend our Island, whatever the cost may be.' – Churchill

It has been said that the British Army has always prepared for the *previous* war. This is a cheap gibe, and a rather unfair one; not being endowed with psychic clairvoyance, no statesmen or generals of any nation have ever been in a position to predict with certainty the exact nature or methods of future wars. Like lesser mortals, they learn the hard way, by trial and error.

Nevertheless there was much irony in the course of events. In 1914, having been conditioned, psychologically at any rate, by experience against the Boers for a contest of rapid movement, the Army found itself pinned down in trench warfare. In 1939 it was widely, if rather vaguely, assumed on the allied side (mainly by the French) that the land war would be mainly a holding battle of position, while British seapower made itself felt, and yet the crucial trial of strength was fought out in the air. When the blow fell, the allies were outmanœuvred and overwhelmed by the speed and weight of 120 German divisions, ten of them Panzers with 2,700 armoured vehicles. The diarist of one RHA battery has recalled how in peacetime he had been taught that the pace of war would be much slower than that of training exercises – and how wrong this proved.

Before the storm broke there were the eight months of 'phoney war' in which, after the fall of Poland, 300,000 French troops sat behind their Maginot Line while people in Britain waited tensely for massive air raids, and Lord Gort's British Expeditionary Force of ten divisions spent a cold, cheerless winter in northern France, with a maximum of digging and fatigues and a minimum of training.

On the artillery side they had some good weapons, which were, however, woefully deficient in numbers. All the principal

First World War types – the 18-pounder, 6-inch gun, 60-pounder, and the 4·5-inch, 6-inch, 8-inch and 9·2-inch howitzers – were all to be used, this time with high explosive only. Among new weapons (not all of which were available at the start of the war) were the 5·5-inch gun-howitzer, firing a 100-pound shell to a distance of 16,600 yards, the 7·2-inch howitzer, and the 4·5-inch gun, which had a 55-pound projectile and a range of 20,500 yards; this gun, however, was never produced in large numbers. Lack of modern heavies was later to be made good from American sources, with the 155-millimetre and 8-inch guns and 240-millimetre howitzers. The anti-tank regiments had nothing better than the 2-pounder, which, though it scored some early successes, was of little use at any distance above 500 yards; the 6-pounder (effective range 800 yards) and the 17-pounder (capable of penetrating 86 millimetres of armour at over 2,000 yards) were still weapons of the future.

The RHA and field batteries, however, had an admirable new arm – the 25-pounder gun-howitzer, with a range of 13,400 yards, or over 7 miles. This tough, hard-hitting gun was to prove its worth time after time, not only against infantry in the open and against prepared positions, but also against tanks. With improvements and modifications to suit different conditions, it was destined to serve brilliantly in every theatre of land warfare, for almost every imaginable task, as one of the most versatile and successful weapons in the fight against Hitler.

On 10 May 1940, the Germans invaded Holland, Belgium and Luxembourg, and flooded on into France. Four days later the Dutch Army surrendered and General von Kluck's spearheads had crossed the Meuse. Through a 50-mile breach in the French line between Namur and Sedan – the hinge of the allied defences – armoured columns were thrusting deep into France and curving northward. As Belgian resistance crumbled in the north, General Gort's force, which had advanced according to plan as far as Louvain, was confronted with a rapidly developing threat of being cut off and encircled. The British had three Territorial divisions, without artillery, whose men had been set to work in the rear areas. These were now hurriedly equipped with guns from reserve stores and sent up to hold the Canal du Nord between Peronne and Douai, but, in a situation that was swiftly dissolving into ruin, improvisations such as this were far too little to check the breakthrough. On 18 May the enemy reached St Quentin; next day they were streaming across the old battlefields of the Somme; Amiens fell on the 20th.

In Albert, according to a German account, the 2nd Panzer Division captured a British battery 'drawn up on the barrack square and equipped only with training ammunition, since nobody had reckoned on our appearance that day'. Soon all hope of breaking through for a British link-up with the French Army that was regrouping farther south had to be abandoned; the most that could be attempted was to establish a corridor through which the BEF could struggle to the Channel ports.

A brilliant example of determined action while the enemy pressed in on the southern flank of the shrinking life-line corridor was the stand of K Battery, 5th Regiment RHA, on 25 May, towards the end of the confused and bitter 'twenty-day blitz'. The battery, with eighty men from a searchlight unit, had been ordered to put the village of Hondeghem in a state of defence. The battery commander, Major R. R. Hoare (later to be a colonel, with DSO and MC), sited two guns just outside the village to guard the approaches, and two in the square to fire at point-blank range on any Germans who evaded or fought past the outer guns and the men with rifles in the buildings on the perimeter.

When the attack came, at 7.30 a.m., two enemy tanks were knocked out almost immediately, but within a few minutes one gun had been wrecked and the detachment serving the other had been wiped out by close-range fire from infantry. Any move to pierce the inner defences, however, was met by a shot at a range of 50 or 100 yards from one or other of the guns in the square, whose detachments wheeled them up and down by hand (these were First World War 18-pounders, rather lighter than the newer equipment). Hour after hour the fight continued, and although buildings were set on fire the Germans made little headway.

At 3 p.m. another tank column was sighted. By this time the artillery ammunition was almost exhausted, three of the four guns of an outlying troop had been knocked out, observers in the church tower had been driven out by shelling, and the village was on the point of being surrounded. At 4.15 Major Hoare gave the order for the survivors to withdraw. St Sylvestre, a village a few miles away, on the road to the main British positions, was chosen as the rendezvous point, but as the gunners drew near they found it full of enemy tanks and infantry.

Deciding to fight his way through, Captain N. B. C. Teacher, troop commander, put two guns into close-range action. Rifle fire and grenades came from Germans sheltering behind the gravestones in the village churchyard, but they were pushed back with the aid of some RASC privates whom the gunners had encountered, and whom Teacher led in a charge.

A tractor was burnt out, a shot smashed one gun, and the other fired its last remaining round. Teacher had this gun blown up. Then he packed all the men who were left into lorries and, in gathering darkness, ran the gauntlet of machine-gun fire through St Sylvestre to escape. Major Hoare, Captain Teacher and Battery Sergeant-Major R. Millard all received decorations, and the battery has since been authorized to add 'Hondeghem' to its title. This is a Royal Artillery honour used only within the regiment, and not officially recognized by the Army as a whole.

Calais fell on 26 May to the 10th Panzer Division. Guderian, the German tank expert, has written: 'We took 20,000 prisoners, including 3,000 to 4,000 British, the remainder being French, Belgians and Dutch, of whom the majority had not wanted to go on fighting and whom the English had therefore locked up in cellars.' The garrison, who had been told that there could be no evacuation by sea and that they must fight to the death, included three Rifle battalions, forty-eight tanks, and the 229th Anti-Tank Battery, Royal Artillery. For two or three days this small force, with French troops, held off several German divisions.

On 28 May, when the fate of the BEF hung in the balance, the Germans were bloodily repulsed in an attempt at an inward turn across the Yser, which would have brought them on to the beaches behind the British fighting troops. Orders were given to the artillery, both field and medium, to use every round they had, without thought of reserve, and, in the words of Churchill, 'this tremendous fire did much to quell the German assault'.

Four days earlier, in a note to General Ismay about the situation in the Calais area, the prime minister had been somewhat critical about the artillery. He wrote: 'Apparently the

Germans can go anywhere and do anything, and their tanks can act in twos and threes all over our rear, and even when they are located they are not attacked. Also our tanks recoil before their field guns, but our field guns do not like to take on their tanks. If their motorized artillery, far from its base, can block us, why cannot we, with the artillery of a great army, block them?' Later he admitted that in this he did less than justice to the troops.

In the final phase of the evacuation, at dawn on 2 June about 4,000 British, with seven anti-aircraft guns and twelve anti-tank guns, remained on the outskirts of Dunkirk with the French forces, still considerable, along the defence perimeter. Between 27 May and 4 June a total of 338,226 troops (including French) were taken to England in Operation Dynamo, thanks to the RAF air cover, the work of the Royal Navy and the Mercantile Marine, and the hundreds of 'little ships' – motor launches, lifeboats, fishing craft, private yachts – that came to save the Army so that it could fight again. But there was room in the ships only for men, not machines. Almost the whole of the heavy equipment, including 2,300 guns, had to be abandoned. Nearly all the new field pieces were lost, hundreds being blown up to prevent their use by the enemy. One senior officer has written: 'It was heartbreaking to see rows of guns with their muzzles splayed out like the leaves of a palm tree.'

By 18 June, the day after Marshal Pétain's Government announced that it had asked for an armistice, the remainder of the British forces in France – 136,000 men, including reinforcements – were moved into Brest, Cherbourg, St Malo and St Nazaire for re-embarkation, this operation being under the direction of General Sir James Marshall-Cornwall, an artilleryman. With them they brought back 310 guns. This still left the field artillery armament perilously low, with a total of about 500 18-pounders, 4·5-inch and 6-inch howitzers, and scarcely any anti-tank guns at a time when it was feared that England must face invasion at any moment.

Churchill has told how, when he was visiting beach defences at St Margaret's Bay near Dover, a senior officer informed him that he had only three anti-tank guns in his brigade, covering 4 or 5 miles in one of the most vital sectors. 'He declared that he had only six rounds of ammunition for each gun, and he asked me with a slight air of challenge whether he was justified in letting his men fire one single round for practice in order that they might at least know how the weapon worked. I replied that we could not afford practice rounds, and that fire should be held for the last moment at the closest range.'

All Britain was scoured for any kind of gun that could be fired. Among those that came to light were 6-pounder Hotchkiss guns from the tanks of 1918, and about a hundred 4-inch and 12-pounder pieces, said to have been found lying under a mountain of coal at a dockyard after being taken out of warships scrapped under one of the naval disarmament agreements. Some of the old guns were mounted in the concrete pillboxes forming the so-called 'stop lines' across England; others were put on the back axles of disused cars to make them mobile.

Luckily other equipment was on the way. As early as 1 June, President Roosevelt had issued orders to the American military departments to report what weapons they could spare for Britain and France. The answers were given within forty-eight hours; on 3 June General Marshall, Chief of Staff of the United States Army, approved the first list; and by the end of the week heavily laden freight cars were rolling towards the docks in New Jersey with 500,000 rifles (·300 calibre), 80,000 machine-guns, 130 million rounds of small-arms ammunition, and 900 75-millimetre guns with more than 1,000 shells apiece. The normal allocation of field artillery for an infantry division in the post-Dunkirk period was seventy-two guns (three regiments, each of three eight-gun batteries) with seventeen as first-line reserve, so that the guns from America would be enough to equip ten divisions.

Certain fastidious experts turned up their noses at the 'seventy-fives', some of which were of the French 1897 model. Churchill has recalled: 'There were no limbers and no immediate means of procuring more ammunition. Mixed calibres complicate operations. But I would have none of this, and during all 1940 and 1941 these 900 "seventy-fives" were a great addition to our military strength for home defence. Arrangements were devised and men were drilled to run them up on planks into lorries for movement. When you are fighting for existence any cannon is better than no cannon at all, and the French "seventy-fives", although outdated by the British 25-pounder and the German field-gun howitzer, was still a splendid weapon.'

One menace with which no field artillery could cope was the build-up of German heavy batteries along the Channel coast of France, the strongest concentration being around Calais and Cape Gris Nez, with the apparent purpose of barring British warships from the Straits of Dover, and also of commanding for Hitler's Army the shortest sea route to England. By the middle of September the enemy had nine heavy batteries along this stretch of coast, with twenty-nine guns ranging from 170-millimetre to 380-millimetre, in addition to thirty-five heavy and medium mobile batteries, as well as seven batteries of captured guns. At the beginning of September, Britain's pre-war coast defence artillery in the corresponding area across the Channel amounted to only two 9·2-inch and six 6-inch guns. As recent additions there were two more 9·2s on railway mountings, and (from the Royal Navy) one 14-inch, two 6-inch and two 4-inch. These were soon reinforced with two 13·5-inch guns from the old battleship *Iron Duke*, on rail mountings, and a battery of four 5·5-inch guns from HMS *Hood*. Many of the additional guns were manned by the Royal Navy and Royal Marines. Britain thus had a powerful concentration, though still inferior in numbers to the enemy.

Here a wise measure of prevision after the First World War stood the Army in good stead. Not all the artillery of 1918 had been scrapped. In a letter to the minister of supply on 10 September 1939, one week after the outbreak of war, Churchill, who was then First Lord of the Admiralty, pointed out that in 1919, when he was at the War Office, he had given instructions for the storing of a mass of heavy artillery, including, as he noted later, thirty-two 12-inch guns, 145 9-inch, a large number of 8-inch, and nearly 200 6-inch howitzers, together with quantities of ammunition; lighter pieces were not mentioned in this context. The minister of supply replied that the use of this old heavy artillery had been under active consideration by the War Office since the September crisis of 1938, and work on reconditioning the guns had been started.

It continued for many months. Churchill, in the midst of all his multifarious responsibilities, took a personal interest in every detail of arming the Dover promontory with guns that could fire across the Channel. In a stream of orders, notes and enquiries addressed to all concerned he relentlessly spurred on the work.

On 8 August 1940, the prime minister was able to write to the First Lord: 'I am impressed by the speed and efficiency with which the emplacement for the 14-inch gun at Dover has been prepared, and the gun itself mounted. Will you tell all those who have helped in this achievement how much I appreciate the sterling effort they have made.'

The enemy batteries first opened fire on 22 August, engaging a convoy and later bombarding Dover. One of the British 14-inch guns replied, and from this date there were cross-Channel artillery duels at irregular intervals, the British gunners' greatest difficulty being accurate observation of fire. Little damage was done by the Germans to convoys. Dover was engaged six times in September, the heaviest day being the 9th, when more than 150 shells were fired.

Before this the prime minister had shown some dissatisfaction. He asked General Ismay and the Chiefs of Staffs Committee: 'What are we doing in defence of the Dover promontory by heavy artillery? Ten weeks ago I asked for heavy guns. One has been mounted. Two railway guns are expected. Now we are told these will be very inaccurate on account of super-charging. We ought to have a good many more heavy guns lined up inside to smaller calibre with stiffer rifling and a range of at least 50 miles, and firing at 25 or 30 miles would then become more accurate. I do not understand why I have not yet received proposals on this subject. We must insist upon maintaining superior artillery positions on the Dover promontory, no matter what form of attack they are exposed to. We have to fight for the command of the Straits by artillery, to destroy the enemy's batteries, and to multiply and fortify our own.'

A few days later, on 30 August, he returned to the charge: 'Some of our heavy artillery – the 18-inch howitzer and the 9·2s – should be planted in positions whence they could deny the ports and landings to the enemy, and, as CIGS mentioned, support the counter-attack which would be launched against any attempted bridgehead. Much of this mass of artillery I saved from the last war has done nothing, and has been under reconditioning for a whole year. Let me have a good programme for using it to support counter-strokes and deny landings, both north and south of the Thames. Farther north I have seen already some very good heavy batteries. . . . I am also endeavouring to obtain from United States at least a pair of their 16-inch coast defence weapons. These fire 45,000 yards, throwing 1¼ tons, without being super-charged. They should therefore be very accurate.'

These American guns did not arrive, it appears, but the 18-inch howitzer (the famous Bochebuster, posted in a tunnel near Canterbury) and a dozen 12-inch were installed. With these additions, the south-east coastal defences should undoubtedly have been capable of bringing down a devastating fire on any landing area. This was never put to the test.

Goering's arrogant bid to smash the Royal Air Force, and the British ground organization and aviation industry, as an essential preliminary to invasion was foiled by the valour of Fighter Command. When the power of the Luftwaffe was switched against London and other cities it met the staunch defence of the RAF and of the gunners of Anti-Aircraft Command, whose story will be told in a later chapter; and for nearly four years, until strength could be mustered for the liberation of the European mainland, Britain remained the citadel, training ground and marshalling area in which an ever-increasing array of units from the artillery and all other arms prepared and waited until the day when they could be launched against the Axis powers in an overseas theatre of operations.

For artillerymen in the British Isles this was a period of much frustration and some tedium but also, for a great many officers and men on staffs and in units, of a vast amount of patient, untiring work in sifting and applying the lessons of the past for the benefit of those who would one day take the field again in Europe. Until 1942, when the invasion threat could at last be discounted, all activity directed towards the training and build-up of a mobile field army had to be closely coordinated at every stage with possible requirements for the defence of Britain itself. One of the biggest and most pressing needs, in general, was for the provision of large numbers of new anti-tank and light anti-aircraft batteries; these were found mainly by the conversion of infantry units.

A wholesale rethinking had to be undertaken not only on unit organization and tactics, but also on the methods for control of artillery in large numbers. One suggestion, from outside the regiment, was that the artillery of a division would never again be handled by its commander as a whole. In modern war, it was argued, the largest tactical formation would be the brigade group; therefore a commander Royal Artillery was no longer required in a division, all that was needed being a colonel RA as *adviser* to the divisional commander, who alone would initiate orders to his gunners through the General Staff. This proposal was defeated, much to the satisfaction of Royal Artillery officers, by whom it had been regarded as imperilling the whole future status of their corps. The successful opposition was largely due to the efforts of Major-General O. M. Lund, who became chief artillery staff officer at General Headquarters, Home Forces, in the autumn of 1940. On this point, as on others, the major-general Royal Artillery received invaluable support from General Sir Alan Brooke, a former gunner officer, who was appointed Commander-in-Chief, Home Forces, in July 1940, and later (as Field-Marshal Lord Alanbrooke) served as Chief of the Imperial General Staff.

During the post-Dunkirk period, almost the only means by which British-based land forces could strike at 'Fortress Europe' was through the amphibious raids for which Combined Operations Headquarters came into existence. Of these the biggest, and the most disastrous, was the Dieppe raid of 19 August 1942, in which little was accomplished and heavy losses were suffered. This operation – it has been described as a reconnaissance in force – was carried out by 5,000 troops of the Canadian 2nd Division, accompanied by about 1,000 British Commando men, who had with them a few Americans and French. In this one day the Canadian Army lost more men as prisoners of war than in all the rest of the European campaign. Many factors contributed to the failure; a German Fifteenth Army assessment put at the head of its list 'lack of artillery support'.

The Canadians had their own group of about 270 artillerymen, with the task of capturing and manning enemy guns, but this proved impossible. All the gunners who were landed were eventually captured (they had left England in the landing ship *Duke of Wellington*). The operation was notable, however, for gallantry which won the VC for a Royal Artillery officer, Captain Patrick Anthony Porteous, while acting as liaison between two Commando groups whose objectives were the heavy coastal defence guns.

In the initial assault Porteous, working with the smaller of the two groups, was wounded at close range, a bullet passing his hand and entering the upper arm. In spite of this he closed with his assailant, killed him with his own bayonet, and thereby saved a British sergeant at whom the German had been aiming. Meanwhile, the larger detachment had been held up, the officer in charge and his second-in-command were killed, and the sergeant-major seriously wounded. Without hesitation Porteous dashed over open ground under fire to take command. Rallying the men, he led them in a charge which carried the German position at the point of the bayonet. Though shot through the thigh he went on to the final objective, where he collapsed from loss of blood after the last of the guns had been put out of action. Porteous was later promoted to the rank of colonel.

The Dieppe raid came shortly before a historic turning point in the British Army's greatest effort of the war outside Europe, the campaigns in Africa which, from a strained defensive start at the gates of Egypt, produced the brilliant desert victories, driving the enemy from the entire northern coastal zone of the continent and leading on to the invasion of Sicily and Italy that, before the end of the struggle, brought men of the Eighth Army across the Austrian frontier after a fighting advance of more than 2,000 miles which can have few counterparts in history.

WAR IN THE DESERT

'No stop; no caution; go on.' – 8th Armoured Division motto, with Green Light badge

In the series of campaigns along the African littoral, from December, 1940, to the fall of Tunis in May 1943, gunners of the British Army, and some of the Australians, South Africans, Indians and Free French who fought alongside them, had to learn a whole new list of techniques. They had to be masters not only of their arms but also of the desert routine of leaguers, the special problems of transport on soft sand, gravel or treacherous saltpan, the art of navigation across vast and almost featureless distances. The wide-ranging ebb and flow of desert action has been likened to war at sea, but there was one great difference; while ships can carry ammunition, stores and food for weeks or even months, armoured land forces were provisioned only for a few days or hours. Long-range forays in Libya were often carried out by men who had to be rationed to one or two cups of water a day.

When Major-General R. N. O'Connor's Western Desert Force took the offensive against Marshal Graziani's Italians, it consisted of 31,000 men with 275 tanks and 120 guns. The British anti-tank batteries were still equipped with the little 2-pounder. With the British armour outgunned, the only effective counter to enemy tanks, at this time and for two years to come, was the 25-pounder.

In six weeks O'Connor's small army advanced 200 miles, took by assault the fortified positions of Bardia, Tobruk and Beda Fomm, and captured 113,000 prisoners and more than 700 guns, using methodical techniques not unlike those of the First World War, with careful artillery preparations. Then logistic problems imposed a halt, together with the decision to divert men and equipment from General Wavell's Middle East Command for the aid of Greece, which had been invaded by Axis troops. The British intervention in the Balkans was doomed to failure after the rapid collapse of resistance when the German crossed both the Greek and the Yugoslav frontiers. A gunner officer, Major C. I. W. Seton-Watson, has described the chaos of a night withdrawal in which his battery managed only 15 miles in twelve hours.

'After dark we started on a nightmare drive. Grevena was full of burning dumps and houses, bewildered Greek troops and confused columns of mules and bullock carts. The road on to the Venetikos was narrow and twisting, sometimes with steep ravines or precipices on both sides. We were a mixed cavalcade. Vehicles were jammed nose to tail for miles, double or even treble banked whenever the road was wide enough. Buses and private cars, Greeks on horseback and foot, were all jumbled in between our guns. Halts were interminable and we crawled forward a few hundred yards at a time. Weary drivers fell asleep in the cabs and had to be roused by cursing officers and NCOs.

'Our route was strewn with all the litter of a retreat: discarded clothing, ammunition and harness, dead mules and horses, sodden papers and office files, and dozens of abandoned vehicles – ramshackle requisitioned lorries from every province of Greece, British 3-tonners side by side with Italian tractors and mobile workshops captured by the Greek Army in Albania and now waiting for their original owners; some bogged down in the ditches, some tipped at crazy angles into bomb craters, others burnt out or shattered by machine-gun bullets. All the time dawn was getting nearer and we could look forward to being caught in the first air sortie like rats in a trap, unable to disperse off the narrow road. As we twisted down into the Venetikos valley, a single Messerschmitt flew along the bottom of the gorge below us. But we were safely in action across the river and well camouflaged before the first air attacks began....

'When we drove through Athens the Greeks lined the streets in thousands, many of them in tears, yet cheering and throwing flowers and shouting: "You will be back; we'll be waiting for you." Few retreating armies can have had such a send-off.'

While General Wavell had been sending 56,000 men and

8,000 vehicles into Greece, Hitler had reinforced the Italians in Tripolitania with a German light armoured division under a little-known general who was to become famous – Erwin Rommel. At the end of March 1941, without waiting for the completion of his build-up, Rommel struck, encircling most of the 2nd Armoured Division near El Adem, south of Tobruk. At dawn the 1st Royal Horse Artillery and some Indian troops broke out, but the rest of the division was captured.

It was decided that Tobruk must be held to deprive Rommel of a forward base for his advance into Egypt. The 7th Australian Division was sent in by sea, with a few tanks but without the divisional artillery. The Australians were reinforced, as the siege of Tobruk began, by the 1st RHA, two other RHA units – the 104th (Essex Yeomanry) and 107th (South Notts Hussars) – and the 51st Field Regiment, RA. For anti-tank artillery, to hold 27 miles of weak and half-completed field defences, there were the 3rd RHA, somewhat unhappily manning small direct-fire guns, and the 2nd/3rd Anti-Tank Regiment, Royal Australian Artillery.

Many of the Australians had not yet been under fire. Soldiers of their nation are not always lavish in praise of the British, but an Australian war historian has paid tribute to the work that was done in preparation for the defence of Tobruk. He speaks of 'the mutual confidence and esteem that in only two days had sprung up between the Australian infantry and the British gunners supporting them'.

One of the first significant attacks in the siege, on 14 April, involved the 1st RHA, and it was appropriate that the opening shots from the artillery should be fired by the senior battery of the Royal Horse Artillery, the 'right of the right of the line' – A/E Battery, RHA; before its amalgamation with E in 1938, A was the famous Chestnut Troop.

When the battery was given the tank alert, about 4 a.m., the gunners set their sights at 400 yards and waited. The main body of German infantry had been checked by fire from an Australian battalion, with the result that the armour came in without infantry support. Having no armour-piercing shot for their 25-pounders, the RHA men used high explosive which, according to accepted theory, might be expected to burst harmlessly on the steel plates. In fact, the first round from No. 1 gun of the

Chestnuts set the leading tank on fire, and the first shot from No. 2 blew the turret off a Panzer Mark IV. Soon five tanks were ablaze.

Next came the turn of E Troop. When the gun position officer had been hit and all members of one detachment had been knocked out, Battery Sergeant-Major Batten took charge and kept the guns firing. (Later he was to be the battery commander.) After this the 5th Panzer Regiment veered off to the east, where they encountered part of the Australian anti-tank unit, in front of whose guns four tanks were left disabled.

Then followed a series of desperate small-scale actions by the infantry, at times with the bayonet. Finally, by 7.30 a.m., the whole of the German force withdrew, in some disorder, through the gap they had made in the wire. Of the thirty-eight tanks employed by 5th Panzer, seventeen were destroyed; 150 German dead were counted, and 250 prisoners were taken. This sharp engagement had clearly vindicated the classic principle of cooperation, with all arms supporting one another and concentrating their maximum effort against one fraction of the enemy—though there were to be many departures from this principle during the increasingly costly gun-versus-tank fights that lay ahead.

An attempt to relieve Tobruk failed in June. Rommel counter-attacked and drove back the 7th Armoured Division at Sidi Omar. The British armour was no match for the Panzer IV with the 50-millimetre gun. German tactics improved; they now tended to stand off and subject British artillery to organized bombardment from medium, field and self-propelled guns, in addition to the cannon and machine-gun fire of tanks. They benefited from skilful use in the anti-tank role of the 88-millimetre anti-aircraft gun, capable of disabling British tanks before these could get their armament within range. The British 25-pounder detachments, deployed in the open, suffered heavy casualties.

Some concern regarding the effectiveness of the artillery about this time was revealed in a note which Churchill, in his capacity as minister of defence, circulated to various senior commanders on 7 October 1941. He wrote: 'Renown awaits the commander who first in this war restores artillery to its prime importance upon the battlefield, from which it has been ousted by heavily armoured tanks. For this purpose three rules are necessary:

'(a) Every field gun or mobile AA gun should carry a plentiful supply of solid armour-piercing tracer shot; thus every mobile gun will become an anti-tank gun, and every battery possess its own anti-tank protection.

'(b) When guns are attacked by tanks they must welcome the occasion. The guns should be fought to the muzzle. Until the approaching tanks are within close range batteries should engage them at a rapid rate of fire with high explosives. During this phase the tracks of the tanks are the most vulnerable target. At close quarters solid armour-piercing shot should be fired; this should be continued so long as any of the detachments survive. The last shot should be fired at not more than 10 yards' range. It may be that some gun crews could affect to be out of action or withhold their fire, so as to have the superb opportunity of firing armour piercing at the closest range.

'(c) It may often happen as a result of the above tactics, especially when artillery is working with tanks, that guns may be overrun and lost. Provided they have been fought to the muzzle, this should not at all be considered a disaster, but, on the contrary, the highest honour to the battery concerned. The destruction of tanks more than repays the loss of field guns or mobile AA guns. The Germans have no use for our captured guns, as they have a plethora of their own types, which they prefer. Our own supplies are sufficient to make good the deficiencies.

'The principle must be established by the Royal Artillery that it is not good enough for tanks to attack a group of British batteries properly posted, and that these batteries will always await their attack to destroy a good proportion of tanks. Our guns must no more retreat on the approach of tanks than Wellington's squares at Waterloo on the approach of hostile cavalry.'

Some points in this, in the light of what is now known, may strike one as rather obvious, and perhaps unnecessary; it may be doubted whether the gun detachments, if they had known of it, would have greeted with enthusiasm the exhortation from Whitehall that they should fight 'to the muzzle'. It was not all so obvious, however, at the time when the defence minister's note was written. General Montgomery (not yet in command of Eighth Army) was not among those to whom the paper was sent, but when he was shown a copy by Churchill, after their meeting in Tripoli in 1943, the general's comment was: 'It is as true now as when it was written.' By the time he spoke the artillery had made its mark.

In 1941 the British gunners in Africa, especially those serving with the armoured divisions, were still largely imbued with the idea of the small raiding groups which became known as the Jock Columns, after their originator, Brigadier J. C. Campbell, DSO and Bar, MC, a thrustful, hard-riding fox-hunter in the true old RHA tradition. It has been said that these raids, in a totally different setting, played much the same role as the trench raids during the static warfare of 1914–18. Each column consisted of a few armoured cars and a company of infantry in lorries or carriers, together with a troop of 25-pounders and perhaps some Bofors guns. Deep penetrations into enemy-held territory were made with the object of reconnoitring, gathering information, and doing as much damage as possible while avoiding involvement with superior forces. The general idea – to maintain the spirit of the offensive and keep the enemy on edge – was excellent in itself, but there were disadvantages.

The columns were too weak to stand much chance once they were pinned down, yet they robbed the divisional artillery of guns that were badly needed. More than once, it was true, they had been remarkably successful in spreading alarm and despondency among the Italians; but this was less likely to work against the seasoned German troops of the Afrika Korps. Above all, the Jock Columns offended against the golden rule of concentration; they stood for a dispersion which, if carried too far, could be extremely dangerous. They fell into disfavour, therefore, and the hit-and-run raids were largely discarded in favour of more complete integration with the divisional support group, and the deployment of artillery in substantial numbers whenever possible. Campbell himself evidently realized that this must happen, for he said: 'As soon as we get the enemy where we want him we must drop dispersed columns and concentrate every available gun.'

On 18 November 1941, Lieutenant-General Sir Alan Cunningham, with the newly-formed Eighth Army, boldly took the offensive. Rommel's force, though larger than Cunningham's, was short of Germans, two-thirds of its total number being Italians; but he was greatly superior in tanks and aircraft, and also in anti-tank guns, of which he had 194 compared with seventy-two on the British side. Major-General J. F. C. Fuller has stressed the enemy's 'ballistical advantage', pointing out that 'Rommel's tank and anti-tank guns were of 50-millimetre (4½-pounder) and 75-millimetre calibre, whereas Cunningham's were 2-pounders, and the effective armour-piercing range of this gun was from 800 to 1,000 yards less than that of the 50-millimetre gun'. The armour of the British 'I' tanks (Matildas) was not proof against the latter weapon, let alone the 75-millimetre with which some of the Panzers were now armed.

For two days a tank battle raged furiously around Sidi Rezegh. Here, in the action that won him the VC, Brigadier Campbell proved that, whatever opinions might be concerning his Jock Columns, he was a fighting leader of superb quality. His small force, including one regiment of tanks, was holding the ridge and airfield. Wherever the fighting was hardest, there he was to be seen with the forward troops, either on foot or in his open car. Standing in the car with a blue flag in his hand, the brigadier formed up tanks under close and intense fire. Twice he helped to man a gun where there had been casualties. During the final successful enemy attack he was wounded, but he remained in the advanced positions, controlling the fire of batteries which inflicted heavy losses on German tanks at point-blank range. Towards the end he acted as loader on one of the guns.

Campbell survived to be decorated with the ribbon of the VC by General Sir Claude Auchinleck, Commander-in-Chief, Middle East, at a parade in Cairo on 10 February 1942, and a few days later his promotion to major-general was gazetted. He was killed in a car accident on 25 February.

Another artilleryman, Second Lieutenant George Gunn, MC, RHA, had won a posthumous VC at Sidi Rezegh while in command of a troop of four anti-tank guns carried 'portee' on lorries. When all but one had been destroyed, he got the last remaining gun into action on its burning lorry, himself aiming it while a sergeant loaded. They shot between forty and fifty rounds, regardless alike of concentrated enemy fire and of the flames which at any moment might have reached the ammunition in the lorry. At least two German tanks were set on fire, and others damaged, before Gunn fell dead, shot through the head.

Early in December 1941, after a great deal of confusion, there was a German withdrawal. The British had lost 18,000 men, but they had inflicted 24,500 casualties and taken 36,500 prisoners. Cyrenaica had been cleared, and the relief of Tobruk had been accomplished. But reinforcements that were expected could not be spared, owing to the war with the Japanese in the Far East, and in January 1942, Rommel, now stronger than ever, returned to the attack, driving Eighth Army back to the Gazala-Bir Hakim line. Frontier garrisons which he established at Bardia and Halfaya Pas fell, but this was followed by a lull.

Auchinleck was ordered by the War Cabinet to open an offensive in May, or June at the latest. Rommel, however, got his blow in first, advancing on 26 May. By this time a number of the new 6-pounder anti-tank guns had reached Middle East Command, and many more were on the way, but the troops had not had long enough to become accustomed to the new weapon before the German drive opened.

In a series of tank battles, with heavy losses on both sides, a determined British attack in the 'Cauldron' failed, partly through lack of sufficient infantry, partly because of the effective German anti-tank guns. Enemy armour poured into Tobruk on 21 June after mass bombing by Stukas; a German account gave as one reason for the fall of the fortress 'the weakness of the defensive artillery fire'. Soon the Eighth Army, battered and rather bewildered, was right back on the so-called Alamein Line – miles of sand, practically indistinguishable from the rest of the desert, but with its flanks resting on the sea and on the almost impassable Qattara Depression.

Hard fighting had fallen to the lot of the gunners. The 28th Field Regiment – almost twenty-eight years after the ordeal at Le Cateau – was overwhelmed in the open. The last stand of the South Notts Hussars unit is one of the most celebrated in the history of the Royal Artillery. The entire support group – the RHA, the anti-tank battery of the Northumberland Hussars (another converted Yeomanry unit) and the Royal Northumberland Fusiliers – fought to the end, drivers, signallers and fusiliers filling the gaps in the detachments as gunners fell. It took the Germans most of a day to subdue them. Last to go under was F Troop, which scored two direct hits on tanks just before it ceased firing. Six months later, when the tide of war swept westward again, British troops found the disabled guns still there, with the layers in their seats and the others lying around them, where they had died.

The 11th Field Regiment, which had arrived from Iraq after a 1,000-mile march, was posted on Ruweisat Ridge, with a battalion of the Essex Regiment, on 2 July after the destruction of the 18th Brigade. The Royal Artillery Commemoration Book says: 'All day long 11th Field bore the brunt of the tank assault. In E Troop, Sergeant Keenan (who had become separated, in the retreat from Mersa Matruh, from his own unit and had joined the troop two nights before) found himself the only man in his detachment who was not a casualty. He continued to fight his gun alone under intense fire and was given an immediate award of the DCM for his gallantry. It was Sergeant Keenan, too, who under a hail of machine-gun bullets gave RSM Clark a lecture on the new No. 29 telescope. The RSM proved such an apt pupil that he stepped into the layer's seat and scored three successive direct hits.

'But of all that devoted band, none displayed more shining and indomitable courage than Bombardier Johnson. Early in the day his left arm was shot off, but he continued to lay and fire with his single arm, refusing all attention. As a result this very gallant soldier died in hospital two days later. . . .

'Seven officers and over eighty men had been killed or wounded out of some three hundred actively engaged. Of the 83rd/85th Battery's nine guns only one was serviceable when the battle ended – that of Sergeant Wilkinson (later awarded the MM) who, twice wounded in the morning, had refused to leave and next day volunteered to take his gun up to join 78th/84th Battery, to bring them up to strength. . . . It is probable that well over twenty tanks were disabled.'

General Montgomery, now in command of Eighth Army, decided that his opponent should no longer be allowed to use his favourite tactics of placing his armour behind a screen of anti-tank guns and waiting to knock out the British tanks as they advanced. 'We would fight a static battle and my forces would not move; his tanks would come up against our tanks dug-in in hull-down positions at the western edge of the Alam Halfa ridge.' There, in a week's battle that started on 30 August, Rommel was repulsed. He attributed this to the weight of the British artillery fire, the intricacy and depth of the minefields, and his own shortage of supplies, especially petrol, through RAF strikes at the lines of communication.

Between early September and late October, Eighth Army prepared. Against General Stumme's force of 108,000 men and 600 tanks (half of which were Italian M.13 'self-propelled coffins'), General Montgomery was able to assemble 220,000 troops with over a thousand tanks, among which were 285 new Shermans with 75-millimetre guns, more than a match for any of the hostile armour except for thirty-eight German Mark IVs. The British had 1,400 anti-tank guns, of which 850 were 6-pounders, in addition to 832 field guns and fifty-two medium pieces.

An important new artillery weapon had made its appearance. This was the self-propelled gun, consisting of a Grant tank with the turret removed and a 105-millimetre gun-howitzer fitted, together with an armour-plated 'pulpit' on which was mounted a Browning anti-aircraft gun, and from which the vehicle took its name of the Priest. The idea of the SP gun was by no means new. An experimental 18-pounder on a tracked chassis had been produced in England as early as 1928, when it was known as the Birch gun, after General Birch who was then master of the ordnance; but the Priests of 1942 marked the first practical success in giving the gunners a combination of mobility and protection in this way. They could now open fire from hull-down positions without having to delay for unlimbering or to dig gunpits.

At last the odds were in the British Army's favour. On the night of 23 October, Montgomery's Army was ready at El Alamein. A Scottish infantry officer, Captain Grant Murray, has described the scene as the men on the start line crouched in their slit trenches, waiting for the battle to begin. As zero drew near I twisted round and looked back towards our own lines. Suddenly the whole horizon went pink and for a second or two there was still perfect silence, and then the noise of Eighth Army's guns hit us in a solid wall of sound that made the whole earth shake. Through the din we made out other sounds – the whine of shells overhead, the chatter of the machine-guns – and eventually the pipes. Then we saw a sight that will live for ever in our memories – line upon line of steel-helmeted figures with rifles at the high port, bayonets catching the moonlight, and over all the wailing of the pipes.'

In the twelve-day struggle before the breakthrough, the enemy suffered 7,000 casualties in dead or wounded according to their own figures (in reality probably far more) and lost 450 tanks and 1,000 guns, at a cost for the British of 12,500 casualties, 500 tanks disabled (but only 150 damaged beyond repair), and 100 guns destroyed. It was the turning point. As Churchill has said: 'Up to Alamein we survived. After Alamein we conquered.'

Now began the long advance in which, this time, there was to be no turning back. On 8 November, while Rommel was saving what was left out of the wreck of his army at Alamein, the British and Americans had landed at Algiers, Oran and Casablanca to trap the enemy between the western and eastern jaws of a giant pincer movement. The Germans left Benghazi on 20 November, Tripoli was captured by Montgomery on 23 January 1943, and in the following month Rommel was facing Eighth Army near the Tunisian border and the old French frontier defences known as the Mareth Line.

In the advance the artillery made good use of its new equipment and methods. At Bou Arada, Lieutenant-Colonel Barstow, commanding officer of the 12th (HAC) Regiment RHA (of which more will be heard in a later chapter) was the first artilleryman to engage a divisional target operationally by the use of new radio procedure. He was able to concentrate successfully the fire of the entire divisional artillery on an enemy battle group, including thirty tanks, which he had seen in the plain below him, moving as though to turn the right flank. This 'Uncle' procedure, as it was called, subsequently became a standard drill.

Near El Hamma, after a check to the frontal assault on the Mareth Line, some of the towed 17-pounder anti-tank guns that had arrived from England showed their mettle. At one point, after German armoured vehicles had been chased across the desert for miles, Brigadier Fowler, the CRA, found it necessary to order the men with the 17-pounders to return to the anti-tank screen and 'stop doing a Prince Rupert'.

The last occasion in North Africa when a British field battery fought tanks over open sights was at Sidi Nsir, where the 155th Battery, 172nd Field Regiment, was overrun after a gallant defence while on detached duty with a battalion of the Hampshires near Hunt's Gap, in a wild country of stony djebels and barren valleys, far beyond the support of other troops.

During one day the battery fired as many as 1,800 rounds per gun. Bren gunners claimed four Messerschmitts. In the final stages, tanks that came on over a ridge in front of F Troop were engaged by three 25-pounders at ranges down to 50 yards or less. The troop, helped a little by the slope of the ground, which made it difficult for the German tank crews to depress their guns sufficiently, fired for more than an hour, with a lieutenant, a fitter, cooks, and all other survivors running from gun to gun, before being silenced. Then the tanks moved on to surround E Troop, which they smothered with gun and machine-gun fire. Some tanks cruised round the position, swivelling on their tracks to crush in the slit trenches. The last radio message from the battery said: 'Tanks are on us', followed a few seconds later by the single letter 'V', tapped out in Morse. Altogether, the 172nd Field Regiment lost one-third of its guns, but twenty-four hours of precious time had been gained.

In the north, where General Anderson's thrust towards Tunis was slowed down by fierce counter-attacks, armoured regiments had to be used for scouting and skirmishing in wasteful 'penny packets' while the artillery was rushed up and down the nebulous line in detached batteries or even troops, supporting improvised forces. Not until 6 May was a way cleared by heavy bombing which, in the words of General Arnold, 'blasted a channel from Medjez el Bab to Tunis'. More than a thousand guns also pounded the defenders.

Two divisions entered Tunis on 7 May, and a few days later over a quarter of a million German and Italian troops in the Cape Bon peninsula, their last foothold in North Africa, laid down their arms. Soon the allies were poised for the next stage – the invasion of Sicily, and after that the long battle northward through Italy.

For Eighth Army and the American Fifth Army, this was to

be a tough struggle, and in many ways a thankless one, with frequent checks and disappointments, in a theatre which could not be the decisive one, and which had to yield priority in man-power and equipment supply to the preparations for invasion of north-west Europe. The Germans, even when all hope of victory had gone, still fought bitterly in their successive zones of strong defences, aided by the natural obstacles of mountains, mud, floods, and line after line of river barriers across the main coastal corridor of the allied advance. Fortunately, the British artillery had the benefit of two innovations, both of which had been used operationally for the first time in North Africa, and which in Italy stood them in good stead. These were the Army Groups Royal Artillery (AGRAS) and the Air Observation Posts.

The AGRAS were formations of field, medium and heavy regiments, under command of an army, though usually allotted to corps or even divisions as required. The way for the introduction of the new groups had been cleared by the decision after Dunkirk to abolish the commanders, Corps Medium Artillery, and their staffs with the exception of counter-battery officers. As they grew, the AGRAS were able to develop a spirit and identity of their own which had been hardly possible for the loose association of units under a CCMA. Perhaps even more important, as definite formations they were better fitted to look after the proper administration of medium regiments, which had tended to be 'nobody's baby', elbowed out, during frequent moves, by the 'solid corporations' of the divisional artilleries.

The Air OPS – 'the eye in the sky' – gave an answer to the problem of how to bring observed fire speedily on to the target in conditions which rendered the use of ground observers impossible or ineffective. With the increased speed of warfare this need became ever more pressing. In spite of many experiments, the RAF, with its other heavy commitments, was unable to produce a satisfactory solution, and it became obvious that what the artillery must have was some form of air observation under its own control.

One of the pioneers was Lieutenant-Colonel H. C. B. Bazeley, secretary of the Royal Artillery Aero Club, which had been formed before the war to assist young artillerymen in learning to fly. In 1942, in the face of a good deal of opposition from some quarters, the RAF agreed to equip squadrons with Austers and to lend ground crews to maintain them, under a dual administrative system which in practice gave the Army full operational control. These light aircraft, relying not on armament or speed but on low flying and use of natural features for such safety as they had, were manned by Royal Artillery officers who filled the double role of pilot and observer, and who did not carry parachutes, as the low altitudes at which they operated would have given no chance for these to open. Taking off and landing almost anywhere, they gave the gunners the advantage of men who really knew their needs and could talk their language. Besides target spotting, the Air OP pilots provided much valuable general information for army intelligence – apart from such semi-official duties as occasional 'flying taxi' trips for VIPs, and the conveyance of the odd bottle of whisky from the rear. One hazard which pilots had to bear in mind, among all the others, was the danger of getting into the line of fire of their own artillery. The need to keep clear may sound obvious enough, but it was not always so easy in practice; one or two air casualties were caused by British shells.

By 1943 twelve Air OP squadrons had been formed. One of them, No. 654, observed seventy shoots in one battle, and in Italy 8,078 sorties of all kinds were flown.

A remarkable instance of international cooperation by artillery took place in May 1944, during the days of hard fighting that led to the forcing of the Gustav Line, a formidable defence system, the pivot of which was the famous abbey of Cassino. Backed by Monte Cairo, over 5,000 feet high, and the Hitler Line, this dominated the Liri valley and the road to Rome. To break through the Liri defences, in cooperation with the Americans on the left, Eighth Army had at its disposal over 3,200 guns, and the total expenditure of ammunition exceeded by nearly half a million rounds that fired at Alamein. On the Army front, in addition to British divisional artillery, fire support was given by Canadian, New Zealand and Italian gunners. Monte Trocchio, a bare rocky hill, extremely exposed, contained almost a hundred allied artillery observation posts.

6th AGRA, which was responsible for coordination on the Army front, used a sixty-line signal exchange in addition to the normal wireless networks. German mortars were particularly hard to suppress, for the crews all had shell-proof dugouts, and most of the mortars themselves were in sunken roads or deep ravines where they could not be reached by shells with an ordinary trajectory. These positions had to be dealt with by 4·2-inch mortars, or by guns firing in the 'upper register', at elevations above 45 degrees.

Cassino town was finally taken by the British, and the abbey, a shattered ruin after RAF bombing, by the Poles. The Germans then fell back on the Hitler Line, where the allies were held up for some days by defences that included gun cupolas emplaced in concrete. The last remaining centres of resistance were almost entirely destroyed by the British artillery, using for the first time a 'William target' – a procedure calling on all available guns of the Army, and concentrating at twenty minutes' notice the fire of 600 pieces.

Rome was entered by Eighth Army on 4 June. Two days later, on the coast of France, the spearheads of 21st Army Group were landing for Operation Overlord, the invasion of German-occupied north-west Europe.

ADVANCE INTO GERMANY

*'**The artillery has been terrific.**' – Field-Marshal Montgomery*

The allied landings in Normandy on 6 June 1944, had fire support of unprecedented volume and variety. So long as the invasion force was still waterborne, the bulk of this inevitably came from RAF bombers and from the Royal Navy, which in addition to the larger warships had many assault craft specially armed with 4·7-inch guns, 4-inch mortars, and barrages of 5-inch rockets. For close-in air defence there were the flak boats, converted landing craft filled with whole batteries of Bofors. But the Royal Artillery also succeeded in contributing to the general bombardment of the shore defences, even before the first wave of infantry leapt ashore. This was made possible by the embarkation of the self-propelled field guns of six divisional regiments, one troop of six guns to each landing craft.

A forward observation officer in a small craft went ahead, and each flotilla of six LCTs was under the command of a naval officer, who by radar and other means kept it heading steadily at a known speed towards the area chosen for the concentration. Each LCT had a 'clock' showing the rate of change of range. Fire was opened 11,000 yards from land and was maintained until thirty minutes later, when, at a distance of about 3,000 yards out, the flotilla had to turn away from shore. Each regiment fired some 1,500 rounds. In the words of Major-General H. J. Parham, who was chief artillery officer of Second Army during the invasion: 'Here was true inter-service cooperation, for the Royal Navy laid our guns for line and we laid them for elevation.'

By 7.45 a.m. (twenty minutes after H-Hour) the first FOOs of the 3rd Division were ashore. The foremost field regiments, landed according to plan at about 8.25, had to come into action on the beach itself, as the bridgehead was too shallow to provide positions under cover inland. Guns of one regiment with the 50th Division, hemmed in between a marsh on one side and a minefield on the other, were at one stage on a road, firing over one another's heads. Luckily the Luftwaffe did not appear, thanks to the work of the Royal Air Force, and the German artillery fire was largely ineffective, though there were exceptions; four 88-millimetres on a ridge caused much damage until the 90th Field Regiment dealt with them.

Some British artillery was in action on French soil before the first assault troops touched down, for gunners had landed by glider on both sides of the River Orne, during the night before D-Day, to aid the 6th Airborne Division's successful operation on the vital left flank of the bridgehead. Comparatively few casualties were suffered by the artillery during the crossing and landing, though two of the subalterns from the 3rd Division who had volunteered for duty as FOOs in support of 6th Airborne had unrehearsed experiences. One of them, dropped at night by parachute, fell into a tree and hung by one foot for several hours until he freed himself by shooting through the parachute harness with his revolver. He was taken prisoner and spent months in hospital. Another, dropped some miles beyond the objective, made his way back in a German vehicle, picking up other men of the division en route.

The 211th Battery of the 53rd (Worcestershire Yeomanry) Airlanding Light Regiment was the first British battery ever to be flown into action. There was only enough glider space for one light battery; the rest of the regiment was to come by sea. The 4th Airlanding Anti-Tank Battery (6-pounders) and one troop of the 3rd, with 17-pounders, were flown in, the remainder of the 17-pounder battery arriving by sea on D-Day.

The first gliders of the Airlanding Light Regiment came in dead on time. Within half an hour of landing the 211th Battery was in action north of Ranville. For some days continuous close support was given to parachute and glider-borne troops, but, excellent as they were, the airborne gunners alone would have been quite inadequate in numbers. Eventually the whole of a field regiment from the 3rd Division was available on call for 6th Airborne. With this aid the division was able to seize and hold the bridges over the Orne, repeated low-level attacks by German planes being beaten off by light anti-aircraft units.

As the Normandy bridgehead expanded, 21st Army Group began to reap the benefits of the British strength in guns, and above all the perfection of the latest methods (in which British troops were definitely superior to the enemy) of handling masses of artillery as single fire units, switched from point to point by radio control. As General Parham has said: 'The enemy within gun range lived under a constant threat of encountering a sudden squall of several hundred shell, all timed to arrive at the target end within a few seconds of each other. . . . The enemy's guns were never able really to assert themselves, and as a result the counter-battery effort which they put up against our positions was negligible. The more persistent nuisance of the Minenwerfer was most difficult to counter, though the development of special counter-mortar organizations led eventually to its suppression. But the task of the anti-tank gunners in the Normandy bridgehead was a far more dangerous one. Casualties, especially in the enclosed "bocage" country and in the wide rolling country west of Caen, were very heavy; so bad in fact that over 2,000 reinforcements had on one occasion to be flown over to make good our losses. However, in this hard fighting great numbers of tanks were knocked out by anti-tank guns of the RA, and it was owing to this among other causes that relatively few enemy tanks were encountered in the final stages of the campaign.'

On 14 June, when a series of heavy enemy attacks developed, great execution was wrought by our artillery. Eleven days later, army and naval gunfire aided in the capture of Cherbourg. But Caen, the principal city and centre of communications in the assault area, was still doggedly held by the Germans; it had proved impossible to take it in the first rush, and adequate artillery support for an attack later in June had been ruled out by shortage of ammunition. This was due to a gale which held up sea transport, and which also severely battered the artificial harbour in the Bay of the Seine, where some of the anti-aircraft gunners on the Mulberry positions narrowly escaped drowning when their floating gun posts were swept by waves.

By early July the supply situation had improved sufficiently for a large-scale attack to be mounted by Second Army. Caen

25. Men of an anti-tank battery get their 17-pdr. into position, 10 September, 1943 (Imperial War Museum)

26. Gliders at Arnhem, 17 September, 1944. In foreground is the headquarters group of an artillery regiment (Imperial War Museum)

27. A camouflaged 5·5-in. gun firing at enemy positions in Normandy, 2 July, 1944 (Imperial War Museum)

28. Self-propelled 25-pdrs., on Valentine tank chassis, in North Africa, with Grenadier Hill in background (Imperial War Museum)

29. Artillerymen preparing to fire an 'Honest John' free-flight missile (Defence Ministry)

was captured by the British and Canadians on 9 July. Among the first to enter the town – perhaps the very first – were two artillery officers, Maurice Hope, then commanding the 191st (Essex and Herts Yeomanry) Field Regiment, and Joe Pearson, one of his battery commanders. After brushes in the streets with German stragglers, they reached the church of St Etienne, where William the Conqueror is buried, and found it crowded with refugees. Hope was induced to mount the pulpit, reassure the French, and lead them in singing the *Marseillaise*.

Before long full vindication was given to Field-Marshal Montgomery's strategy of pinning down on the allied left-centre the greatest possible number of enemy formations, including armour, so that the American divisions, which on D-Day had landed farther to the west, could swing out in a vast right-hook movement to threaten Hitler's forces with encirclement. In August the time was ripe, the pincers closed in on the St Lambert Gap, turning an orderly German withdrawal into helpless rout, and offering to the artillery targets beyond their wildest dreams in the Falaise pocket, where crippling losses were inflicted on the enemy. Then followed the memorable forward swoop which in a few days advanced the allies by hundreds of miles – to Paris on 23 August, Brussels and Antwerp in the first week of September.

About a fortnight later, in a bold operation aimed at striking right through Holland into the north German plains, the newly formed First Airborne Army was sent in to seize the bridges on all the river barriers lying across Second Army's line of northward advance. The British 1st Airborne Division, veterans of Africa and Italy but not yet used in north-west Europe, were allotted the place of honour, and danger, at Arnhem in the north, where they were to capture the vital bridge over the Lower Rhine. This division's artillery resources were small. It had the 1st Airlanding Light Regiment, armed with 75-millimetre howitzers, the 1st and 2nd Airlanding Anti-Tank Batteries, with 6-pounders and 17-pounders, and the 1st Forward Observer Unit, consisting of parachute parties. To make good the shortage of divisional guns, elaborate plans were made for Second Army to bring medium artillery well forward, so that its fire could support the men at Arnhem long before ground troops could complete the link-up to relieve them.

Two thousand aircraft carried the troops from England. A few of the big Hamilcar gliders overturned on landing in rough fields, but even from these, lying on their backs, 17-pounders and tractors were successfully removed. After a sharp fight the bridge fell to the British and 6-pounders were in action at its northern end; but the main body of 1st Parachute Brigade had not reached the bridge, and by the middle of next day the enemy had definitely blocked its advance. In the meantime, one light battery had moved to a position at Oosterbeck, 3 miles away, from which fire support could be given to the parachutists at the bridge.

Repeated attacks, supported by all guns of the Light Regiment, failed to capture the rest of Arnhem or to get through to the beleaguered parachutists. By 20 September, the fourth day of the operation, they were completely cut off, and though a troop of anti-tank guns which was with them did great execution against enemy vehicles attempting to cross, they were unable to prevent four Tiger tanks from forcing their way through. On the 21st those who were left at the bridge, with food and ammunition all but exhausted, tried to fight their way out. All were killed or captured.

Once all attempts to relieve the defenders of the bridge had failed, the gunpits of the Light Regiment at Oosterbeck became part of the front line of the divisional perimeter. Here Lieutenant-Colonel W. F. K. Thompson, commanding officer of the regiment, displayed outstanding leadership in collecting, rallying and redeploying parties of infantry and anti-tank gunners who had withdrawn in some confusion into the area, the defence of which was reinforced by glider pilots. In spite of the almost complete failure of airborne ammunition re-supply, the Light Regiment, under nearly continuous mortar and machine-gun fire, and frequent attacks backed by tanks, fought as field gunners, giving indirect fire in support of the division as a whole; in the anti-tank role, over open sights at ranges down to 50 yards, manhandling their guns among the ruined buildings; and as infantry, in defence of gunpits and command posts, and in counter-attacks led by battery and troop commanders. For two days Captain John Walker manned an observation post in a house well in front of the line, with the garden full of Germans. Wounded later, while acting as second-in-command of an infantry company, he returned after medical attention and took over as adjutant of the battalion.

On the afternoon of the 21st, a Forward Observer Unit representative, Captain McMillen, was able to report that he had at last made contact by radio with artillery of Second Army. The division was through to 64th Medium Regiment, deploying with the leading troops of the advancing force at Nijmegen, 10 miles to the south, and separated from Arnhem by two major rivers. Within a few minutes the first shells from the medium guns crashed into a German tank concentration which the light howitzers of the airborne regiment had been unable to damage.

It was heartening for every man in the division to feel that they were no longer entirely without support from outside. During the remaining four days of 1st Airborne's fight, the aid of the XXX Corps artillery, firing at almost maximum range, was beyond price. Major Philip Tower, DSO, who was brigade major RA with the gunners at Arnhem, has written: 'Never was confidence in their artillery shown so clearly by the infantry. On the last day the CRA himself directed a 155-millimetre shoot on an enemy company which had penetrated to a wood actually within the divisional perimeter. The wood was 200 yards south of divisional headquarters, the guns were 20,000 yards south of the wood!'

But the end was near. The main axis of the XXX Corps line of advance had twice been cut, once by a German thrust from the east and later by one from the west. On the ninth day after the landing of the airborne division, Field-Marshal Montgomery, facing the unpleasant facts, ordered the withdrawal of the survivors. To cover this, an intensive artillery fire plan was arranged over the tenuous radio link. As fire was opened, on the night of 25 September, the defenders began to steal down to the river, where Canadian troops with boats awaited them. Last of the division to leave were the artillerymen of the Light Regiment, after removing the breech blocks of their guns and dropping them into the river. Boats were sunk by enemy fire, and many of the men had to swim. Of 1st Airborne Division as a whole, 7,000 had been killed or taken prisoner in this tragic defeat which came so close to victory.

The next major operations of the campaign were the battle of the Maas pocket and the clearing of the Scheldt estuary, to make possible the use of Antwerp as a supply port. The assault on Walcheren from the sea, and the capture of Flushing, set the imprint of success on this hard struggle.

In the attack on Flushing, a brigade of the 52nd (Lowland) Division had under command one battery of the 1st Mountain Regiment, RA, with jeeps in place of the pack animals that had been left behind in Scotland. Even in the unmountainous surroundings of Walcheren these gunners showed that they had not forgotten how to manhandle a gun up an awkward ascent. An account by Captain Vincent Cohen, MC, second-in-command of the 452nd Mountain Battery, tells how one gun was brought into action from a first-floor bedroom window in Flushing to deal with a concrete pillbox, built into the wall of a reservoir, which had previously been engaged without decisive effect.

Captain Cohen writes: 'Carrying the heavy parts of the gun up a narrow staircase was made more difficult by the discovery that the key which unlocks the two parts of the barrel had been left behind, and the breech, chase and slipper had to be carried in one piece – a weight exceeding a quarter of a ton!

'An upstairs bedroom is by no means an ideal gunpit. At the first round the crack in the ceiling became an alarming gap. At the eighth, the trail legs began to disappear into the room below. But direct laying had scored eight hits. Just as we decided to risk one more round, a white flag appeared at the pillbox and fourteen dazed Germans filed out.'

Four days of gallant fighting towards the end of October at s'Hertogenbosch, where Germans were clinging tenaciously to outlying parts of the town, were marked by the devoted work of D Troop, 381st/116th (Royal Welsh) Light Anti-Aircraft Regiment – the 'front-line Bofors' men. This troop, under Captain Donald Lever, had been ordered to give all possible assistance in a ground role to the infantry in the sector. With one self-propelled Bofors brought right forward, the gunners managed in spite of heavy Spandau fire to flush out Germans from houses, cellars and dugouts, capturing a number of prisoners and weapons.

On the last day, when progress was held up after it was found that a small bridge over a dyke had been blown, Captain Lever crossed over by a plank, followed by three infantrymen who took up covering positions while he tackled enemy weapon pits with a

Bren. He had collected seven prisoners before he was hit by a burst of fire. Under cover of a smoke screen he was brought back across the dyke with the aid of a ladder, but died shortly afterwards. Several awards for gallantry were made to men of the troop. Captain Lever received no decoration (the VC is the only award that can be made posthumously); but he is remembered by many in the Royal Artillery as one of the bravest men who fought in the Second World War.

After the failure of the Germans' desperate midwinter counter-offensive, the brunt of which fell upon the Americans in the Ardennes, Operation Veritable, for the clearing of the Reichswald area, was carried out in February 1945. To smash the upper end of the Siegfried Line, XXX Corps, under First Canadian Army, had well over a thousand guns, including five AGRAS and two anti-aircraft brigades. In the worst possible conditions of thick woodland and waterlogged tracks, field batteries fought desperately, often in the closest contact with the British infantry, and against stiff resistance. For considerable periods some of them were firing as many as five rounds a minute. On the night of 28 February, the 76th (Highland) Field Regiment, with 3rd Division, fired 450 rounds a gun; others must have expended nearly as many, and at times ammunition ran dangerously short. But the objectives were gained, giving a jumping-off ground for the last great battle – the crossing of the Rhine.

This operation had the backing of more than 3,000 guns. It was notable for the smooth cooperation between the British and American artilleries (in spite of many differences in procedure and phraseology); the excellent communications established by the forward observers dropped by parachute beyond the Rhine; and the number of guns that were flown in during the four and a half hours of the landings on the far side of the river by two airborne divisions, the British 6th and the American 17th.

The moves for concentration of some 1,300 guns in the XII Corps and XXX Corps areas for the crossing between Wesel and Emmerich had been concealed by vast smoke-screens along a front of 50 miles. Wesel itself was captured by the 46th Commando, helped by the sturdy screw-guns of the 1st Mountain Regiment, RA. At about 5.30 p.m. on 23 March the massed guns opened their counter-battery programmes, followed throughout the night by bombardment and covering fire in support of the assault troops. Many of these went over in Buffalo amphibious vehicles, which carried them, with artillery observers, all the way from the marshalling areas down to the river and across. As the preliminary objectives were well within range of 25-pounders on the west bank, the ferrying of artillery was not a high priority apart from some anti-tank units, and light anti-aircraft guns to protect bridging sites. One RHA regiment, however, crossed on rafts at an early stage for a special task in support of a mobile column.

By dawn on 24 March British troops were well established on the east bank, and bridges were under construction in most sectors. The anti-aircraft brigade commander responsible for their defence also had to take on the unfamiliar task of protection against waterborne attack. His composite force, which included CDL tanks (with searchlights) and anti-tank guns, accounted for fifty mines floating in the stretch of river between Wesel and Zanten, the legendary birthplace of Siegfried.

All was soon ready for Operation Varsity, the airborne assault to extend the bridgehead and seize outlets from it. Never before had large-scale airborne forces had to attack objectives within range of massive artillery support from guns already deployed. This called for the most accurate coordination and precise timing in balancing the need for counter-flak fire with avoidance of risk to their own aircraft from British guns. During the artillery preparation proximity fuses were used against enemy in the neighbourhood of the landing and dropping zones, so as to give air-bursts and avoid cratering of the ground.

After withstanding heavy counter-attacks, the airborne divisions were strengthened by their 'land tails' as soon as bridges were available, and two field regiments were placed under command of 6th Airborne. The division's own light airlanding and anti-tank artillery units had suffered heavy casualties in the assault.

Two days of build-up and regrouping were followed by the breakout from the bridgehead. Some hard fighting still remained to be done in the advance into north Germany, but within six weeks the British had reached the Baltic, contact had been made with the Russian spearheads on the Elbe, Hitler was dead in the ruins of Berlin, and on 8 May 1945, the German armies surrendered. The war in the west was over.

The Germans in Italy had given up the struggle a few days earlier. More than three months went by before the Japanese admission of defeat, after the dropping of the atomic bombs on Hiroshima and Nagasaki, and the formal surrender of General Kimura in Rangoon did not take place until 24 October. This marked the end of a long, arduous fighting return by the 'forgotten men' of Field-Marshal Slim's Fourteenth Army, some of whom in 1942 had come out of Burma grimly covering the rear-guard, and who fought their way back step by step in the face of difficulties unsurpassed in the history of the Royal Artillery.

The Arakan campaigns, from Maungdaw to Rangoon, are without parallel for ingenious unorthodoxy in the deployment and use of artillery. Guns of every type from 2-pounders to 7·2-inch howitzers were moved by rafts, country boats and landing craft of all kinds, before being taken into action over mud and mangrove swamps (sometimes with motor transport, but often by sheer muscle power) through the efforts of British, Indian and West African gunners.

In the words of Lord Slim: 'For artillery it was the most difficult theatre of all. The immense effort of moving guns through jungle, the problem of clearance, of an often meagre ammunition supply, the lack of visibility and the constant threat of Japanese infiltration might have reduced the guns to comparative impotence. Yet all of these, and a dozen other handicaps, were overcome by brains, brawn and determination. Gunners developed new techniques of cooperation with infantry, tanks and air. They became adepts at close defence. They took on any job – road-making, lorry columns, air supply. They acted as infantry, and more than once artillery officers took command of infantry units which had lost all their own officers. They packed themselves and their equipment into aircraft as readily as they undertook a move by road. They mounted their guns in ships and manned them. Nor did three years in the jungle make them slow-moving or static-minded. When we broke out in the plains of central Burma, they without hesitation adapted themselves to almost desert tactics and mobility.'

To these men might also have been applied, with equal justice, the tribute that Field-Marshal Montgomery paid to the gunners of 21st Army Group, whose 25-pounders had fired since the Normandy landings more than 13 million rounds. From his headquarters in Germany he wrote: 'The gunners have risen to great heights in this war; they have been well commanded and well handled. In my experience the artillery has never been so efficient as it is today; it is at the top of its form. For all this I offer you my warmest congratulations.

'The contribution of the artillery to final victory in the German war has been immense. This will always be so; the harder the fighting and the longer the war, the more the infantry, and in fact all the arms, lean on the gunners. The proper use of the artillery is a great battle-winning factor.

'I think all the other arms have done very well too. But the artillery has been terrific and I want to give due weight to its contribution to the victory in this campaign.'

ANTI-AIRCRAFT COMMAND

'Thou shalt not be afraid for any terror by night; nor for the arrow that flieth by day.' – *Psalm XCI, v*

The many thousands of the Royal Artillery who manned the guns, instruments and searchlights of Anti-Aircraft Command in the defence of Britain, from before the Blitz right up to the end of the fighting, were cast for a role which had no counterpart in any previous war. While others won fame and glory on distant battlefields, their share was necessarily a subordinate one, subsidiary to the brilliantly planned and gallantly executed work of the Royal Air Force; but all who found a place in it could take satisfaction in the knowledge that it was an essential one, though often frustrating and sometimes underrated.

Before the time of trial by ordeal, in the massive air raids on London during the autumn of 1940, the dreary period of waiting through the first cold, miserable winter of the war set a test for morale in the gun sites spaced out around the outskirts of the capital – not the most vital target of all, perhaps, but certainly the largest, the most populous, and in many ways the most vulnerable. Equipment in those early days was far from perfect, and the capabilities of some of the Territorial units, inevitably, may have left a good deal to be desired. Some odd things happened.

One Londoner, who had been a temporary member of a searchlight unit during the crisis of September 1938, and who had put his name down for a Heavy Anti-Aircraft Regiment long before the outbreak of war, waited for months without receiving any reply. In November 1939 he received by post instructions to report for enlistment at a Territorial regimental headquarters in a requisitioned house near Dulwich. There, still not sworn in, and without a single item of army clothing or equipment, he was immediately sent to a gun site, where for about a fortnight, in a town overcoat with a civilian gas-mask in its cardboard box slung over his shoulder by a piece of string, he fell in with the rest for parades, and also for successive night turnouts on the guns – practice drills or 'unidentified aircraft' alarms, in which no shot was fired, though all the laborious routine of removing semi-frozen tarpaulins, checking instruments, and bringing out ammunition had to be performed. At the end of this period the embryo artilleryman, having stumbled through at least a dozen turnouts, and having earned through his civilian garb the jocular nickname of 'the battery spy', was finally taken to an army centre where he was given a medical examination, the oath was administered, and a tin hat and army respirator were subsequently issued.

At the beginning of the winter, the troop occupying this site possessed a couple of army huts, but some of the men had to be accommodated in a semi-derelict cricket pavilion, separated from the main camp by fields which when, not snow-covered, soon became an ocean of mud. In the 'annexe' there were no beds, except for a few which gunners had knocked together for themselves out of oddments of timber and wire netting; the rest laid their straw-filled palliasses on the floor. Heating was limited to one or two small and unreliable oil stoves. As the weather grew more severe all the pipes froze, and those who were sybaritic enough to require hot water for shaving had to beg or steal it from the cookhouse and carry it precariously across the icy fields. Discomforts of this kind were, of course, trivial in comparison with what men underwent elsewhere; but they were scarcely what might have been thought likely in static defences within 7 or 8 miles of Charing Cross.

Anyone who joined a Heavy Anti-Aircraft unit in the expectation of an easy time was liable to disillusionment. Fatigues were many, from interminable filling and piling of sandbags to 'spud bashing', exposed to all the winds of heaven, outside the sacred precincts of the cookhouse. These chores, of course, were in addition to the work on the guns; and it should be noted that, at this time, despite mechanization and the progressive introduction of advanced scientific devices, the duties of a 4·5-inch detachment depended on sheer muscle to a surprising extent. Although figures for bearing, elevation and fuse setting were electronically transmitted from the predictor to dials which the gunners followed with their controls, the ammunition numbers still functioned very much on the lines of the old days. Every round had to be withdrawn from steel-doored recesses in the emplacements, removed from its protective fibre case, placed with others on a trolley, and wheeled round to keep station with any movement of the gun. The shell was then placed on a roller, inserted into the fuse setter, and afterwards hoisted up to the loading numbers, who pushed over the tray, ready for the ramming numbers to drive the shell home into the breech by heaving on a somewhat primitive arrangement of wires with wooden handles. Each complete round of 'fixed ammunition' – shell and propellant cartridge in one piece like an enormous bullet – weighed about 80 pounds.

Some of the experiences of one unit – the 312th Battery, 54th (City of London) HAA Regiment, RA, TA – are no doubt typical of others. In May 1940, while ominous news was beginning to come in from France, this battery became due for practice camp. On the day before their departure, orders were received that all ammunition on the site must be 'chamber gauged', meaning that every round should be checked beyond any possible doubt as to size and fit by actual insertion in the guns. For most of the day, and in relays well on into the night, the gunners toiled, uncasing the hundreds of rounds, lugging them to the 4·5s, and hoisting them up to be placed in the breech, then reversing the process to remove, recase and stack them all. After a few hours' sleep for the luckier ones, next morning the artillerymen had to complete final details of packing, ready to entrain for the firing camp at Aberporth on Cardigan Bay.

On their return to the London area, now presumably as fully-fledged AA gunners after having shot at towed targets with 3-inch, 3·7 and 4·5, they discovered to their infinite disgust that there was no site available for them to man. Their own guns had been taken over by another battery, which was remaining for the time being; whether this was part of some deep-laid plan, or simply a marvel of staff ineptitude, the 312th had no means of knowing. They were told that until further orders they would be on permanent guard duty at 'vulnerable points'.

So, at a time when the battle of France was drawing to its close and every trained gunner might be needed for the defence of England at any moment, the battery was split up into small detachments for infantry duties. Among others, the 'battery spy' (in uniform now) found himself taking his turn as sentry, for no very obvious reason, outside a house in a back street of Eltham. After a few days this particular detachment was moved out to guard a large underground ammunition dump not far from the mental hospital at Banstead. There, while the sounds of battle across the Channel could be heard on the still night air above the Surrey downs, the disconsolate gunners, rifles on shoulders, paced the cinder path behind the rusty barbed wire, patrolling one half of the perimeter while the other was the responsibility of an infantry platoon.

Relations between the two groups were not over-cordial. Whatever their military potential may have been, the infantry (most of them young National Service men from the East End) were frankly out of their element in the countryside. The hooting of owls disturbed them and, in the night watches, they had little patience with orthodox ideas of silent vigilance, preferring to reassure themselves, and anyone else who might be within earshot, by a lively whistling or brisk scuffling of feet. Rather unkindly, they complained through their sergeant that Gunner So-and-so tended to alarm them by his manner of 'creeping up' quietly towards their sector while on sentry duty. As the National Service boys had bayonets, while the artillerymen did not, the gunners were in fact more likely to be the sufferers in any mistaken chance encounter which might have occurred in the dark.

This spell of irksome duty (briefly enlivened by a false alarm of a landing by German parachutists) did not last long. Perhaps there was some overriding necessity for it; but few things could be better calculated to dishearten gunners than to take them away from their guns in an hour of crisis.

The battery detachments were gathered together and returned to their original gun site. A few days later, early in June when the Dunkirk evacuation was at its height, two or three men of the troop were ordered to pack their kit and be ready to leave within an hour. They had no idea where they were going, or why, except that all of them, for one reason or another, had recently been medically down-graded after re-examinations. The gunners piled their kit, a truck bore them away, and set out on a long circuitous tour of west London, picking up en route men from other batteries who were in the same plight. Under a new order, it appeared, all those below a certain medical category were no longer considered acceptable for duty on the gun sites. The bespectacled 'battery spy' had been downgraded from A.1 to B.3, solely on account of defective sight.

Eventually the small group of gunners were set down to mingle with other rejects in the spacious grounds of Kneller Hall at Twickenham, home of the Royal Military School of Music. Here they were given a meal, marched hither and thither, allotted tents, and told to draw beds from the stores – still completely unaware of what the Army intended to do with them, except that it seemed unlikely they would be turned into bandsmen. Just as they were about to settle down for the night, amidst much grousing, word came that they were to pack again at once for a further move. This took them to St Paul's School at Hammersmith, where, in an atmosphere of harassment tinged heavily with confusion, parties of soldiers from units of every description were arriving, being sorted out, and finding sooner or later a place to lay their heads. The famous school was in fact undergoing an uneasy transformation for the role it was to fill for a long time to come as 'S.P.'—General Headquarters, Home Forces.

The Ack-Ack men – small unhappy islands lapped by an alien sea of humanity – bedded down for the night on the floor of one of the classrooms, amidst Guardsmen, kilted Scots, and North Country soldiers, several of whom had lost almost all their kit during the retreat to Dunkirk or the evacuation from the beaches. In the morning they were paraded to be detailed for their future duties. Some of the gunners, including the 'spy', were set to work as batmen for junior officers attached to headquarters; others, among whom were men who had put in years of service in the Territorial Army, became orderlies under the camp commandant. For several days at least, these individuals sat on chairs in corridors, outside the closed doors of staff offices, morosely reading old magazines or paperbacks until such time as an officer or chief clerk might require them to carry a message to some other part of the building. Before long, by luck or initiative, a number of the outcasts from Ack-Ack contrived to make their way into slightly more congenial, and more useful, forms of military activity; some even became officers, but most of them had seen the last of the guns.

The men who remained with the batteries were soon in action. For fifty-seven days in succession, from 7 September to 2 November, London was under attack by an average of 200 bombers every night. On 18–19 September, the Luftwaffe dropped 350 tons of bombs, more than fell on Britain in the whole of the First World War. In July, Anti-Aircraft Command had totalled close on 160,000 men, with nearly 1,750 guns and 4,000 searchlights, but the preliminary raids on provincial cities during August caused a considerable dispersion of high-angle defence arms, and when London first became the main target there were only ninety-two guns in position around the capital. As anti-aircraft artillery techniques were still in such an imperfect stage, it was thought best, for the time being, to leave the air free for the night fighters – six squadrons of Blenheims and Defiants working under No. II Group at Uxbridge.

For three nights from 3 September the people of London, in their homes or in the shelters, lay wondering why the guns were silent, why they must endure what seemed to them an unresisted onslaught. But the night fighters, weak in numbers, had their own problems, and the casualties they could inflict on the enemy at this stage were few. It was therefore decided that British planes must be kept out of the way, and the artillery must be given its chance. Within forty-eight hours General Sir Frederick Pile, Chief of Anti-Aircraft Command, doubled the number of guns in the London area by withdrawals from the provinces. On 10 September the word was given and the guns spoke, under orders that every possible round was to be used.

'Fire was not to be withheld on any account,' General Pile has written. 'Guns were to go to the approximate bearing and elevation and fire. Searchlights were not to expose. RAF fighters were not going to operate over London, and every unseen target must be engaged without waiting to identify the aircraft as hostile.

'The result was as astonishing to me as it appears to have been to the citizens of London – and, apparently, to the enemy as well. For, although few of the bursts can have been anywhere near the target, the heights of aircraft steadily increased as the night went on, and many of them turned away before entering the inner artillery zone. . . . It was in no sense a barrage, though I think by that name it will always be known.'

The thunder of the cannonade, which was to become so familiar a part of wartime life in London, was at this period a tonic not only for the gunners, released from inaction, but also for the civilians, who could feel that at last the nation was hitting back, that the Luftwaffe was not having things all its own way. Even if the number of bombers destroyed by Ack-Ack fire in 1940 was small, the deterrent effect was considerable, and also the influence on public morale, though this itself was not without its adverse angle; there must have been many who were uneasily conscious that 'what goes up must come down'. Certainly it could not have been pleasant to have to take temporary shelter from tinkling showers of their own shell fragments, to say nothing of the occasional unexploded round which descended through some luckless person's roof.

The batteries now fired regularly, with intervals from time to time while the night fighters, whose technique was rapidly progressing, took over. Slowly, by dint of constant practice, ingenuity, and urgent need, the shooting of the artillery improved. That the percentage of kills was extremely low at first is scarcely surprising if one bears in mind the problems involved in hitting a fast-moving aerial target (perhaps unseen) that might take evasive action at any unpredictable moment before or after the actual bombing run. Assuming that all data had been correctly given, and accurately applied to the gun, the target, even without changing course, would inevitably have travelled a mile or two in the fifteen or thirty seconds that elapsed between the moment when the shell left the muzzle of the gun and its arrival at the height at which the bomber was flying. Without the predictor, any serious attempt to engage modern aircraft with artillery would have been utterly hopeless.

Months before the Blitz, mysterious pieces of apparatus, shrouded under canvas covers from the eyes of inquisitive gunners except when under adjustment by skilled artificers, had made their appearance on certain Ack-Ack sites. These were the radar sets, the new marvel of British science that was to enable the guns to 'lock on' to unseen targets, day or night. The first came into use in October 1940, but many months passed before all the defences were equipped with radar.

By May 1941, the monthly bag claimed by the gunners had risen to over a hundred aircraft. The strength of Anti-Aircraft Command had increased to 312,500, with 2,477 guns (1,247 of them static) and 4,500 searchlights, functioning under the general control of a central operations room in close cooperation with the RAF. General Pile, a commander always open to new ideas, had taken, or at least accepted, the revolutionary step of giving women from the Auxiliary Territorial Service a share in operational duties with the artillery. This move, which would certainly have horrified bygone artillery worthies, and which was viewed with mixed feelings by men on the gun sites, produced a total of 3,500 women on battery establishments and 3,000 others on headquarters and administrative staffs, releasing men from static duties. Women took over predictors and other instruments, while men provided the gun detachments. The first mixed battery came into service in August, 1941.

Churchill himself had evidently foreseen difficulties and opposition. He wrote to the secretary of state for war: 'I fear there is a complex against women being connected with lethal work. We must get rid of this. Also there is an idea prevalent among the ladies managing the ATS that nothing must conflict with loyalty to the ATS and that battery *esprit de corps* is counter to their interest or theme. No tolerance can be shown to this. The prime sphere of the women commanders is welfare, and this should occupy their main endeavours.

'The conditions are very bad and ugly, and I expect will get worse now that large numbers are being brought into the War Office grip by compulsion or the shadow of compulsion. A great responsibility rests upon you as secretary of state to see that all these young women are not treated roughly. Mrs Knox and her assistants should be admirable in all this, but do not let them get in the way of the happy active life of the batteries or deprive women of their incentives to join the batteries and to care as much about the batteries as they do about the ATS. . . . Every kind of minor compliment and ornament should be accorded to those who render good service in the batteries.'

With his sure instinct for the little things that are so important to morale, the prime minister said it was quite wrong that ATS girls should be forbidden to wear, in addition to their own badges, the insignia of the artillery with which they served.

In the ranks of the ATS with the batteries were some very brave women. One of them was Violette Szabo, a bright, diminutive young Frenchwoman, wife of a French officer who was killed later at Alamein. After leaving Ack-Ack, Mme Szabo volunteered to be parachuted into occupied France on a particularly dangerous mission in April 1944. Twice she was arrested, but each time managed to get away. Finally, surrounded with a resistance group by German forces, and fighting Sten gun in hand until she fell exhausted, she was captured and executed after being tortured by the Gestapo. She was posthumously awarded the George Cross. A Royal Artillery officer, Lieutenant-Colonel J. W. Naylor, has written: 'I shall always be very proud to be able to say "I was her battery commander".'

Towards the end of 1941 new anti-aircraft weapons were introduced. These were the UP (unrotated projectile) batteries, also known as Z guns, some of which were taken over by the Home Guard.

In his book *The Second World War*, Churchill has remarked on the extreme difficulty of achieving really accurate shooting with anti-aircraft guns. He wrote: 'A wide yet intense burst of fire round the predicted point was an answer. Combinations of a hundred guns would have been excellent, if the guns could have been produced and the batteries manned and all put in the right place at the right time. This was beyond human power to achieve. But a very simple, cheap alternative was available in the rocket, or, as it had been called for secrecy, the unrotated projectile (UP). Even before the war Dr Crow, in the days of the Air Defence Research Committee, had developed 2-inch and 3-inch rockets which could reach almost as high as our AA guns. The 3-inch rocket carried a much more powerful warhead than a 3-inch shell. It was not so accurate. On the other hand, rocket projectors had the inestimable advantage that they could be made very quickly and easily in enormous numbers without burdening our hard-driven gun factories. Thousands of these UP projectors were made, and some millions of rounds of ammunition. General Sir Frederick Pile formed these weapons into huge batteries of ninety-six projectors each, manned largely by the Home Guard, which could produce a concentrated volume of fire far beyond the power of AA artillery....

'By the middle of 1941, when at last the rocket batteries began to come into service in substantial numbers, air attack had much diminished, so that they had few chances of proving themselves. But when they did come into action the number of rounds needed to bring down an aircraft was little more than that required by the enormously more costly and scanty AA guns of which we were so short. The rockets were good in themselves, and also an addition to our other means of defence.'

There were about fifty UP batteries in 1941. Another project which appealed strongly to the fertile brain of the prime minister was to shoot up explosive charges which would float down on parachutes to dangle from long wires in the path of hostile bombers – in effect, the laying of a minefield in the sky. It was not possible to pack the mines and parachutes into shells, but a rocket provides more room, as its walls do not have to be made so thick to stand the shock of discharge. A certain amount of 3-inch rocket ammunition, intended to lay an aerial minefield on wires 700 feet long at heights up to 20,000 feet, was made and held ready for use against mass attacks on London. It was hoped that if the wing of an aircraft fouled a wire at any point this would pull up the mine until it reached the plane and exploded. In fact, however, these devices were never brought into use on any considerable scale; by the time they were ready in large numbers mass attacks by bombers had ceased.

Between December 1942, and June 1943, Anti-Aircraft Command had to cope with a series of hit-and-run attacks on coastal towns by low-flying planes, and early in 1944 with a renewal of heavy raids on London. These died out in March, but the allied invasion of France coincided with the launching of the first V1s ('buzz-bombs'), making necessary a rapid redeployment, and the adoption of new techniques and methods. The first system that was tried – an artillery zone of 1,640 guns on the North Downs – failed to stop more than one in three of the robot bombs, which travelled low at 350 to 400 miles an hour. By 19 July 1944, General Pile had moved all available guns (a total of 1,596) to the south coast.

Somewhat later, when the Germans began to launch robot

bombs from planes over the North Sea, as well as from sites in France, Belgium and Holland, the artillery zone had to be extended north to cover the Thames Estuary and East Anglia, an extension which eventually included 1,050 more guns. Before September, when flying bomb attacks were reduced by the capture of the last remaining launching sites in the Low Countries, Anti-Aircraft Command was destroying three out of every four sent over. Its total for the entire period of attack was 1,978 destroyed out of 9,250 launched. In August attacks with V2 rockets began, and continued until March 1945; no effective defence against these weapons, with their speed of over 2,000 miles an hour, was ever achieved.

During the war as a whole, 5,823 V1s and 1,054 long-range rockets came down on the British Isles, in addition to more than 64,000 tons of bombs. By the end of the flying bomb attacks, an almost completely automatic chain of operations had been perfected for the artillery. A heavy anti-aircraft site was equipped with radar which followed the target automatically (except for range-finding) once it had been put on target by the operators; an automatic predictor; remote-controlled guns, thus eliminating possible errors by layers; automatic loading and firing mechanism; and radio proximity fuses. Thus the human factor was practically eliminated once the radar was on target.

The proximity fuse, which was largely responsible for destroying hundreds of 'buzz-bombs', was one of the cleverest scientific developments of the war. It cut out the need to score a direct hit, or even to achieve the almost impossible accuracy involved in setting a time fuse so that the shell exploded at the exact moment when it was passing the target. (An error in timing of one tenth of a second might cause a shot to miss by a couple of hundred feet.) At the Admiralty in 1940 work was directed towards the invention of a fuse which would detonate automatically as a rocket passed near the target. Photo-electric (PE) cells were used which produced an electrical impulse whenever there was a change of light, such as the shadow cast by a plane. A working model was made, but by the time the PE fuses were ready in quantity the need for them was, for the moment, not so pressing.

Attempts were made in 1941 to design a similar fuse, working through a miniature radar set to explode the warhead.

Preliminary tests were successful, but before the device had been fully developed in England the Americans, to whom British technologists had passed on their information, managed not only to perfect the instrument but to reduce its size so much that it could be inserted in the head of a shell instead of a rocket. The proximity fuse, first used by ships, and manufactured in the United States, was used in great numbers in the last year of the war, and proved effective not only against the V1s but against Japanese aircraft in the Pacific.

Right up to the end of the war, Anti-Aircraft Command remained to a large extent a separate organization, almost an army on its own. There were, of course, links with the rest of the gunners through the Directorate of Artillery and other sections at the War Office, but contacts with field force units were few. It had been impressed upon General Pile from the highest quarter that purely static defence must be kept to a minimum, and that as large a proportion as possible should be available to give mobile anti-aircraft cover to home defence units if necessary. However, as the invasion danger receded, and plans were made for a return to Europe, the isolation of AA Command became emphasized. The officers of the Major-General Royal Artillery at GHQ Home Forces were not officially concerned in any direct way with the main home defence Ack-Ack effort, though they had their own staff section dealing with the anti-aircraft side of the gunner units which, slowly and with infinite pains, were being built up and prepared in Britain for service overseas. It was perhaps inevitable, if regrettable, that artillerymen who belonged to the field armies (though still far from the action for which they were intended) should have given the impression of regarding with a certain scepticism, not unmixed with condescension in some cases, the efforts of the home Ack-Ack men, with their odd devices, their women in uniform and Home Guard rocketeers.

The task of the anti-aircraft gunners was in many ways a thankless one. Not for them was the glamour of the fighter pilots or the verve of the dashing RHA. There were months of drab monotonous routine between the spells of heavy firing. But the men and women in the batteries could at least feel that they were carrying out, under extremely skilful direction, a job that had to be done. At the height of the Blitz, they knew that, behind the outnumbered squadrons of the sorely tried Fighter Command, they were the final line of defence, the last hope of preventing the rain of fire and steel from falling on the thousands of little houses, some of which, if they were still standing, sheltered their own families. If ever soldiers fought in defence of their homes, they did.

THE SENIOR TERRITORIALS

'We are but warriors for the working day.' *– Shakespeare*

The Honourable Artillery Company, which served with distinction in 1939–45 and in two major wars before that, has been described in the *Encyclopedia Britannica*, venturing for once on to highly debatable ground, as 'possibly the oldest regiment in the world'. This depends upon the definition of 'regiment'. Less contentiously, it can claim to be senior of all among the citizen soldiers grouped under the general name of Territorials. Possibly a word of explanation concerning its title may not be out of place. Although it has produced so many excellent artillerymen, the Company is by no means exclusively a fraternity of gunners; the word 'Artillery' in its name bears the old original meaning of missile weapons, which pre-dated artillery as we now understand the term.

The known history of the Company can be traced back to the charter of incorporation granted by Henry VIII on 25 August 1537, to three overseers of the archery fraternity or guild of St George. As bowmen of all kinds were still classified as 'artillery', this guild was henceforth known as the 'Artillery Company'. Soon it became the main training centre of the City of London when troops were required. In the year of the Armada it not only instructed citizens in the science of 'small artillery', but sent many of its members, as officers, to other parts of the kingdom to organize trained bands.

As crossbows and longbows gave way to pikes, muskets, and more modern firearms, so the infantry battalion of the HAC changed its composition accordingly. It was not until 1781 that the City authorities presented to it a couple of brass cannon which, at first used as battalion guns, formed the nucleus for a field battery in 1853. A light cavalry squadron, formed in 1861, was converted into a horse artillery battery in 1891; this and the field battery combined to continue an unbroken existence in the 1st Regiment HAC (RHA). During the South African War an artillery battery and infantry and mounted detachments from the HAC served with the City Imperial Volunteers. In 1914–18 five HAC batteries and two infantry battalions went overseas, and in the Second World War four artillery regiments (three of them RHA and one Heavy Anti-Aircraft). In each of the World Wars the Company provided from among its members more than 4,000 officers for other units.

Few regiments' men can have figured during the Second World War in roles so varied as those of the Company, which, in addition to gunners, also produced infantry, national defence companies, special constables, and officers of their own cadet battalion, besides forming an Officer Cadet Training Unit by the conversion of the old HAC infantry battalion, which suffered so heavily in the First World War. This multiple contribution is pointed out by Major-General Sir Julian Gascoigne, Colonel Commandant, HAC, in a foreword to Brigadier R. F. Johnson's war history, *Regimental Fire!*

During the first eight months of 1939, the artillery component of the HAC, which had consisted of a two-battery regiment, was expanded to three RHA regiments. The final wartime total amounted to fourteen batteries, of which all but one served overseas. Meanwhile, artillery and infantry alike kept up their flow of officers to other branches of the service. Long before any HAC units were in battle, they had contributed officers in numbers far exceeding their own original total strength.

The 11th (HAC) Regiment RHA first went into action with the Jock Columns in Libya in January 1942. Its offshoot, the 12th Regiment, started its fighting career with the First Army in North Africa. In April 1942 the 11th was transferred from the

Eighth Army to First Army, and the 'parent and child' units fought side by side in the final battles of the Tunisia campaign, under command of the 6th Armoured Division. Then their roads parted, the 11th going on to Sicily (they were the first gunners to land in the southern invasion of Europe), while the 12th remained in Africa. Later, after a short period of service close to each other in North Africa, the two regiments again went their separate ways in the advance up the Italian peninsula. The 13th (HAC) Regiment RHA was formed around five officers and about 360 other ranks from the 12th. Its first battle was at Caen.

Although the 11th moved out of Armoury House, London, as soon as war was declared, they had to wait more than two years before it was possible for them to function realistically as an artillery unit. In the days of the invasion threat, half-trained men were 'whisked away' to guard curiously chosen vulnerable points. At last, on 6 December 1941, the regiment landed in Egypt as part of the Support Group, 1st Armoured Division. In the first action on 18 January 1942, some 30 miles from the Gulf of Sirte and about 100 miles south of Benghazi, they were engaged, a battery at a time, in support of three columns, each of which had also an anti-tank and a Bofors light anti-aircraft troop.

Gun tractors stuck in soft sand. One subaltern, as soon as he had fired his first round, found that his gun could neither be traversed nor run up. After three-quarters of an hour's firing every gun of C Troop had its firing platform so twisted and buckled that the wheels would not stay in position on it. Stukas came howling down to dive-bomb. By dint of much effort, some equipment was saved, but the support group had to make a hasty withdrawal, in the course of which some of the artillerymen became widely separated. One officer, who had been taken prisoner, returned at the wheel of a German truck, which he had driven off while the attention of his captors was diverted. Two dishevelled figures in Arab robes, seen hobbling painfully across the desert, approached a troop position and identified themselves as Major J. R. E. Benson and Lieutenant L. R. Drage.

In March, after the remnants of B and E Batteries had been merged and re-formed with new guns and vehicles, a troop was sent to support a Free French column west of Bir Hakim. General Koenig reported later: 'Captain Colley's troop was engaged without warning on the morning of 16 March and overwhelmed by a column of German tanks while it was in the act of moving forward to a position in which . . . it could attack with greater effect a column of Italian tanks which had previously been reported. . . . It continued to fire right up to the end. An inspection of the battlefield has shown that some enemy tanks were forced to continue firing to within 100 yards of Captain Colley's guns.'

Another spell of reorganization followed. Then, in May and June, came the battle of Gazala (the Cauldron), in which B Battery, who with the Sharpshooters had been opposing a thrust near Knightsbridge, were caught in a devastating attack by dive bombers while moving east to support the Bays. About fifty men were killed or wounded.

After the withdrawal past Tobruk, when the enemy had reached the sea beyond Mersa Matruh, orders were given that a breakout must be made. How this was done has been told by Captain de Boinville of the 11th: 'Dear old Christchurch (my Honey tank with ninety-nine lives) had to do a lot of towing. . . . The journey through enemy leaguers was little short of a miracle. We were shot at by everything, and never have I seen such a firework display. . . . The drivers and NCOs of our battery were incredibly cool. Though I could see machine-gun bullets bouncing off wheels and pouring through quads [four-wheel drive gun-towing vehicles], they never lost station, but all came steadily on.'

For a fortnight the battle swung to and fro. On 17 July in repulsing the final attack, the HAC battery felt they were getting their own back when they received the order for 'twelve rounds gunfire' (independent fire) seven times over.

Before Alamein, the 11th were honoured by selection as the first regiment to use the new Priest self-propelled guns. Brigadier Johnson records that the batteries were now utilizing a new technique, firing air burst and bouncing high-explosive shells so as to explode a few feet from the ground, with telling effect against troops in slit trenches. They also employed for the first time the American white phosphorus smoke. The Germans fired somewhat similar smoke shells into British lines as markers for the Stukas. The British batteries always kept one gun loaded with smoke shell. As soon as forward observation officers spotted dive bombers on the way, the order 'Stuka' was given over the radio, the gun was fired, and 'the troops had the satisfaction of seeing the Germans bombing their own troops'. This went on several times a day for a week before the enemy grasped what was happening.

After the victory at Alamein and the onward drive to the Mareth Line, on 24 April 1943, the regiment had their first encounter with the Panzer Mark VI (Tiger), mounting an 88-millimetre gun with all-round traverse. Two direct hits were scored, setting tanks on fire, but it was noted that no shot penetrated the frontal armour, which had a thickness of 102 millimetres.

Two months later, with Sicily in allied hands after just over a month's fighting in the island, the 11th were in the Messina area. Major Morris was determined that they should be able to take part in the bombardment across the straits. In a local workshop, with the help of Italian fitters, he put together an Italian 140-millimetre gun which on 3 September fired seventy-six rounds in company with the bombarding American artillery. Montgomery slipped across the Straits of Messina two divisions which met little resistance, and in less than a fortnight the whole of the toe of Italy had been overrun; but the 11th was ordered back to Bizerta, and it was not until 24 May 1944, that it embarked for Italy as part of the 1st Armoured Division support group.

Before the regiment saw further action the enemy had fallen back to the Gothic Line. On 12 September the entire artillery of the division opened up, continuing during the night attack that followed and throughout the next day. The HAC batteries fired 225 rounds per gun. In the broad spaces of the desert a regimental target had been rare; here, in the cramped corridor between the mountains and the sea, even a divisional concentration was by no means uncommon, neutralizing a whole area within five minutes of the call from an observation post for 'Uncle'. It was during this stage that one battery captain had an embarrassing experience. Ordering more ammunition, he used the unofficial but widely known artillery term of 'bricks' for shells. Evidently the message was not taken down by an artilleryman, for the captain was horrified to see lorries arrive laden with real bricks made of clay.

Later the regiment came under a number of different commands – the 56th Division, the 1st Canadian, the 8th Indian Division, and then the newly arrived Jewish Brigade, which was relieved by a regiment of Italians, now on the allied side. For a time, with one battery kept ready for action, the rest sweated as navvies, making roads in the Villanova area. A few rounds across the Po near Pollesella were the last fired by the regiment in the war against Germany.

The 12th (HAC) Regiment RHA came into existence on 8 May 1939, a few weeks after the decision to double the Territorial Army. At first they had no artillery equipment at all. They spent the winter of 1939–40 on guard duties, and it was as infantry, responsible for defending a large slice of Lincolnshire, that the code word 'Caesar' gave them warning of an imminent invasion that did not materialize. Like many others, they had only ten cartridges a man. By March 1941, with the issue of 25-pounders the regiment's equipment was at last brought virtually on to a war footing, though one 18-pounder and one 4·5-inch howitzer troop still had obsolescent weapons. In November 1942, the 12th left for Algiers in Operation Torch.

During the fierce counter-attacks against General Anderson's spearheads in December, the regiment roved Tunisia, 'stopping holes'. Often they were working with the Guards Brigade, so that, as the Guards had the First Army nickname of the 'Plumbers', the 12th became known as the 'Plumbers' Mates'. In the following month, near the road from Robas to Pont du Fahs, D and F Batteries, with a troop of the 72nd Anti-Tank Regiment, were in action against tanks, including Tigers. In a few hours, 3,600 rounds were fired. The bag included one Tiger which was recovered, and which was examined during a special visit by General Sir Giffard Martel, Director, Royal Armoured Corps.

Disaster was near in February 1943, when the Germans broke through an American regiment, drove into the Kasserine Pass, and threatened communication centres. The British armour fell back, F Battery conforming. Near Thala, while the weary tank crews were in leaguer at night, armoured vehicles approached. At first it was thought that they were probably

British tanks, returning from detached action, but Sergeant T. B. Ainslie, No. 1 of T Troop's nearest gun, was suspicious about one that halted, apparently to deal with some slight mechanical trouble. Creeping forward, he heard German voices. In the gun position a plan was quickly made. Captain John Pirie would send up a Very light; Ainslie would lay his gun on the tank while Lieutenant John Bagnall, with a Bren, was to prevent any German from showing his head.

With his opening shot Ainslie scored a direct hit, following this with a second to knock out another German tank which had crept up behind the first. Machine-gun fire was now sweeping the position. Sergeant J. C. Lawrie, who was with his detachment in half-completed slit trenches, saw the silhouette of a passing tank. Jumping up, he laid, loaded and fired the detachment's gun himself, and disabled the tank. Seldom can three 25-pounder rounds have exercised such effect. If the tanks had passed unscathed through the battery lines, Le Kef might have fallen, and the whole campaign would have suffered a grave setback.

In April 1943, the artillery transport faced great difficulties as IV Corps grappled with its task of closing the Fondouk Gap, where a wide valley narrowed into a defile leading down to the coastal plain in which stood Tunis. Quads, trailers and 3-ton ammunition lorries in particular found it increasingly hard to keep pace with the Sherman tanks in the many tricky little wadis. On 12 April a dusty reconnaissance car, painted a dirty pink, pulled up at regimental headquarters north of Sbika. It was the regiment's first contact in the link-up with Eighth Army. During the final stages before the fall of Tunis the 12th, with the Guards Brigade, formed an anti-tank screen on the right of the 6th Armoured Division's axis of advance. A new lesson was now driven home; that if observation in support of armour was wanted, the artillery observer officers must be given tanks.

When the 12th were rearmed in August, after being out of the battle for ten months, they were supplied with the Priests, with Shermans as mobile observation posts. Fortunately the 11th Regiment, back from Sicily, were stationed near enough to give some tips on the new equipment. In the long, hard-fought advance through Italy the gunners were tested almost to the limit. Past Florence the going became even less suitable for armour. In places where bulldozers could not clear the roads quickly enough, detachments poised on mountain ledges had their rations carried up on mules. In one position 'each round had to be manhandled for a mile, the nearest any troop could get after torrential rains, completing the wreckage the enemy had left behind them'.

On 9 April 1945, the regiment began their last battle of the war, on the Senio. Until the forcing of the water barriers ahead – a dozen or more parallel rivers, all swollen into torrents – the 6th Armoured Division could only remain in reserve. The 12th Regiment, however, had an important role both in preliminary fire plans and in support of infantry assaults. Before the surrender in Germany ended the European war, the gunners had crossed the Austrian border into the beautiful province of Carinthia.

The 13th (HAC) Regiment RHA, formed on 13 November 1940, had little, apart from the limited number of officers and men from the 12th, to denote any outward connection with the Company. Of the few hundred raw recruits who were collected at Denbigh, many were labourers from Manchester and Liverpool, with a high percentage over thirty years of age. In March 1941 the regiment moved to the West Riding to join the 11th Armoured Division, with which its future was to be linked.

More than three years later, on 12 June 1944, the 13th embarked at London docks to join in Operation Overlord. They landed in Normandy, on the western edge of Juno Beach, on D-Day plus nine, in time to take part in the struggle for Caen. The day of their first experience of enemy shellfire also brought the first decoration. Near St Mauvieu, E Troop was in action when an armour-piercing shot went through the front of a self-propelled gun mount and into the engine compartment, killing three men. Gunner L. F. Adams dashed into the burning vehicle and, with ammunition exploding all around him, for five minutes struggled to rescue the crew. Only when ordered by an officer to abandon the hopeless effort did Adams leave the wrecked gun. He was awarded the MM.

After the breakout from the bocage, the advance as far as Antwerp – about 350 miles by the route that was followed – took the gunners exactly a month. The regiment entered Holland by way of Heeze, Someren and Geldrop, over open marshy ground where coppices offered good cover for enemy snipers. On the Helmond road, when Captain Young's tank was knocked out, Gunner Adams was killed.

A section of H Battery, deployed along the Milheeze-Oploo road on 25 September was the first RHA unit, and the first regiment in the corps, to fire a salvo into Germany. In the north-east corner of Brabant the 13th spent three strenuous if unspectacular months, helping to clear up the line of the Maas. They were among those engaged in a hard slogging match in October, supporting first the United States 7th Armoured Division and then the British 3rd Division for the capture of the village of Overloon.

In the bombardment before the first British troops crossed the Rhine, the regiment made their contribution in the counter-battery role. For ten hours on 23 March their guns fired without respite, then on at intervals until the middle of the next morning, when they moved up to within 1,500 yards of the river to cover the bridgehead that had been established during the night. In just over fifteen hours they shot off 16,800 rounds – 420,000 pounds of high-explosive shell.

Advancing into Germany, on 15 April the regiment heard, and saw, evidence of horrors as they passed through the area in which lay Belsen. Major Charles Chapman, commanding officer of the light anti-aircraft battery accompanying the 13th, was in charge of part of the death camp after the British entered. On the autobahn outside Lübeck, in the last few days before enemy resistance ceased, G Battery in a single night took 600 prisoners, including a U-boat commander and his crew; altogether, the division captured 15,000 in a day.

The first HAC to come into action during the war had been not one of the RHA units, but the 86th (HAC) Heavy Anti-Aircraft Regiment. After five years of trying and often exasperating service in the air defence of Britain they had nine months overseas, in which they functioned not only as heavy and light AA, anti-tank, coast defence and field gunners, but even as infantry, as well as interludes of arduous but less warlike labours. In the first year alone this regiment provided no fewer than 801 officers, either by the grant of direct commissions or through OCTU.

The first rounds were fired by the 273rd Battery from Hackney Marshes at a lone raider on 22 August 1940. For more than two years the regiment were on duty – armed successively with 3-inch, 4·5 and 3·7 guns – at sites on the northern and eastern approaches to London, with frequent changes of station.

On 2 June 1944, the men went on board ship at Tilbury for Normandy; they landed with the Canadian 3rd Division on Juno Beach on D-Day. With other AA units, for nearly a month they gave cover for the landing areas, ensconcing themselves between raids in dugouts, as the beaches were still commanded by one German long-range gun at Merville, away to the east. In August, for the capture of Le Havre, the 86th were given the task of deploying for coast defence, to prevent the enemy escaping by sea. This particular role did not have to be fulfilled, but the silencing of hostile anti-aircraft batteries was carried out with efficiency.

In October there was an issue of American radar and predictors, the latest of their kind, and the regiment moved to Zandhoven, 10 miles east of Antwerp. Although the city had been taken in September, no effective action had been staged to secure possession of the 70-mile channel leading from it to the sea; also, in wooded country east and south-east of Antwerp, the Germans had started in desperate haste the building of new launching sites for flying bombs. Officially, the task of the regiment was in defence of Brussels, but the gunners were in the corridor through which as many as fifty VIs a day were heading for Antwerp. Guns picked up the flying targets at 8,000 to 10,000 yards, and took them on at a ground range of 5,000 or 6,000 yards. With a buzz-bomb of average speed, this gave about fifteen seconds to fire the first round, and roughly forty seconds to bring it down before it passed out of range. Between 1 November 1944, and 14 March 1945, the regiment shot down seventy-eight 'divers' for an expenditure of 9,600 rounds. One bomb fell in the midst of a battery, killing one man, wounding three, and wrecking ten vehicles.

Later the 86th were called back into the Antwerp defence ring, for the Germans, after their penetration in the Ardennes, now had a new VI site in Holland, so close that every bomb that got through was deadly. This time was the peak of activity for the regiment. Never before had the batteries been deployed so near together, in a 3,000-yard line of guns. They claimed eighty-nine kills out of ninety-one targets engaged, with an average of ninety rounds for each buzz-bomb destroyed.

An offshoot of the 86th Regiment, before the invasion of Europe, was the 275th (HAC) Heavy Anti-Aircraft Battery. After having shared the parent unit's career in England for over two years, the 275th left in October 1941 to become part of the 118th HAA Regiment, and later the 165th. The main body of the battery disembarked, through heavy surf, on Mike Beach in Normandy on D-Day plus seven. Later they formed part of the barrier which was hastily assembled by Montgomery to block the line of the Meuse against the mid-winter thrust through the Ardennes.

DEFENDERS OF MALTA

'These men are born and bred to the sound of artillery. Noise will not frighten them.' *– Dragut Rais during the Great Siege, 1565*

In the course of its history the Royal Artillery has set down roots in many lands, some of which are now independent countries, where gunner regiments on basically British lines have been established. First and foremost that come to mind are the great dominions of Canada, Australia and New Zealand, whose gunners have made such fine contributions in time of world war. Other artillery forces with which the Royal Regiment still retains 'alliances', as they are officially called, are those of India, Pakistan, Ceylon, Malaysia, Hongkong and Fiji. Another regiment which deserves a closer glance, both by reason of the intrinsic interest of its record and the fact that until recently it formed an integral part of the British Army, is the Royal Malta Artillery, which now composes the regular element of the Malta Land Force, the small army of the central Mediterranean islands which since 1964 have been an independent state within the Commonwealth.

The first Maltese artillery units were formed in 1801. Some years before that, while Malta was still under the rule of the Knights of St John, companies of gunners from the islands were raised for the service of King George in Corsica, when that territory was under British protection, and about the same period approximately 1,600 Maltese were serving with the Royal Navy.

In 1798 Napoleon, on his way to the invasion of Egypt, landed troops in Malta. The régime of the knights rapidly collapsed, with no effective resistance, but the islanders rose in revolt against the French, who were virtually besieged within the fortresses. Not long afterwards Lieutenant James Vivion, RA,

30. A farewell parade, at Woolwich in 1960, to mark the disbandment of 57 Heavy Anti-Aircraft Regiment, R.A. In the foreground is a Thunderbird missile (*The Times*)

31. The King's Troop, Royal Horse Artillery, gallops past during a Hyde Park review in May, 1967 (*The Times*)

32. Firing the 105 mm. pack howitzers, highly mobile weapons in use by Light Regiments, in July, 1969 (*The Times*)

33. Abbot 105 mm. self-propelled guns firing during Royal Artillery Day at Larkhill, Salisbury Plain, September 1970 (Defence Ministry)

at the head of a small detachment of gunners, made a landing to aid the Maltese guerrillas, some of whom had raised the British flag, but who had few arms save muskets, short swords and knives. With the British came two heavy mortars, which were used to bombard French ships in harbour. The first artillery regiment composed entirely of Maltese rank-and-file, and established under the auspices of Britain, came into existence in January 1801, about a year before the Treaty of Amiens, which contained a paragraph stating that half the garrison of the islands was always to be recruited from among the inhabitants, with Maltese officers. Vivion, who had been promoted to captain and appointed inspector of Maltese and other troops in the islands, took command of two militia companies of coast artillery, with some Maltese officers under him.

Uniforms were almost identical with those worn by the Royal Artillery at this period, but rates of pay appear to have been slightly lower. They worked out at six and two-thirds pence a day for a private, eightpence-halfpenny for a corporal, and tenpence for a sergeant.

During the latter part of the Napoleonic Wars a number of artillery units from England did tours of duty in Malta. Some men belonging to one of these became involved, against their will, in an extraordinary mutiny that broke out among non-British troops. Owing to their chronic shortage of men to face the conscript armies of France, the British were reduced, not for the first time, to enlisting almost any foreigners who were available and willing, without too nice a regard for quality or reliability. In Malta a certain Count Froberg, described as a Frenchman, offered to raise a regiment of Greeks for Mediterranean service. His offer was accepted, and he organized a miniature Foreign Legion which included not only Greeks but also Albanians, Sclavonians and Turks, under the name of Froberg's Regiment.

An account of the mutiny in April 1807 was given in a book written towards the end of the nineteenth century by Major A. G. Chesney, an officer of the South Staffordshire Regiment who was adjutant to the Royal Malta Militia. According to this work, most of the officers of Froberg's Regiment were Germans, who deemed it necessary to enforce harsh discipline for the control of their motley collection of men. The immediate cause of the outbreak was an incident in which an officer struck a drummer across the face with a cane. Mutiny spread like wildfire among the foreign troops in Fort Ricasoli, which stands at the tip of a headland facing Valletta, the capital, across the entrance to Grand Harbour.

Two officers were killed, the gates of the fort were barred, the drawbridges raised, and the Russian colours were hoisted above the walls. The choice of flag may perhaps be explained by the fact that the Tsar had been the ally of England against the French; he may also have been regarded by some of the men at Ricasoli as their patron in a more special sense as protector of the Greek Orthodox faith. (It was under the Tsar's protection that the Knights of St John sought temporary refuge after their flight from Malta in 1798.)

Among the troops in the fort, in addition to the foreign soldiers, were a detachment of British gunners, commanded by Captain Fead. One gunner was killed while trying to prevent the mutineers from gaining access to the powder magazine. The rest were forced, at the point of the musket, to load several guns and mortars, which were aimed towards Valletta.

The fort, under the control of the mutineers, held out for about a week. A few shots were fired across the water at Valletta, without doing a great deal of damage. Eventually, after other measures had failed, loyal troops made their way into Ricasoli by escalade. Some of the foreigners escaped, but they were rounded up before long. The mutineers were tried and condemned to death. On the Floriana parade ground (now known as the Independence Arena) fifteen of them were shot, and fifteen hanged.

It may be noted that no Maltese soldiers were dishonourably involved in the strange affair of 1807. Their loyalty, before and since, has been above suspicion. The Royal Malta Fencibles, who in origin had been principally an infantry unit, changed to an artillery role in 1861. Their first overseas service was during the Egyptian campaign of 1882, when a battery, made up entirely of volunteers, fought side by side with the British. The work of these few Maltese, about a hundred in all, won from Queen Victoria the grant of the battle honour 'Egypt, 1882'.

Detachments from the Royal Malta Artillery (the 'Fencibles' part of the title was dropped in 1889) were sent to Egypt on various other occasions. Between 1900 and 1905 a company of Maltese soldiers formed part of the small garrison stationed midway between Alexandria and Port Said. During the First World War another company was attached to British troops in Egypt, and between 1940 and 1943 several anti-aircraft sites, as well as the coastal defences of Port Tewfiq, were in the hands of men of the RMA. During the First World War the regiment had been entrusted with coastal batteries protecting Malta itself, but there they were not called upon for action. However, hundreds of Maltese, many of whom were already in the ranks of the RMA, volunteered to serve overseas, and soon found themselves in France or Gallipoli.

On 23 August 1939, before the outbreak of war, the people of Malta witnessed general mobilization in the islands for the second time within living memory. By 1942 the Royal Malta Artillery was to expand from one regiment to five, with a detached battery in Egypt. On the military side of the defence of Malta, the RMA and the King's Own Malta Regiment shared responsibility with their comrades of the Royal Artillery and several British infantry battalions, notably the Devonshire Regiment.

The episode which is regarded by all concerned as the finest hour of the RMA took place on 26 July 1941, when the coastal batteries beat off with heavy losses a determined attack on Grand Harbour by Italian E-boats and torpedo-carrying craft. The raiders were sighted close offshore at 4.30 a.m. The Maltese, even at normal times, are early risers, and on this occasion throngs of them, far from taking shelter, hurried out to find the choicest vantage points on the old bastions.

An eye-witness, describing in *The Times of Malta* what happened when the RMA opened fire, wrote: 'Hundreds of pounds of lead must have smashed into the leading E-boat simultaneously. It blew up with a roar. A large black column of water spouted up. Overhead the whine of shellfire was mingled with the roar of aircraft engines as RAF fighters dived and zoomed down to add their quota to the defence of Grand Harbour. The excitement of the hundreds of people on the bastions overlooking the harbour and breakwater was contagious. It seemed to have caught hold of the men behind the guns, for they fired like madmen – but ever such accurate madmen. . . . The attack was beaten off with a zest, accuracy and fine frenzy that indicated how keenly the men had been awaiting the chance to use their guns in real earnest.'

A gap, which can still be seen, was blown in the breakwater viaduct beyond Fort St Elmo, but it is believed that of seventeen enemy craft that took part in the raid not one returned safely to base in Sicily. This was, in fact, the most outstanding defensive action by coast artillery in any theatre of the war. It proved the efficacy of 6-pounder twin mountings, which were in operational use for the first time.

Never again did the Italians venture an attack of this kind and on a comparable scale; but as the war continued, Malta, which has seen so many invaders and lived through so many ordeals, from long before the Great Siege by the Turks in 1565, was to find stern tasks for the gunners, and her other defenders, in the dark days when the supply convoys suffered terrible losses, food ran short, and the bombs rained down on the docks, the ships, and the little narrow streets. Casualties were heavy for the Maltese gunners, and the British too. Among other service memorials in the Anglican church of the Holy Trinity at Sliema is a tablet bearing the names of fifty officers and men of the 10th Heavy Anti-Aircraft Regiment, RA (later designated the 68th) who died between 1940 and 1945 in defence of the islands.

In April 1942, Malta's worst month of the war, the RMA accounted for more than ninety enemy aircraft, while other artillery units shot down twelve more. It was in this month that King George VI awarded the George Cross to the island fortress to commemorate 'a heroism and devotion which will long be famous in history'. A more personal honour, for the gunners, was the king's acceptance of the appointment of colonel-in-chief of the RMA, 'in recognition of their skill and determination'. Later men of the regiment were to have the privilege of mounting guard over ships of the Italian fleet which had come to surrender.

In August 1942, gunners of the Royal Maritime Artillery, which furnished detachments for the defensive armament of so many merchant ships, were on board the tanker *Ohio* when, with her decks awash after being torpedoed, she was towed into Grand Harbour, one of the few survivors of the famous convoy from Gibraltar that ran the gauntlet with petrol, ammunition and food at a time when the islands' stocks were desperately low.

After the war the RMA was reduced to two regiments, some of whose men served for a considerable time with the Royal Corps of Transport on lines of communication in the British Army of the Rhine. In 1970, with Malta now independent, they returned from Germany, and it was decided that in future the regiment should form part of the Malta Land Force. A ceremonial parade to mark the farewell to the British Army was held on the Independence Arena on 26 September 1970, in the presence of a number of senior officers from England, among whom was General Sir Robert Mansergh, Master Gunner of St James's Park. In a speech before the gunners marched off to their quarters in Fort St Elmo, General Mansergh announced that the Queen, who like her father before her was colonel-in-chief of the Royal Malta Artillery, had consented to retain that appointment after the regiment's incorporation in Malta's own forces.

Gifts were exchanged between the regiment and the Royal Artillery. The RMA presented two silver statuettes, made by Maltese craftsmen, of soldiers wearing the uniform of the Malta Fencibles in the 1840s, and of the RMA in the 1890s. From the Royal Artillery they received a silver model of the 13-inch mortar that was brought to Malta by Lieutenant Vivion, and from the British Army in general a painting of the E-boat attack in 1941. The presentation was one of the last public duties performed by General Mansergh, who died on 8 November 1970.

The main armament of the RMA at the time of the handover consisted of rather elderly Bofors guns. In Malta, which has echoed so often to the sound of cannon, it is now rare to see artillery weapons of later date than antiques from the seventeenth or eighteenth centuries outside public buildings. Many pieces have vanished completely; according to Royal Artillery figures, in 1849 there were as many as 486 guns in Malta – but only two companies of artillerymen, totalling about 180. Before the First World War, one of the most prominent British officers in promoting the efficiency of coast artillery was General Sir John Owen, who as Royal Artillery commander in Malta had been a pioneer of night firing practice.

The Victorian heyday of heavy coastal ordnance has left

scarcely a trace, but there is one notable exception – the 100-ton gun of the Rinella Battery, a short distance along the coast from Ricasoli Point, not far from Bighi where a naval hospital was established in Nelson's days. This massive piece, one of the biggest of the Armstrong rifled muzzle-loaders, was an object of interest during a visit to Malta in October 1970 by Mr Austin Carpenter, Superintendent at Plymouth for the Ministry of Works, whose responsibilities included the preservation of old cannon. Mr Carpenter stated that, apart from the Rinella gun, there now existed only one other of the same size and type, complete with mounting, at Gibraltar. He knew of another, much smaller, but also still on its own carriage, in Ascension Island.

The Rinella gun, which looks out over the sea from a high-walled emplacement resembling a small fort, has been 'adopted' by a Maltese youth group whose members, with praiseworthy industry, have sand-blasted the metalwork and painted it a rather light shade of battleship grey. The battery is open to the public from time to time.

Thousands of miles from the shores of Malta, on the fringe of the vast Asian mainland, there existed during the first half of the present century a remarkable little unit of gunners, some of whose members have also given wartime service in the Royal Artillery. This was the field battery forming part of the Shanghai Volunteer Corps, the part-time citizen defence force of the municipal council that administered the International Settlement in the days when nationals of foreign powers still enjoyed extraterritorial rights in China, and the possibility of Communist rule over the whole of that enormous country was as yet hardly imaginable.

The SVC – now almost totally forgotten, no doubt, save by a few 'old China hands' – was a small self-contained international army long before the first United Nations peace-keeping force was planned. Although it was customary for a British officer to be made available as commandant, and help was also given with equipment, the corps was never part of the British Army. Its allegiance was to the flag of the Shanghai Municipal Council, with the motto *Omnia juncta in uno*; its duties were to assist in maintaining law and order during periods of unrest, to defend the perimeter of the Settlement whenever it was infringed or endangered by civil or international war, and, if necessary, to protect the inhabitants, both foreign and Chinese, until the arrival of regular troops from Britain or one of the other powers involved in the great commercial interests at stake in Shanghai.

Besides the field battery, the SVC included armoured cars, machine-gun sections, engineers, a troop of light horse, and infantry companies, among them the Shanghai Scottish. In the ranks were to be found Englishmen, Americans, Germans, Scandinavians, a few White Russian refugees who acted as a maintenance nucleus, and – officially – even a Japanese company at a time when, as in 1932, a Sino-Japanese local war was being fought on the outskirts of the city. The French, having their own separate Concession, were not represented in the corps.

Most of the gunners were young British employees of big Shanghai firms, though a few Scandinavians also joined the battery. Its members wore British-style artillery uniform, with khaki tunics, bandoliers, breeches, puttees, and ankle boots complete with spurs, although the course of duty never set them astride a horse. Every man had a Lee Enfield rifle and ammunition, which were kept at home, ready in case of emergency. In times of peace the battery was a cheery social group, with parties almost as frequent as gun drills; when tension arose the work could be serious enough, though the artillerymen, owing to the conditions of their service in a densely populated built-up area, were more likely to be used as infantry than in the gunners' true role.

Firing practice was a problem. As it was impossible to find any suitable place to use live ammunition in the Shanghai area, hemmed in by Chinese territory with many villages and sacrosanct grave mounds, from time to time the men of the field battery were put on board a British destroyer and shipped down the coast to Hongkong, where facilities for a shoot could be provided by the garrison.

BALANCE OF TERROR

'War is nothing more than the continuation of politics by other means.' – *Clausewitz*

After 1945 it was widely believed that the days of limited warfare of the old kind were over, that the advent of atomic weapons meant that conventional arms, perhaps including artillery of the traditional type, were obsolete, and that any future war was likely to expand swiftly into a global conflict between the superpowers, wielding bombs and missiles with nuclear warheads. This is among the many assumptions that, so far, have not held good. Atomic weapons have not been used in action since 1945; the so-called balance of terror has contributed (as many think) to preventing an all-out struggle between the west and the Soviet Union; but in Asia and Africa there has been a succession of military actions, varying in scale and intensity, in which British artillery, armour and infantry have been engaged on lines not vastly different from those of the past.

As the east–west confrontation developed, Britain's main responsibility as regards land forces within Europe rested with units of the British Army of the Rhine, which from their original role as occupation troops in Germany became transformed into an important, though numerically small, factor in the strength of the North Atlantic Treaty Organization. It was also the period of the rapid reduction of Britain's overseas possessions, usually under political or armed pressure for independence, and the curtailment of imperial commitments east of Suez – though this latter process was hedged around with reservations and doubts, some of which persist.

To maintain the Nato contingent, and to keep in being even a small strategic reserve, taxed to the utmost the available

British manpower after the ending of the National Service system, which meant that the Army must now rely entirely on voluntary recruitment of regulars. The postwar rundown of the forces, followed by the amalgamation of many famous regiments of cavalry and infantry, was drastic. The Royal Artillery, by its nature, escaped the worst upheavals and heartburnings of the forced amalgamations, and in 1950 it still had, for the time being, sixty-nine regiments – a number greater than that of the infantry battalions of the line. Of the artillery's total, fourteen regiments were still grouped with Territorial units in Anti-Aircraft Command. Half of the remainder were field artillery units, one quarter medium and heavy, and the other quarter field force anti-aircraft. On paper, the number of gunner units might have seemed at least adequate; but the shortage of infantry was so acute, and the calls for intervention in distant theatres were so many and so varied, that time after time artillerymen had to be used as infantry, in which role, unwelcome as it may have been, they performed service of the greatest value.

Fortunately, Britain managed to steer clear of the worst morass of all – the Vietnam tragedy, which has taken such heavy toll of American resources and morale; but, apart from the United Nations operations in Korea from 1950 to 1953, there have been about a dozen widely separated scenes of action where more than twenty Royal Artillery regiments have been engaged, some of them for considerable lengths of time and on a number of different occasions, though not all of these units are listed as officially on active service. Among them were: security action in Palestine during the final period of the British mandate before the emergence of the independent state of Israel; Suez Canal Zone duty from 1948–55; the years of bitter struggle with terrorists in Malaya; the Cyprus campaign of 1957–58 against the Eoka guerrillas; the suppression of the Lanet mutiny in Kenya; support for British troops and the Federal Army in South Arabia and Aden, and against tribesmen on the Yemen frontier; and months of exacting service in the jungles and riverlands of Borneo and Sarawak during the time of Indonesian aggressiveness. No fewer than fourteen artillery regiments and four independent batteries took part there.

In many cases the terrain and the nature of the tasks –

internal security and anti-terrorist work – militated against the use of artillery as such, quite apart from the chronic shortage of infantry. In Malaya – a guerrilla's paradise, as Gregory Blaxland terms it in his recent book *The Regiments Depart* – 26th Field Regiment went into action as foot soldiers. During the Cyprus operations gunners proved themselves worthy replacements for the Commando men and parachutists whom they relieved. Members of 50th Medium Regiment, in the extreme north-west of the island, displayed notable 'swiftness on the draw'. On four occasions their patrols inflicted heavy losses on terrorists who tried to ambush them, and in their own ambushes the artillerymen in the infantry role captured three Eoka leaders.

Batteries linked with famous names of the past appeared in unfamiliar settings, on duties that could scarcely have been in sharper contrast with their earlier exploits. The strife-torn streets of Haifa were patrolled day and night by self-propelled guns of the Chestnut Troop, 1st RHA, later to figure in Aden. Men of the 14th Regiment on internal security duties at Karachi in 1947 included the 5th Battery which served in the defence of Gibraltar, 1779–83. Among the field artillery units employed in Malaya were the 2nd Regiment, with L (Néry) Battery, N (The Eagle Troop) and C (Rocket Troop); the 25th, represented by the 54th (Maharajpur) and 93rd (Le Cateau) Batteries; the 26th, with the 16th (Sandham's) Company, the 17th (Corunna) and 159th (Colenso) Batteries; and the 34th Regiment's 11th (Sphinx) Battery.

In the midst of the bleak rugged hills of Korea, gunners distinguished themselves in the battle of the Hook in the autumn of 1953, the Pusan operations, and the fighting at the Nakton River, for which the 27th (Strange's) Battery of the 20th Field Regiment received a special citation from President Sygman Rhee of South Korea. An outstanding action was the Imjin River battle, in which the Gloucestershire Regiment made its famous stand in defence of a vital ford, after Chinese forces, crossing the border to aid the North Korean Communists, had attacked on an 80-mile front with Seoul, the capital, as primary objective. During fierce fighting the VC was won by Lieutenant-Colonel J. P. Carne of the Gloucesters. Steadfast support by the 45th Field Regiment, RA, was recognized by a United States presidential citation, and the honour title of 'Imjin' was conferred upon the regiment's 170th Battery.

Some of the later post-1945 operations, such as those in Aden and Borneo, were carried out under severe limitations of manpower, for the cuts that followed the Second World War, though somewhat delayed so far as the gunners were concerned, went deep when they came into full effect, between 1956 and 1965. As Gregory Blaxland writes: 'The Royal Artillery suffered the heaviest mauling of all, being slashed by twenty regiments and the equivalent of one more in minor units. This was on top of the disbandment of AA Command, which had been ordered in 1954 and involved the disbandment of fourteen regiments, leaving the gunners with responsibility only for the air defence of field units. All that remained after these cuts were thirty-four regiments and a battery, barely one-third of the total in 1949. This was the price to be paid for the increase in striking power in the nuclear-armed Honest John and the even more powerful Corporal.'

Changes in artillery equipment since the war against Nazi Germany have been far-reaching, and some of them are still controversial. Development in the immediate postwar period centred on improved anti-aircraft weapons; guns capable of firing atomic shells; and rockets able to carry either atomic or 'conventional' warheads. The first test of an American gun designed to fire high-explosive or atomic shells took place near Las Vegas in Nevada on 25 May 1953. This 280-millimetre weapon, which had a maximum range of about 20 miles, weighed 85 tons, almost as much as the static giants of coast defence in late Victorian days; but it was transportable. Suspended between two truck units, it could be moved over good roads at 35 miles an hour.

Later research was directed towards smaller and more mobile atomic artillery. By 1957 the United States Army had developed an 8-inch atomic shell. The Americans introduced the Corporal as their first combat-ready guided missile for ground-to-ground use, and the Honest John as an unguided rocket with atomic or high explosive warhead. The Honest John was 27 feet long, weighed 4,830 pounds, and had a range of over 15 miles.

In the British Field Army the emphasis (still the subject of some debate within the regiment) has been on guns of larger calibre, combined with the greatest degree of mobility that can be achieved. One easing of commitments, though a controversial one, came with the decision, in view of the increasing power of direct-fire weapons, to transfer the anti-tank role to the Royal Armoured Corps, a switchover that was completed in 1950. So far as the units earmarked for Nato are concerned, the staunch old towed 25-pounder now belongs to a bygone era. British field units in Germany entered the 1970s equipped with the close support 105-millimetre self-propelled gun (Abbot), the medium SP 155-millimetre (M. 109), and the heavy SP 175-millimetre (M. 107). A replacement for the 5·5-inch medium gun had at last been found in the towed 155-millimetre (FH 70).

The acceptance for service of a new 105-millimetre gun for light regiments was announced in August 1971. This weapon, which will be issued by the mid-seventies to units in the United Kingdom mobile force and east of Suez, replaces the Italian – designed 105-millimetre pack howitzer, which did well in Borneo and Aden. The change was described as the first step in a complete replacement of all present artillery equipment by the end of the decade. Additional range is the most important feature of the new gun. With a maximum of over 10 miles, it fires a 35-pound shell 4,000 yards farther than anything in the same class, and 6,500 yards farther than the 105-millimetre pack howitzer. In appearance the newcomer resembles the 17-pounder anti-tank gun of the Second World War, but it is much lighter, and can be lifted by the Puma tactical transport helicopter.

The Abbot, which came into service during the sixties, can fire a 35-pound shell for 17,000 metres (about 10 miles) at a maximum sustained rate of six rounds a minute. It has all-round traverse; the tracked mounting is capable of good cross-country performance, and can reach speeds of up to 25 miles an hour. This SP gun can 'swim', and can be fully closed down for protection, but it has no chemical or nuclear ammunition. Each battery of six Abbots needs for its regular back-up some thirty other vehicles to carry men, ammunition and supplies. All information on bearing, range and angle of sight is calculated by Field Artillery Computer Equipment (Face). For reliability and ease of handling the Abbot certainly ranks among the best in the world, despite some criticisms, mainly on the score of insufficient range.

Plans have been made for the arming of all close support regiments in BAOR with 155-millimetre guns, a move which would accentuate the already existing need for a reassessment of the tactical handling of self-propelled guns. The 155-millimetre SP howitzer already in service fires 95-pound shells to a maximum distance of 14,600 metres at a rate of two a minute; the model used by the Americans has an increased range of 17,000 metres, and also chemical and nuclear ammunition.

The Honest John rockets of the missile regiments, and the heavier Corporal under the control of higher formations, can add formidable destructive power. On the other hand, they tie up large numbers of men to serve and maintain them while, it has been argued, they might never be brought into play, either because the general order for nuclear release was not issued, or because their yield was considered too high for the conditions that exist in Germany.

Anti-aircraft defence in the field depended at medium ranges on the Thunderbird 2 guided missile, and for lower-level action on the Rapier (small, light and effective) and the Blowpipe; but some doubts have been expressed about an air defence that rests solely on missiles, not guns. As regards the protection of the United Kingdom itself from air attack, the decision to scrap Anti-Aircraft Command, which had fallen on evil days, was taken in the evident belief that the heavy AA guns, whose continued existence might have been justified against manned bombers, could no longer be considered a worth-while investment in face of the onslaughts by ultra-swift high-altitude nuclear missiles which must now be held possible. Save for the deterrent effect of retaliatory power (and anti-missile missiles in the case of the United States), no realistic means of defence against such attack exists, so far as can be judged from information that has been made public. The disbandment of the heavy batteries was the more striking as a break with the recent past because in the early 1950s some magnificent fully automatic 5·25-inch anti-aircraft guns were available in England. Across the Atlantic, in 1953 the United States Army disclosed its Skysweeper, a 75-millimetre gun fitted with radar that could spot planes miles away, follow their course in daylight or darkness, and automatically aim the piece. It could fire 11½-pound shells with proximity fuses at a rate of forty-five a minute.

The new rockets that followed had the advantage that they could be directed on to their targets by electronic remote control even if planes took evasive action. The Nike, a 20-foot long liquid-fuelled missile, was announced by the Americans late in 1953. Britain's Thunderbird 1 was introduced in 1958, Thunderbird 2 being completed in December 1964.

At present the state of air defence of the field army is a source of concern among some artillery officers. An outspoken article by Major A. M. Child (*Journal of the Royal Artillery*, March, 1970), went so far as to state that the regiment had rendered a disservice to the Army in the past by regarding anti-aircraft artillery, perhaps unwittingly, as an inferior branch.

'By the 1970s,' Major Child wrote, 'the British Army will be unique in being the only major army to rely on missiles alone for its air defence. It may be that our Army is one technological step ahead of the others. It may be that we have failed to realize the limitations of missiles. . . . In the air war over North Vietnam and the continuing Arab–Israeli conflict missiles of every type have not shown up too well and in some cases have been discarded in favour of simpler weapons. . . . The gun is simple, reliable, easy to operate and based on well-proven technology. The disadvantages of the gun, in the air defence role, that have discredited it in this country are inherent inaccuracy and poor lethality. There is good reason to believe that these defects can be overcome. The gun has a chance once the aircraft has committed itself to an attack. When the aircraft has complete freedom of manœuvre, then missiles are the only effective weapon.'

A good many gunners think that the BAOR artillery, still short of fully adequate firepower, needs a better capacity to deal with both aircraft and armour. Some hold that the artillery should be given a chance to fill the gap left by the disbandment of the anti-tank regiments.

Besides its technical problems, the Royal Artillery continues to be harassed by the old bugbear of employment on tasks remote from its primary function, and sometimes of doubtful validity as legitimate duties for any soldiers. In 1971, after the completion of cuts ordered in 1968 and modified two years later, the artillery had twenty-nine regiments plus three batteries. Among troops who have done police duty, and suffered casualties, in the Ulster disorders have been several gunner units. A dispatch from Bielefeld, West Germany, in *The Times* of 17 May 1971, which referred to 'this apparently wasteful use of trained technical troops', said that men of the 27th and 45th Medium Regiments, RA, were being trained with rifles and truncheons for Northern Ireland internal security duties, and were being reinforced for this purpose from guided missile units, as well as from two tank regiments. Under a new Ministry of Defence policy, many of the troops required in Ulster were being taken from the Rhine Army rather than from the strategic reserve based in the United Kingdom.

One reason given for this policy is that if the Northern Ireland commitment were left to the infantry alone, the Rhine Army battalions, all of which have tracked personnel carriers and a wide range of technical equipment, would be unable to keep themselves up to the mark for their main military purpose. Another consideration is that in previous years the use of spear-head battalions from the strategic reserve has robbed that force of much of its capability as a world-wide 'fire brigade'.

At the end of June 1971, when a further 900 soldiers were about to be sent to Northern Ireland for border patrol or riot control duties, it was stated that two of the three units involved were artillery regiments, the 3rd RHA and the 42nd Medium, both of which had already served in Ulster. The 3rd RHA, 400 strong, were going from Colchester to Belfast, and the 42nd Medium, with another 400, from Devizes to Antrim. When first-line units are moved from Germany arrangements are made for their return at short notice should the situation in Europe degenerate to a point necessitating the declaration of a certain state of readiness, from which moment alone the British Army contribution to Nato would come into practical effect. Nevertheless, it would be hard to imagine any more thankless and galling situation than that of professional soldiers taken away from their own rightful jobs and sent out with shields and protective jerkins in the streets of Belfast, where they become the targets not only for snipers' bullets, nail bombs and IRA gelignite charges, but also for the provocative jeers and insults of angry partisan mobs, whether Catholic or Protestant.

At the time of writing the military commander in Northern Ireland is a gunner officer, Lieutenant-General Sir Harry Tuzo, formerly Director, RA. His new appointment came soon after the loss of two young artillerymen in Belfast – Gunner R. G. Curtis of the 94th Locating Regiment, killed on 5 February 1971, and Lance-Bombardier J. D. Laurie, 32nd Heavy Regiment, who died of wounds on 15 February. Troops serving in Northern Ireland were still not officially classed as on active service – a state of affairs which may seem ironical, but which at least offers the advantage that dependants of soldiers who are killed or wounded are entitled to claim compensation. Mrs Joan Curtis, the pregnant widow of Gunner Curtis who was killed by the IRA, was granted £500 in a Belfast court as an interim award. At that time the Government at Stormont was facing compensation claims in respect of seven British soldiers killed and nine injured.

TODAY AND TOMORROW

***'In war there is no room for two mistakes.'** – Lamachus, Athenian general*

Anyone who tries to unravel the tangled skein of military history is likely to be left with a certain scepticism. After a brief venture into the past of the artillery, and of the Army as a whole, a cynic might be tempted to wonder, on a superficial view, how Britain ever won a battle, let alone a war. Bravery and devotion have so often been frustrated, or at least sorely handicapped, by shortcomings in organization and supply, and sometimes by the blunders of those in high places. Yet, in spite of all, the victories themselves are beyond dispute. Time after time, in the face of almost incredible difficulties, the quality of the men and the leadership of their officers have achieved the seemingly impossible. Few who study their record can fail to be imbued with a deep sense of respect, bringing with it a sober but real hope for the future. Such hope is badly needed at a moment when so much relating to the nature of any future warfare is uncertain, and even the practicability of a continued role for fire support of the traditional kind has itself been challenged.

Considerable discussion, and some criticism, has been aroused by an article by Mr G. Ashcroft of the Institute for Strategic Studies (*Royal Artillery Journal*, March, 1970). In this he wrote: 'If direct fire weapons, such as armed helicopters and new means of longer range and infantry anti-tank weapons at shorter range, offer a reasonable variety of measures to apply against APCs (Armoured Personnel Carriers), the case for an artillery capability to supplement these weapons becomes less strong, particularly if a complete replacement of guns and ammunition reserves might be involved.' Mr Ashcroft suggested that the right answer would be to give priority to the introduction of armed helicopters and more effective minefields. His lowest priority would be for rockets, and he would sacrifice improved guns, in the short term, if this were necessary to make possible the provision of helicopters.

But he also had a good deal to say for the indispensability of the gun. He wrote: 'It seems that consideration of massive nuclear firepower has pushed conventional fire support considerations into the background. This is a great pity. And if the now fashionable doctrine of flexible response is to mean anything, then the scope and capacity of conventional fire support must receive its fair share of constructive analysis. . . . For the immediate future at least, guns have qualities which rockets cannot match and the two are not wholly interchangeable. . . . In its present state of development the rocket does not seem to be a wholly satisfactory weapon for traditional artillery use. It is relatively inaccurate. It poses significant logistic problems which its extra range does little if anything to ameliorate. . . . Recent military history is littered with precedents warning against a too hasty and a too enthusiastic changeover from guns to untried missiles.' (Russia still has large numbers of conventional artillery.)

In the same issue of the *Journal*, Major M. J. Woodcock, in an article on 'Reshaping the artillery for the seventies', said: 'Some have questioned the value of close support artillery because theoretical studies have shown that indirect fire weapons have a low probability of immobilizing AFVs [Armoured Fighting Vehicles]. But now that Nato has rejected the "tripwire" theory for the "flexible response", the ability to slow an attack with conventional forces is most important. The Nato Governments need as much time as possible to assess the situation and to decide when nuclear release can be given. Close support artillery would be a vital component in the delaying battle. It remains, as it has always been, an essential part of any combat force.'

Writing on 'Space age artillery' in the *Journal*, March, 1971, Major P. D. Williams stated that a whole series of new surveillance and target acquisition devices, extending the capability of observation posts to include engagement of targets at night or other times of poor visibility, would be coming into service. The OP would probably have a doppler radar coupled to a device such as a thermal imager, image intensifier, or thermal pointer. There would be stay-behind parties, pre-placed sensors to report on enemy movements, and drones (small pilotless aircraft) transmitting information direct to battle group or brigade headquarters. In twelve or fifteen years' time, OP, command post and guns would be almost completely automatic. Bracketing must be a thing of the past, everything being done to ensure a lethal opening burst of fire from the battery, followed swiftly by a change of ground to avoid retaliation. The total time from identification of target to the delivery of the first rounds could be as little as fifteen seconds, all data being 'untouched by human hand'.

'All guns will fire simultaneously, and thirty shells weighing in all over 1¼ tons will be in the air together – and before the first one hits the ground the guns will be moving.'

Major Williams added a word of warning: 'We should strongly resist the temptation to introduce new technical gadgets merely for their own sake.' This is a matter on which some artillery officers feel keenly. They see dangers in excessive perfectionism which, by insisting on incorporation of every new scientific refinement, can delay by many months the completion of an item of equipment, and greatly complicates the work of officers and NCOs who are responsible for seeing that gun detachments are at all times fully instructed in their armament and accustomed to its use.

At the moment, so far as can be gauged, the danger of a full-scale war in Europe between the major powers appears to have receded since the first onset of tension with the Soviet Union, though no statesman or military leader would be justified in assuming that this state of affairs is bound to continue. Most of the endless and voluminous commentaries on the subject have tended to assume that if a continental war broke out this would almost inevitably involve the battlefield use of tactical atomic weapons, perhaps after a comparatively short period of fighting with conventional arms, and that in all probability this would be followed quickly by an all-out exchange of inter-continental nuclear missiles, causing millions of deaths, with havoc on a scale which might render vast areas of the earth's surface uninhabitable for years, perhaps for ever.

The plain fact is that nobody knows. The complexities of missiles and anti-missiles, first strike potentials, ripostes and deterrents have now reached a stage at which the most highly skilled experts can do little more than grope hazardously in a maze of theories and possibilities, guided by a compendium of known facts in which, for obvious reasons, many of the most vital must be kept secret. Certainly on the western side no living person – neither the Pentagon generals nor the custodians of the American 'think tanks' – is in a position to predict with any real certainty what form a future world conflict would take; and even the men in control at the Kremlin, if they chose to unleash the hideous powers of nuclear weapons with the advantage of striking first as an aggressor, would be venturing into an uncharted field bristling with pitfalls.

In such circumstances, two things may be taken as reasonably sure. One is that for the immediate future land forces in Europe will have to be kept available, and at the highest pitch of efficiency for which the will and the means can be found, for Nato in case of need. The other is that, while the likelihood of global war may be comparatively remote, fairly recent experience has proved that Britain, even with her reduced commitments, still stands in constant need of land troops for deployment at short notice in defence of her remaining possessions against external attack or internal disorder, or as part of a United Nations force. In both these roles, perhaps more especially in that of the 'small wars', artillery still has a part to play.

One of the lessons of the past is that in war it is usually the unexpected that happens. So many confident forecasts have been falsified, and so many painstaking schemes robbed of any but precautionary value, that common sense inclines us to feel that something of the same kind may happen again. Before the outbreak of the Second World War one of the weapons that was most keenly dreaded by millions of people, as a probable agency of unparalleled suffering and loss of life, was poison gas. It was not used.

During the same war, the remarkable development of air power led many to believe that in future artillery would be totally ousted and made obsolete by massive bombardments from aircraft. Yet it is now known that, for all its great achievements, the Royal Air Force was over-optimistic in some of its claims regarding the effects of bombing. After the end of the war it was fairly generally accepted that, for precision attack with high explosive and for the methodical battering of prepared positions, the artillery offered an accuracy, flexibility and reliability that could not be equalled by the manned bomber. In a similar way, it is at least possible that a survival value may be maintained by the guns (with atomic shells for some of them) in relation to nuclear missiles at medium ranges, even if the baffling and horrific realm of intercontinental-rocketry must lie outside the scope of land artillery as it is now understood.

One of the maxims taught to generations of young gunners is that 'the weapon of the artillery is the shell' – not the gun, it will be noted. Perhaps the time has come when the wording should be changed from 'shell' to 'projectile', which would also include the rocket and the guided missile. It is the projectile with its explosive charge, conventional or nuclear, that counts, not the equipment for delivery, which is only a means to an end.

An outstanding characteristic of the British gunners, which cannot fail to strike any open-minded person who examines their record, is adaptability. Down the centuries, in good times and bad, they have constantly been altering their methods to suit new conditions, new weapons, and new tactical doctrines. Scarcely a decade has gone by without some degree of internal reorganization of re-equipment. Whether all these changes have been necessary, or whether the inevitably unsettling effect has sometimes outweighed the benefits of modernization, is a matter of opinion, on which no layman can be qualified to pass judgment, and on which unanimity is unlikely to be found among the professionals. But there can be no doubt that an impressive store of experience and expertise has been built up. Today the standard of the men is high, training is thorough and well thought out, and the weapons are good and efficiently handled, whatever divisions of opinion there may be on the desirability of new equipment and tactics.

Possessing such qualities, the Royal Artillery is surely well fitted to adapt itself once again, and to continue to give invaluable service amidst the complexities and deep uncertainties of the nuclear age. Any move, in the name of military rationalization, that would jeopardize the separate identity and importance of a specialist corps of such a description, with the traditions which it so rightly cherishes, should not lightly be contemplated.

Put in its simplest terms, the case for the artillery as a twentieth-century arm is a strong one. For any foreseeable length of time ahead, there is at least a probability that there will be wars of one kind or another. In any war such as men now living can possibly envisage, there will be a call at some stage of operations, even in an all-out nuclear conflict, for soldiers on foot – men to carry out the tasks of patrol, occupation and consolidation which no machines, however ingenious or deadly, can perform.

We come back to bedrock fundamentals, which are unchanged. So long as men fight on land, infantry will be essential, and to support them they will require the firepower of artillery weapons, whatever form these may take. The gunners will be needed.

Sources

Bidwell, Brigadier R. G. Shelford, *Gunners at War*, Arms and Armour Press, 1970.

Blaxland, Gregory, *The Regiments Depart*, Kimber, 1971.

Callwell, Major-General Sir Charles, and Headlam, Major-General Sir John, *The History of the Royal Artillery from the Indian Mutiny to the Great War*, R. A. Institution, 1931.

Carey, G. V., and Scott, H. S., *An Outline History of the Great War*, Cambridge University Press, 1928.

Chapman, Guy, *A Passionate Prodigality*, MacGibbon & Kee, 1933.

Chesney, Major A. G., *The Maltese Corps in the British Army*, W. Clowes & Sons, 1897.

Churchill, Sir Winston S., *Marlborough, His Life and Times*, Harrap, 1934.

The World Crisis, 1911–1918, Thornton Butterworth, 1923–31.

The Second World War, Cassell, 1948–54.

Duncan, Colonel Francis, *History of the Royal Regiment of Artillery* (3rd ed.), Murray, 1879.

Falls, Captain Cyril, *The First World War*, Longmans, 1960.

Fortescue, Sir John, *A History of the British Army*, Macmillan, 1899.

Glover, Michael, *Wellington as Military Commander*, Batsford, 1899, 1968.

Graham, Brigadier-General C. A. L., *The Story of the Royal Regiment of Artillery* (5th ed.), R.A. Institution, 1944.

Grinnell-Milne, Duncan, *Mafeking*, Bodley Head, 1957.

Hargreaves, Reginald, *This Happy Breed*, Skeffington, 1951.

Hime, Lieutenant-Colonel H. W. L., *History of the Royal Regiment of Artillery, 1815–1853*, Longmans Green, 1908.

Howarth, David, *A Near Run Thing: the Day of Waterloo*, Collins, 1968.

Jocelyn, Colonel J. R. J., *History of the Royal Artillery, Crimean Period*, John Murray, 1911.

Johnson, Brigadier R. F., *Regimental Fire!: the Honourable Artillery Company in World War Two*, HAC, 1958.

Lawson, Cecil, *A History of the Uniforms of the British Army*, Peter Davies, 1940.

Macrory, Patrick, *Signal Catastrophe*, Hodder & Stoughton, 1966.

Mercer, Captain Cavalié, *Journal of the Waterloo Campaign*, 1870.

Montgomery, Field-Marshal Viscount, *Normandy to the Baltic*, Hutchinson, 1947.

A History of Warfare, Collins, 1968.

Pile, General Sir Frederick, *Ack-Ack: Britain's Defence Against Air Attack during the Second World War*, Harrap, 1949.

Royal Artillery Commemoration Books for the two World Wars, compiled for the R.A. Association, G. Bell & Son, 1920, 1950.

Sheppard, Major E. W., *A Short History of the British Army* (4th ed.), Constable, 1950.

Smyth, Brigadier Sir John, VC, *The Story of the Victoria Cross*, Frederick Muller, 1963.

Young, Brigadier Peter, *World War, 1939–45*, Arthur Barker, 1966.

Dictionary of National Biography: Entries on Granby, Sackville, Dundas, Wellington, Shrapnel, Raglan, Wolseley, and others.

Index

INDEX

INDEX